MW00781967

PASTOR'S

HANDBOOK

John Bisagno

www.BHPublishingGroup.com

ISBN: 978-1-4336-7149-4

Published by B&H Publishing Group
Nashville, Tennessee

Dewey Decimal Classification: 253
Subject Heading: PASTORIAL THEOLOGY \ MINISTRY \
CHURCH ADMINISTRATION

2 3 4 5 6 7 8 9 10 • 16 15 14 13 12

CONTENTS

Part 3: The Pastor as Spiritual Leader

Part 4: The Pastor as Organizational Leader

Part 5: The Pastor as Preacher

Part 6: Worship Services

Part 7: Programs and Ministries

Part 8: The Church Staff

Part 9: The Church Finances

FOREWORD

I was seventeen years old when I first read John Bisagno's classic book *How to Build an Evangelistic Church.* My life was permanently impacted. As a young man just beginning a life of ministry, I devoured John's wise and practical advice about pastoring and leading a local congregation. Over the years I reread the book many times, gleaning new insight each time I read it. Bisagno was a long-distance mentor to me. He modeled pastoring with a big vision and loving with a big heart.

Of course, I am only one of thousands of pastors who have been marked by the ministry of this wonderful, creative man. John has been, and continues to be, a pastor's pastor. He has loved those of us in ministry, so we couldn't help but love him back.

Now John has finally put in print all the insights, all the lessons, and all the wisdom he's gathered from a lifetime of faithful service to Jesus Christ. This book is a gold mine! It represents a virtual seminary education in a single volume. And it is classic Bisagno—clear and simple, convicting yet loving, practical and profound, humorous, and, above all, biblical. If you've never read Bisagno, you are in for a treat.

John was innovative before innovation became cool. He has never been afraid to shake up the status quo. He was always more interested in being effective than in holding to the party line. As a result, he grew one of the greatest churches in the world.

Some great pastors excel in one particular area. But John has excelled at everything—preaching, leading, evangelism, discipleship, planting churches, transitioning churches, leading worship, raising money, doing world missions, resolving conflict, motivating members, and loving everyone. Thank God he took the time to write it all down in this book.

My prayer is that an entire new generation of pastors and church planters will use this book to develop the necessary perspective, convictions, character, and skills needed for ministry in the twenty-first century from this giant of the twentieth century.

Rick Warren, author
The Purpose Driven Church

INTRODUCTION

For over half a century, it has been my joy to serve the Lord. I began as a traveling evangelistic singer, directing worship for the popular weekend youth revivals of the 1950s that produced men like Jess Moody, Freddie Gage, Homer Martinez, Ron Dunn, and others who are legends in my denomination.

I had the privilege of traveling with Dr. Hyman Appelman, the most prominent evangelist on the scene between the ministries of Billy Sunday and Billy Graham. I served as crusade planner, public relations man, program director, platform manager, and music director for three years. It was one of the most important training periods of my life. I have since had the opportunity to organize and lead numbers of citywide evangelistic crusades as well as preach in hundreds of them including thirty-seven internationally.

Just out of college, I served as associate pastor in charge of worship, education, and students at First Baptist Church of Sallisaw, Oklahoma. Since that time I have pastored five years at First Southern Baptist Church, Del City, Oklahoma, and thirty years at First Baptist Church, Houston.

I received a bachelor of fine arts degree with a major in music from Oklahoma Baptist University, never dreaming I was not preparing for what I would ultimately do in life.

In most ways I only learned by experience what I'm going to share with you. With the help of the Holy Spirit and the good counsel of pastor friends of many denominations, it has been my joy to successfully pastor two wonderful churches.

First published as *Letters to Timothy*, these truths were produced in the crucible of trial and error and refined at both the cost of failure and the surprise of success. For years I have longed to see something in print that would spell out the ABCs, the practical "what-to-do's" and "what-not-to-do's" of the ministry, which could have made it so much easier. Now I've had the opportunity to revise and embellish the original book.

I shall never forget my first experience in serving the Lord. I became a Christian August 1, 1952, being called into vocational ministry simultaneously with my conversion. Six weeks later I went to Pryor, Oklahoma, to lead worship at a weekend youth revival at Emmanuel Baptist Church with evangelist Paul McCray, who would later be the best man in my wedding.

As the bus arrived at the station in Pryor, I picked up my trumpet, Bible, and suitcase and stepped into the aisle to leave the bus. Then it hit me, "Oh, my goodness! I wonder what they do in revivals."

It has been nearly six decades since that bus station in Oklahoma, and I often feel I still have more questions than answers. But here is straightforward information—practical, tested, and written from a heart of conviction and love for the Lord, His people, and my fellow pastors.

Only one in five seminary graduates are still in ministry eight years after graduation and nine in ten pastors say they were inadequately prepared for life in the pastorate.

I have attempted to anticipate and address the issues that will confront a pastor in his ministry. They have not been treated exhaustively. To do so would require a volume of books—not just one. These pages provide an encapsulation, an overview, and answer the most obvious and difficult questions under each title. The chapters are short and succinct. They are tried and proven. I pray they will be helpful to you.

I think of this handbook as my "Letters to Timothy." Like the apostle, I have a beloved son in the ministry named Timothy, whose tender ministry to at-risk young people is the most effective I know. Unlike the apostle, he is my own flesh and blood. To my son Timothy, and all the Timothys out there, who will follow in the footsteps of the Master for years to come, I dedicate this book with a prayer and a heart of love.

> "But as for you, continue in what you have learned and firmly believed. You know those who taught you, and you know that from childhood you have known the sacred Scriptures, which are able to give you wisdom for salvation through faith in Christ Jesus." (2 Tim. 3:14–15)

Part 1

THE CHURCH

Chapter 1

GOD'S GLORIOUS CHURCH

Before the world was formed, God planned the church to be His instrument of redemption in the world. The word *church* is the Greek word *ecclesia*, meaning "called out ones." The idea is a town hall meeting where issues were discussed and announcements made.

Jesus referenced Himself, when He said in Matthew 16:18, "On this rock I will build *My* church." Jesus is saying the church is "My called out-ones, *My town hall meeting*" and is the only institution He established on earth.

The word *church* in the New Testament is used in two different ways. The first is the universal or invisible church. When you become a Christian, the Holy Spirit baptizes you into oneness, not only with Jesus but with all other believers everywhere. It is a church that exists beyond buildings, denominational lines, and international borders. It is the body of Christ, the family of God on earth.

Ninety percent of the time, however, the New Testament use of the word *church* refers to a visible, locally assembled body of baptized believers, honoring Him, worshipping together, edifying one another, and winning the lost.

The church is less than perfect. Naysayers and charlatans, like Simon the sorcerer, would buy the power of the Holy Spirit and use the church for their own selfish ends and financial gain. Let them be accursed.

Perhaps it is a just commentary on the failure of some of us within the church that so many extracurricular and parachurch organizations have developed in the kingdom. Most call themselves extensions of the church, or arms of the church, and I am grateful for each. But far too often, parachurch organizations give only lip service to their commitment to the local church.

When Christ came, He established the church. He died for the church. He loved the church. Today He continues to indwell the church, and one day He will come to receive His church. She is His bride, and He is her groom. The old spiritual song, "Let the Church Roll On," says it well:

> There's a woman in the church,
> and she talks too much.
> Tell me, what we gonna do?
> Let the church roll on.
> There's a singer in the church,
> and he won't sing right.
> Tell me, what we gonna do?
> Let the church roll on.
> There's a deacon in the church,
> and he won't "deac" right.
> Tell me, what we gonna do?
> Let the church roll on.

God's church has grown and flourished and will do so until Jesus comes to take her to heaven. *Let the church roll on.*

Throughout your ministry you will be confronted with many avenues of service. Some may indeed be God's perfect purpose for your life. You will seek His heart, hear His voice, and do His will. As you do, consider this: that which is not truly birthed of the church, emanates therein, extends there from, and culminates therein, is doomed to make little lasting impression for God and for good in this world.

Well over a century ago, the YMCA was born, a soul-winning organization to win young men to Christ and train them in the Word of God. Is that the purpose of the YMCA today?

The church is flawed, imperfect, wrinkled, and blemished, but her end is not yet. He is her unfailing strength, and you will do well to commit your life to serve through her.

Today God is greatly expanding His church. In spite of persecution from the Middle East to China, God is at work. The rate of the growth of the church in Brazil is three times faster than the birth rate. At the present rate of kingdom growth, the entire continent of Africa may be Christian by 2020. On a recent Sunday afternoon, 18,250 new believers were baptized in Red Square in Moscow.

For nearly sixty years I have loved Christ and His precious church. My ministry was always centered in His church. I'm so happy I did it that way and would do so again in a minute.

Missionary C. T. Studd said it well:

> Only one life, 'twill soon be past,
>   only what's done for Christ will last.

Let me say it a bit differently:

> Only one ministry, 'twill soon be past,
>   only what's done *through Christ's church* will last.

When Flight 92 went down in Pennsylvania on 9/11, Todd Beamer called his wife, Lisa, from the bathroom of the plane. Together they prayed the Lord's Prayer. His last words to Lisa were, "Let's roll." Sounds good to me.

> "Husbands, love your wives, just as Christ loved the church and gave Himself for her to make her holy, cleansing her with the washing of water by the word. He did this to present the church to Himself in splendor, without spot or wrinkle or anything like that, but holy and blameless." (Eph. 5:25–27)

> "To Him be glory in the church and in Christ Jesus to all generations, forever and ever. Amen." (Eph. 3:21)

Chapter 2

GREAT GROWING
CHURCHES

In the mid-1970s, Adrian Rogers of Bellevue Baptist Church, Memphis, Tennessee, and Edwin Young of Second Baptist Church, Houston, Texas, independently of each other, and unknown to each other, conducted a study of the twenty-five largest, fastest growing churches in America to determine whether there were common ingredients in each.

Some churches were in the north; some in the south. Some were African-American, some Anglo. Some were Hispanic, some Asian. Some were charismatic; most were not. Some facilities were modern; many were old. Each had five factors in common.

1. *They were strongly pastorally led.* Boards, sessions, deacons, elders, and committees abounded. There was a large variance in ecclesiastical structure. But in each case they reported, "It didn't take long, analyzing the inside workings of the church, until it became obvious where the power center was."

But it is essential to understand: *Leadership is not demanded; it is deserved.* Pastoral leadership is taught in Scripture and must be granted by the people but *earned by the pastor.* When you have to start telling them, *"I'm the pastor,"* you no longer are.

God's people are better *led* than *driven.* The wise pastor will seek counsel and work with his leaders while humbly assuming the position of leadership with which God has entrusted him.

2. *They were strong Bible churches.* Each pastor believed the Bible to be inerrant and infallible, the unflawed, perfect Word of God—not just a record of God's Word but God's Word itself. These men were not attempting to be apologists. They were not defending the Bible, debating it, or trying to prove it. They were *preaching* it. And it was happening throughout the entire life of the church.

3. *They had celebration worship.* This is not to say the Sunday services were a hootenanny or the atmosphere carnivalistic. It is to say, they were happy churches with bright, warm, friendly atmospheres. The people felt the freedom to laugh, to cry, and to respond. Remember, *you can't hatch eggs in a refrigerator.* A warm, fluid service that allows for the freedom and spontaneity of the Spirit is conducive to tender response to the Spirit of God. Such services are often mistakenly considered to be only emotional, and decisions made therein naturally shallow. Such is not the case.

Jesus said to love the Lord our God with all our mind, heart, and soul.

In love we respond to His love with the totality of our being, including our emotions.

We thwart the stirring of the Lord when we stifle the freedom of the Spirit with stilted, overly formal services.

"Where the Spirit of the Lord is, there is freedom" (2 Cor. 3:17).

This is not, of course, to suggest an inherent lack of planning. An order of service can be directed by the Holy Spirit and still be printed in advance. But the freedom and ease with which it should be carried out can and *must* be allowed.

4. *They were churches in unity.* The people gave a high priority to their oneness in Christ. Racial, social, and economic diversity are a great plus in the church. Ideally your church will be a cross section of your city and one which celebrates its diversity in unity.

When a church is in harmony with itself, it becomes the beautiful body of Christ on earth, through which the Lord Jesus in heaven expresses His presence and person every time the people of God gather. Songwriter Lanny Wolfe said it well: "I love the thrill that I feel when I get together with God's wonderful people."[1]

5. *Each church had an indomitable spirit of conquest.* There was a holy drivenness about the congregation. They would not be satisfied. Each pulsated with an atmosphere of more, more, more.

They must cross the next river, climb the next mountain, give the next dollar, build the next building, send the next missionary, and win the next soul. They would not be stopped.

The Nissan Motor Company, formerly the Datsun Motor Company, once had a marvelous PR slogan: "We Are Driven."

Pastor friend, we, too, are driven.

God's children are a driven people. We are driven to the ends of the earth by the Great Commission, driven to the end of ourselves by the love of Christ, driven to the end of time by His imminent return.

These many years later, the same five principles are consistently present in America's great churches. Young pastors today "get it," and more. And I'm grateful.

And never forget the tone of each of these five ingredients is clearly set by the pastor. It all starts in the pulpit. Keep your eyes on the Lord. Keep your ears open to the Great Commission. Keep your chin up, your knees down, and keep going. Never stop. The best is yet to come.

> Onward, Christian soldiers, marching as to war,
> With the cross of Jesus going on before.
> Christ, the royal Master, leads against the foe;
> Forward into battle see His banners go![2]

"I looked, and there was a white horse. The horseman on it had a bow; a crown was given to him, and he went out as a victor to conquer." (Rev. 6:2)

Endnotes

1. Larry Wolfe, "God's Wonderful People," © 1974.
2. Sabine Baring-Gould, "Onward Christian Soldiers."

Chapter 3

THE OFFICES
OF THE CHURCH

E very home needs a dad; every team, a coach; every nation, a president. Every church needs a leader, and leaders don't have two heads, let alone five or ten. Church government by committee has no place in the biblical record. The purpose of committees is to offer counsel *to* the pastor and/or make decisions and implement projects as requested *by* the pastor. God calls one person to lead a local congregation, and that person is the pastor. But remember, leadership is never demanded. It is deserved and it is shared.

God has placed deep in the heart of every woman a desire for a man she can look up to as the head of the home and spiritual leader of the marriage. In the same way, He has put in the heart of every congregation the desire for an undershepherd to lead and for them to respect and follow.

Shepherds don't follow the flock; they lead the flock. But that leadership must be deserved, earned, and won by integrity, faithful ministry, true humility, godliness, ministry, and feeding the flock the Word of God. And that takes time. The longer you pastor a congregation in that spirit, the more freedom you will be granted to lead.

The pastor may be called bishop, elder, rector, or some other title, but the purpose of leadership is to lead, and the function of leadership is to get things done.

Some New Testament churches may have had several pastors, but I am inclined to think there was a chief shepherd and others who participated with him, more in the vein of today's executive pastor, staff, and deacons or elders.

Whatever else may be wrong about the way we do church, the concept of an earthly shepherd as pastor/leader is right. And, remember, we are talking about a concept, a position, an office, *not just a person*. The person may fail and even need to be removed by the congregation, but *the office* itself is always to be honored.

A delicate balance exists between pastor, deacons, committees, and congregation, but the office of pastor must be regarded as the ultimate position of leadership in the church.

A young private greatly disliked his sergeant and threatened not to salute. "Soldier," the sergeant said, "you're not saluting the man; you're saluting the office."

Deep in the heart of His people is a God-given desire to salute both the man *and* the office. I have found when we *earn* our leadership, God's people are more than willing to *grant* it.

As I read the New Testament, while there are many gifts, there are only two offices in the local church: pastor or elder and deacon.

But a wise pastor will have a group around him on whom he depends for wise counsel in the decision-making process. Participatory leadership is biblical. Autocratic leadership is not. They might be called the trustees, the session, the deacons, the leadership team, or the elders, but a New Testament-minded pastor will embrace their help and counsel. The book of Proverbs says, "In many counselors, there is much wisdom."

Unfortunately, conflict between pastor and deacons for leadership exists in far too many churches.

Large numbers of Baptist churches are named Unity, New Way, New Harmony, New Freedom, or New Fellowship, suggesting they came from a divided congregation.

Deacons too must earn their right to be part of the participatory leadership style of the pastor, not by demanding it but by serving the people, preserving the unity, and protecting their pastor.

Sadly, many Southern Baptist churches still haven't figured out the issue of church governance. We can and must do better. We'll try to get the process moving forward in subsequent chapters.

Chapter 4

GOD'S GIFT TO THE CHURCH

God gave three categories of spiritual gifts to the church: the gift of the gifted leader, the body-edifying gifts, and the evangelistic sign gifts for unbelievers.

As the gift of God to the local congregation and to the church at large, gifted persons not only *have* spiritual gifts; they themselves *are* the gift. They are the prophet/preacher, evangelist, pastor/teacher, or pastors who teach. Certainly pastors must be teachers, and the correct title may well be pastor-teacher.

"And He personally gave some to be apostles, some prophets, some evangelists, some pastors and teachers, for the training of the saints in the work of ministry, to build up the body of Christ" (Eph. 4:11–12).

New Testament apostles were personally commissioned by Christ and eyewitnesses to His bodily resurrection. No such persons exist today.

Regardless of the title, God gave pastors as gifts to the church first and foremost to be His undershepherds. Just as those who participate in the leadership of the pastor may have many different names—*deacons, elders, trustees, the session,* etc.—the pastor himself is called by five names: *pastor, elder, bishop, overseer,* and *shepherd.*

In the book of Revelation, God calls pastors His "stars."

Jesus promises a special crown for faithful pastors: "And when the chief Shepherd appears, you will receive the unfading crown of glory" (1 Pet. 5:4).

The greatest joy you will know is to "shepherd God's flock among you" (1 Pet. 5:2). Treasure each moment as a special gift and sacred trust. As God's gift to your congregation, your pastorship is also God's precious gift to you. Remember, it is at once valuable and fragile. Handle with care.

I am constantly amazed by pastors who confess how much they dislike what they do and can't wait to get out of the ministry. Can you imagine how much our Heavenly Father, our Great Shepherd, the Lord Jesus, loved His sheep when He laid down His life for them? Can you comprehend the honor and the privilege that is yours in being entrusted by our Lord Jesus to shepherd His little flock?

A cross is an *I* crossed out and is the heart of the Christian faith. And certainly at the heart of ministry stands a life of selfless service and giving. It is often said, "You can't out give God." Neither can you out give *the people of God*. Pastoring a church is like looking into a mirror; it tends to give back what it gets. If you truly love your people, pour out your life for them and serve them with all your heart. They *will* love you back.

Yes, there will be some phony Simons along the way and some traitorous Judases and doubting Thomases. But the overwhelming majority of God's people are good people. They will love you, bless you, support and follow you as they see the integrity and selflessness of your devoted service and ministry to Christ and to them.

I don't know any congregations that despise Jesus. Why do some seem to despise their pastor? Is it because they do not see Jesus in him?

Unrelenting, unavailable, proud, ambitious, self-serving, unapproachable, unprepared—words used far too often in describing some pastors.

Some of you might be reading this book as a last hope. Perhaps you're greatly discouraged, looking for a way out, and you've hoped to get enough encouragement within these pages to hang on just a little longer.

You've got to go back, way back, all the way to the cross. Go back to where the journey started and kneel before the Lord Jesus. Let the words of "The Old Rugged Cross" well up again within your soul. Ask our Lord once again to form His heart, His character, and His love within you.

If you can't get there, you should probably get out of the ministry. It is not impossible that you have missed God's call altogether. Something is desperately wrong when pastors hate the body of Christ that our Lord loves and calls us to serve.

Be the gift of God you truly are to your people. Don't make them think they won the booby prize.

Herschel Hobbs was a patriarch of the faith. He served as president of the Southern Baptist Convention and pastored the First Baptist Church of Oklahoma City for thirty years. He died at nearly ninety years of age, still preaching every day.

In his book, *Preacher Talk* he wrote, "If I had 10,000 lives to live, I should want to spend every one of them as a pastor."[1] And I say, "Me, too, Dr. Hobbs. Me, too."

May God grant us the faithfulness and integrity to be worthy gifts of His grace to His wonderful people.

Early in ministry I was often discouraged, speaking only before small congregations and living on tiny love offerings. One Sunday afternoon riding around in my car, I felt overwhelmed. I turned on the radio as Bev Shea began to sing,

> I'd rather have Jesus than silver or gold;
> I'd rather be His than have riches untold.
> I'd rather have Jesus than men's applause;
> I'd rather be faithful to His dear cause.
> Than to be the king of a vast domain,
> And be held in sin's dread sway.
> I'd rather have Jesus than anything,
> This world affords today.[2]

I kept driving.

Endnotes

1. Hershael Hobbs, *Preacher Talk* (Nashville: Broadman Press, 1979), 72.
2. Rhea F. Miller, "I'd Rather Have Jesus."

Chapter 5

ELDER RULE

There are two kinds of leadership: participatory and autocratic. Autocratic rule, with one person making all the decisions with the participation of no one else, is neither New Testament nor smart.

First, none of us are *that* smart. There is indeed much wisdom in many counselors. Where only one person holds autocratic leadership—or a tiny handful of two or three have all authority—you not only tend to cultism but also sacrifice the wisdom and counsel of your people.

Second, you forfeit buy-in spiritually, prayerfully, and financially from the people. What people have input into deciding, they support with their prayers, their presence, and their resources.

Third, you fail to train leaders. If you fail here, your church can fall apart when you leave. We pastors love to talk about what happened *since I came*. The test of your leadership is what happens *when you leave*.

Autocratic rule is fraught with much potential danger.

Fourth, participatory leadership is the New Testament way and is the *best* way.

INSIDE INFORMATION! It does not matter what you call them, you need a team to help you lead.

You may call them by different names. Some churches call them simply deacons, the board; others, elders; still others, trustees, the session, leadership team, or church council. It doesn't matter what you call them. The important thing is that you are not supposed to do it *by yourself*.

He who does not practice participatory leadership, solicit the advice and opinion of others, and is not accountable will regret it.

Before you adopt or change any system of church governance, ask yourself some questions.

These are the leaders of our church. Says who? How are they dismissed? Are they self-perpetuating? Who appoints new leaders and for how long? Does the church never vote on anything? We shall clearly see that any governing system with just you, or you and two or three others holding all of the authority, is not the way the New Testament church did business.

Every church needs a constitution and bylaws. The bylaws must be well thought out and followed, and they must address the issue of *how decisions are made*. All of them being made by one or two people is neither New Testament nor smart.

There are some things about which we may not be certain regarding the structure of leadership in the New Testament. We *do* know that these names are used interchangeably: elder, pastor, shepherd, overseer, and bishop.

When the apostle Paul addressed the elders and sent Timothy to appoint elders, we cannot be certain whether it was one elder in each church or a plurality of elders in one church, but I think we can safely assume that because the Bible teaches there is much wisdom in many counselors—experience has borne out the fatal flaw of autocratic leadership—there were others who were elders, serving by whatever name in each church, while one—the pastor—served as chief elder.

The Dallas Theological Seminary-trained Bible church pastors have used the elder-led system for many decades. I recently spoke with three of their more prominent pastors and professors. They all agreed: it is essential that elders be elected *by* the church, are accountable *to* the church, rotate, and that the church votes on *some things* as we shall see in another chapter.

They all emphasized one word: *balance*—consisting of pastoral leadership, elder board, committees, and congregation.

The New Testament way is a group of leaders working together, with the pastor or chief elder making most decisions, with the congregation, the *ultimate authority,* voting on only *some* things not scripturally addressed and of significant importance.

Again remember, *it doesn't matter what you call them*: deacons, elders, the session, trustees, or whatever. You need a group of people to help you who are elected *by* and accountable *to* the church, who do not serve in perpetuity.

So my fellow Baptist pastor, before you change your system of church government, throw out the deacons, dismiss congregational government, and move to a system you may call elder rule (and probably split your church in the process), I encourage you to think a long time. It's far better to make the system work you already have, *and you can*.

As I write these words, I am preparing to preach in one of the great churches in the Convention, decimated by an ill-fated attempt by the pastor to move the church from deacon led to elder rule. It cost him three thousand members in six months.

There's a better way.

> For since there is envy among you, are you not fleshly and living like unbelievers? For whenever someone says, "I'm with Paul," and another, "I'm with Apollos," are you not unspiritual people? What then is Apollos? And what is Paul? They are servants through whom you believed, and each has the role the Lord has given. I planted, Apollos watered, but God gave the growth. Now the one planting and the one watering are one in purpose, and each will receive his own reward according to his own labour. For we are God's coworkers. You are God's field, God's building. (1 Cor. 3:3–9)

Chapter 6

DEACONS AND THEIR MINISTRY

I n Acts 6, we have the first record of deacons. Though only actually called deacons in Philippians 1 and 2 Timothy 3, the seven men named in Acts 6 were the first to serve as such.

Simply stated, the preachers needed help. Overwhelmed with ministry needs, Peter and the other disciples were spending too much time meeting the physical demands of the people and too little time in preparation to teach and preach the Word.

God's answer? Set aside deacons. The catalyst was the distribution of daily food to the widows. The Grecian widows complained that the Hebrew widows were getting priority while they were being neglected. Dr. Luke says it this way: "There arose a complaint by the Hellenistic Jews" (Acts 6:1).

Even a cursory reading of the text indicates the most important issue was not the food but the *argument* over the *distribution* of the food. The fellowship was divided. The church was split, and divided fellowships *go nowhere*. Perhaps Dr. Luke's statement, "Select from among you seven men of good reputation, full of the Spirit and wisdom, whom we can appoint to this duty" (Acts 6:3) should be interpreted, "Find seven men whom we may appoint over this *mess*."

Clearly the apostles were disturbed over the division of the fellowship. The primary purpose of deacons was not to do the physical work of the church but to preserve the fellowship of the church that was being destroyed over the *issue* of the work.

Division within the church is devastating. The unity of the body of Christ is everything. The unbeliever may disbelieve God and doubt the Bible, but when he comes into the presence of Jesus, created through the lives of a unified people, something wonderful happens. And in that presence, there is life. People are drawn to Christ and receive Him. Unity in the church must be preserved at all costs. Unity attracts. Disunity repels.

And to whom is the responsibility given of preserving the unity of the congregation? That responsibility is placed squarely on the shoulders of the deacons. Never forget, deacons were ordained not just to meet the physical needs of the congregation—serving tables—*but primarily to preserve the fellowship* that had been broken over the *issue* of serving tables.

Unfortunately, in some churches the deacons, far from maintaining the fellowship of the church, however, *are themselves* the *cause* of disharmony within the church. I speak bluntly here, perhaps even harshly, but I do so in the context of honoring the deacons of the churches I served as pastor. They were masters at maintaining the fellowship.

But I must say, the most consistent problem with which I have helped young pastors deal through the years has been deacons creating a power struggle with the pastor. They were actually *dividing* the church rather than *unifying* it. Running off pastors, administering budgets, fighting over secondary issues, and creating power struggles are not what being a deacon is about.

Frankly, in far too many churches, the whole issue is indeed a mess, and churches are desperately hurt, going nowhere, even declining because of it. But where deacons do what deacons are supposed to do, the church prospers and the deacons are happy. The deacons should protect the fellowship, assist the pastor, minister to the congregation, and consult with the pastor as requested.

The word *deacon* is the Greek word *dia-kanos*, which means "servant." He is not primarily one who leads; he is one who serves. And through that service he earns the privilege of participation in the leadership of his pastor. Nothing is more biblical than the concept of participatory leadership.

First Timothy 3:5 says, "If anyone does not know how to manage his own household, how will he take care of God's church?" But the deacon, as well as the pastor, is in a place of *earned* leadership. He leads only because he serves. If I do not serve, I cannot lead—nor can he.

Too often deacons think they can participate in leadership without participating in service. Deacon, seize the initiative! Find a problem and fix it. Find a need and meet it. Go to the hospital. Win the lost. Mow the yard. Empty the trash. Take food to the widows. Say to the pastor, "I'll do this. Here, I'll handle that. Let me . . . Don't worry about it. We'll take care of it." *That is to be the attitude of the deacon.*

Deacons who don't serve, but want to lead, are unhappy deacons, and their churches are dying. Deacons who protect the fellowship, honor their pastor, have a humble servant's heart, and love to work are deacons who are happy and whose churches are alive and well.

My best friends are deacons. I have worked with the best deacons in the world. They supported me, and I supported them. For thirty years Houston's First worked in harmony and went forward.

And I say to the credit of my deacons and the glory of my God, "Thank the Lord for deacons who understand the ministry to which God has called them, serve and protect the fellowship of the congregation, and *have their pastor's back.*" Make your deacons your best friends. You'll need them.

Chapter 7

DEACONS AND DIVORCE

Let's talk first about the oldest controversy surrounding the positions of pastor and deacon. I speak, of course, of the issue of divorce.

First Timothy 3 lists qualifications for bishops and deacons, among them the controversial verse 12, "Deacons must be husbands of one wife."

The issue of the ordination of divorced church leaders has been greatly debated through the years. The general assumption has been that it simply means one may never have been divorced. Others have suggested it is a reference to bigamy—one wife at a time. We do speak, do we not, of a former wife as an "ex-wife"? Then there is the question, must a deacon be married? Is this a prohibition against a single deacon? The answer, of course, is no.

Other problems abound. What of the man who remains married to a woman who is a practicing lesbian? Is he qualified under this obvious exception if he divorces her? If he divorces his wife, does he then denounce his pastorate or his deaconship? And what of the grace of God?

Are we or are we not new creatures in Christ Jesus? Are old things passed away, or are they not? And what if the divorce occurred before a man became a Christian, or he is the classic innocent party? On and on goes the controversy.

Did our Lord intend such confusion when he inspired these words through the apostle Paul? I think not. No New Testament issue has racked Baptist churches with more confusion than this, and our Lord is not the author of confusion.

The apostle Paul said we are to "correctly teaching the word of truth" (2 Tim. 2:15). The Greek word means "cutting it straight." Paul was a tent maker. He knew the importance of "cutting it straight." If each piece is not cut to the original pattern, each successive piece becomes more deformed than the last. The issue has become more bizarre today because we have failed to see the original pattern correctly.

The best thinking today of Greek scholars is that it is impossible in the Greek, for the expression "husband of one wife," to refer to a *status*. It is not a *status*. It is a *trait*. It is not what one *is* (i.e., married or divorced); it is what one *is like* (i.e., faithful to his wife).

Commentator John MacArthur writes:

> The overseer or elder must first be above reproach in relation to women. He must be *the husband of one wife*. The Greek text literally reads "a one-woman man." Paul is not referring to a leader's marital status, as the absence of the definite article in the original indicates. Rather, the issue is his moral, sexual behavior. Many men who are married only once are not one-woman men. Many with one wife are unfaithful to their wives. While remaining married to one woman is commendable, it is no indication or guarantee of moral purity.[1]

Nor is it a reference to a mistake made in high school when a boy got married for six weeks and then divorced. God never intended that we split the hair that finely.

And what, after all, is marriage? Some people have taken vows that were never sexually consummated and then signed divorce papers. Does this apply to them? What about the bigamist? What about the man who was divorced before he became a believer? What about the innocent party? What about homosexuality? What about a man who never legally divorced but whose wife left him a week after they got married, never to see her again?

Or one who lives in pornography? Is he qualified to be a pastor or a deacon? Bizarre to the point of the ridiculous are the extremes to which we may go when we don't *cut it straight*.

The Greek does indeed mean a "one-woman man." Not only the Greek but also the simple principles of hermeneutics demand such an interpretation.

Contextualizing the passage, you find that every other qualification is an "inclination toward," not a "hard and fast" *state*. Each is not a *status* but a character *trait* of which Paul writes.

The text doesn't say the prospective deacon never once failed to be watchful; it says he is vigilant. It doesn't say he never once had a belly laugh at a good joke; it says he is sober or serious. It doesn't say he never once misbehaved; it says he is of good behavior. It doesn't say he never once turned down a request to let the visiting preacher spend the night in his home; it says he is inclined to hospitality. It doesn't say he never once messed up a Sunday school lesson; it says he is apt to teach. It doesn't say he never once had a drink at the senior prom; it says he is not given to wine. It doesn't say he never once demonstrated impatience; it says he is patient. It doesn't say he never once got into a fight in grade school; it says he is not a brawler. It does not say he never once really wanted his neighbor's new Lexus; it says he is not characterized by a covetous spirit.

A good hermeneutic demands that, in context, the "husband of one wife" qualification must also be an *inclination* or *tendency*, not a fixed status.

In my denomination and probably yours, traditions die hard. We hear sermons on the "Tradition of the Elders" and the "Immovability of the Pharisees," whom Jesus criticized because they set tradition above truth, and say *"Amen."* But when *our* traditions are challenged, it can be most difficult for us.

Far too often, unqualified deacons and other church leaders remain in office while good and godly men who have proven their faithfulness to their wives for thirty and forty years are excluded from service. Try to transform the thinking of your people at this point from *tradition* to *truth*.

Endnotes

1. John MacArthur, *1 Timothy* in The MacArthur New Testament Commentary (Chicago: Moody, 1995), 104.

Chapter 8

THE CHURCH COMMITTEES

Church committees, teams, or groups (it doesn't matter what you call them) are a vital part of a healthy church. A wise pastor will respect and appreciate official groups in the church, commissioned to help him do the work of the ministry.

Various teams or committees to implement the many facets of a growing church are most important. Varying degrees of authority/leadership are assigned to five different entities within the church: pastor, staff, deacons, committees, and congregation. There is an important place for each in the life of the church, and each should consider the other more important than itself.

The pastor must be the vision caster. This means he must have a vision to cast, which presupposes time with God to receive the vision. It is important that each team or committee sense this in the heart of their pastor.

The purpose of committees, teams, or groups is to give counsel and input to church leaders in helping make decisions. The purpose of the deacon body is to refine and recommend, and the responsibility of the congregation is to affirm and commit.

When the body of Christ feels uneasy about a decision, a wise leader will back off and reassess. Committees, deacons, and congregation are a marvelous insulation and support to the pastor in the decision-making process. Good committees will think of things you haven't thought of and view from different perspectives the various aspects of an issue.

And don't stack the deck with committee members who always agree with you. Your committees are not to be your "rubber stamp." While you do not want committee members who are obviously not supportive of their pastor, it is still profitable to hear from all sides. Good leadership is secure enough to be challenged and not threatened. The other opinion just might be the one you need to hear.

The wise pastor will use committees as a sounding board to refine and massage major decisions before implementing them.

But committees are not only recommenders; they are also enactors. Often, as a pastor, I would take an issue to a committee and say: "I really don't care what you do about this, and I trust your wisdom completely. Make your decision and implement it. Just get it done."

Conversely, in an average week I would make many decisions and just say, "This is what we're going to do." Most of the time I did not feel the need to bring a committee into the matter. It is neither feasible nor prudent to call your committees into session a dozen times a week to help make every little decision that comes along.

Sometimes, however, there were decisions I felt the need to refer to the deacons for approval and support. Again, very often, the decisions will stop there, but occasionally major things need to go on to the congregation for final approval.

Doctrinal issues are never decided by congregation or committee. They are defined and articulated by the pastor.

If the congregation does not have confidence in the pastor at this point, they should call a new pastor in whom they have such confidence. But doctrinal stance by committee is not an option. Sometimes it takes courage. Sometimes it will cost. Sometimes you will lose members. But the people will support you.

The obvious questions then are: Which decisions should a pastor make? Which should he ask a committee to assist in making? Which should be referred to the deacons? Which should be taken to the entire congregation?

It is not possible to predetermine categories for every decision and define in advance at what level each will be made.

That issue arose in my fifth year in Houston, and I went to our deacons with this proposal:

"Give me the authority to be the one to determine at which of the four levels issues will be resolved as they arise. In a year let's review and see how the system is working. If you're not pleased, we'll find another."

They agreed. Years later another issue arose over who had the authority to do what. Again I went to the deacons, reminding them of their earlier decision, and asked if it was their pleasure to reaffirm the policy. They chose to do so, and the church continues to live by that policy today.

When I am uncertain, I always err on the side of caution. I would rather have too much input and too much support than too little in the arena of an important issue.

Ninety-nine percent of the time, the committees and the church will follow what you believe the Lord would have you do. Be respectful of the input of your committees. It's a wonderful way to do God's work.

> Give my greetings to Prisca and Aquila, my co-workers in Christ Jesus, who risked their own necks for my life. Not only do I thank them, but so do all the Gentile churches. Greet also the church that meets in their home. Greet my dear friend Epaenetus, who is the first convert to Christ from Asia. Greet Mary, who has worked very hard for you. Greet Andronicus and Junia, my fellow countrymen and fellow prisoners. They are noteworthy among the apostles, and they were also in Christ before me. Greet Ampliatus, my dear friend in the Lord. Greet Urbanus, our co-worker in Christ, and my dear friend Stachys. (Rom. 16:3–9)

Chapter 9

APPOINTING THE COMMITTEES

A church can have many committees. Houston's First has one pastor, one staff, one deacon body, and a host of committees. Currently the church has the following committees: committee on committees, finance, personnel, properties, children, preschool, youth, benevolence, recovery, Christian life center, resource center, social, baptismal, Lord's Supper, missions council, scholarship, First Place Council, First Kids Council.

The two most important committees in the church are the finance committee and the personnel committee. Depending on each church's individual needs and priorities, other committees will run a close second, third, or fourth. This will, of course, vary with each church.

In Houston's First, the missions committee is also important. In previous years the media committee, handling radio and television, was important. Ministries come and go and priorities change, but the crucial importance of the personnel and finance committees remains constant.

The purpose of the finance committee is to prepare the annual budget, review it monthly, and monitor expenditures. Consistent overages in any line item must be addressed. But generally it is best to raise the budget across the board on a percentage basis in good times and even lower it the same way in difficult times. And don't panic when seasonal expenditures are over budget.

The air-conditioning bill will always be higher in the summer. The church budget must be prepared and administered in faith.

Unproductive ministries should be considered for termination. New money should be allocated to ministries that are enjoying the blessing of God in great measure.

Absolutely no person should serve on the finance committee unless he or she tithes *to the church*. And it goes without saying, that the same is true of the staff. We must not tolerate a situation in which those who live by the tithes of the people are not themselves tithers.

The personnel committee will aid the pastor when called upon in the hiring and dismissing of staff, appraisal of job performance, and related issues. At Houston's First I had the right to hire and fire, but I always did so, particularly at upper-level positions, in consultation with the personnel committee. Not only was their counsel and input of great value, but they were a buffer when the release of a person was handled as a personnel committee matter.

The personnel committee and finance committee, as well as all church committees, should be appointed by a *committee on committees*, which is the other high-priority committee in your church. The question obviously arises, Who appoints the committee on committees? Who names the persons who will name the persons who make up the committees? Therein, friends, is the kicker. Ideally, it should be the pastor. In some cases it is the committee on committees itself.

When the committee on committees names the committee on committees, they obviously become a self-perpetuating body. This can only work when you have a pliable, sensitive, mature, wise, unselfish group of committee members who truly want to work with their pastor, have the best interest of their church at heart, and have no interest in naming their friends or themselves in perpetuity.

For nearly three decades at Houston's First, we were blessed with a great group of men and women who comprised our *committee on committees*. They were wise enough and gracious enough to consult with their pastor before naming any other members to the committee on committees, as well as the other major committees of the church.

Under no conditions should a pastor be saddled with a group of people on the main committees of the church with whom he cannot work. It is the responsibility of the *committee on committees* to honor the position of pastor by seeking his input and blessing on all potential committee members for their own committee and others.

And by all means, no person should ever be asked to serve on any committee until the pastor has approved. The committee on committees should never put their pastor in an embarrassing position by saying: "Pastor, we've asked Bill Smith to serve on the building committee. Is that OK with you?" If it's not OK with you, you're a dead duck. You can't say no, or you will be at odds with a good member of the church. The committee can't go back to Bill Smith and say, "The pastor doesn't want you," or, "We've changed our minds."

Another possibility is that the chairman of your deacons and three or four other important committee heads can work with the pastor in naming the committee on committees.

Or they may be elected from the floor of the church. The problem with this is that some people might be nominated who are unqualified to serve, leading to unpleasant discussion, hurt feelings, and other problems.

Committees should rotate. Ideally, there should be one-, two-, and three-year-term members on each committee.

From time to time it will be necessary to appoint ad hoc committees. This is normally done by the pastor for a stated purpose, for a short time, and with a stated termination date.

Chapter 10

CHURCH DISCIPLINE

Discipline was practiced in the early church, and the problem is still with us. Sadly today, it is occasionally necessary to carry out discipline within the church. For both pastor and people, nothing is more difficult. Fortunately, we have biblical instruction for dealing with the flagrant sins of unrepentant church members.

The disciplinary procedure within the church is different from the civil and criminal measures carried out in secular society. Unlike the secular world, church discipline is administered with a view toward redemption, in a spirit of grace. The goal is never to *punish* the offender but to *restore* him to fellowship within the church.

In our church our deacons wisely established a policy designed to insulate the pastor against having to deal with this difficult issue. Our procedure has been to have a designated staff member, such as an associate pastor or minister of counseling, join three or four mature deacons and deacons' wives in comprising the disciplinary committee.

Resist the urge to reach a negative conclusion too quickly against a church member who has been accused of wrongdoing. Remember that Golden Rule. Instead, ask your disciplinary committee to explore the matter fully, interviewing all parties involved in the dispute. This can be a lengthy and burdensome task, but it must be done to assure total fairness to the accused party. And beware of the person who brings an accusation but is unwilling to have his or her name associated with the accusation.

Perhaps the most difficult problem you will encounter is dealing with the person who is viewed with a sense of discomfort within the body but against whom there is no hard evidence. Foreseeing these kinds of situations, the Holy Spirit wisely placed within the body of Christ those believers who are gifted with the gift of *spiritual discernment*. Select those kinds of persons for the disciplinary committee.

Through the years I have forbidden service to individuals about whom there was a spirit of "dis-ease" within the heart and soul of my most mature and sensitive people. Give serious heed to the spiritually discerning church member who says, "Pastor, I just don't feel good about this individual or that situation." Whatsoever is not of faith is sin. When in doubt, don't do it.

The Quakers call it "minding the checks." When there is a "check mark" in the spirit of your most mature people, you need to listen and take heed. Deacons' wives as committee members will be of great assistance here. Mature Christian women often have a heightened sense of spiritual discernment.

Several years ago the deacons of Houston's First adopted a "morals and ethics policy." The policy is based on the Matthew 18 model and deals with accusations and responses to accusations within the church. It contains the following elements:

1. The accuser is asked to go to the accused and seek his repentance. This encounter is then reported to the disciplinary committee.

2. If the accused refuses to respond to the accuser, the matter is referred to the disciplinary committee which, in turn, manages the matter *as designated agents of the church*. Our policy is to authorize the committee to act on behalf of the church rather than dealing with the matter before the entire congregation.

3. If the accused is determined to be guilty, he is removed from any place of service or leadership in the church until such time as the disciplinary committee determines that complete restoration has occurred.

4. In the event the accused is determined to be guilty and is resistant to disciplinary guidelines imposed by the committee and, further, if he continues in his sin or wrongdoing, the guilty party may be asked or directed to leave the church.

A second part of the "moral and ethics policy" relates to those of unsavory reputation. The scriptural qualifications for church leaders require that they not only be good people but also "of good report" or "of good reputation."

Should various spiritually discerning members of the church, independent of one another, report a feeling of "dis-ease" regarding an individual member, such situations should be referred to the disciplinary committee for prayer and consideration. If the feeling of "dis-ease" persists, it may be assumed that God is speaking in a delicate and sensitive area through His body, the church.

In such cases direct accusation and confrontation may not be necessary. The disciplinary committee should privately communicate with key church leadership about persons who are objects of concern, toward the end of not using such persons in places of service. There is no need to remove such persons from the congregation however. Given time, the Word of God and the Holy Spirit will ultimately do what they do best.

To minimize the potential for church disciplinary problems, it is important that all candidates for any type of church leadership be reviewed by the pastor and senior staff. Sometimes the pastor or another minister will know something in confidence about an individual that would make his or her appointment to a leadership position inappropriate.

I pray the wisdom of the Father, the love of the Son, and the discernment of the Holy Spirit for you as you undertake the task of dealing with this difficult matter.

Chapter 11

THE CHURCH PRAYING

A fter each plateau in the history of Houston's First, the church again began to grow.

The reason was twofold:

1. The people didn't panic. They stayed the course and did what they do best. They knew who they were and understood their unique purpose.
2. The church turned up the prayer thermostat by several degrees.

Prayer became more important. New prayer groups were formed—some inside the walls of the church, some outside. Today there are many weekly prayer meetings across the city in the life of this great church. Early on there was only one. Additionally, the church began giving priority to prayer in the weekly staff meetings and worship services.

Most Protestant churches call their Wednesday night gathering "prayer meeting." Yet in most, prayer is what we do the least. We take prayer requests, write prayergrams, sing hymns about prayer, and talk a lot about prayer. We even have devotionals and Bible studies on prayer. In an average one-hour "prayer meeting," however, we usually spend only five to ten minutes actually praying.

Invite the people to the front, get on your knees, call on three or four to pray first, and ask the people to pray one after the other, leaving no time between prayers. When they have finished, close. But, whatever you do, spend at least twenty to thirty minutes actually praying.

Rotate among the various prayer meetings of your congregation. Join them in their homes. Be seen. Be heard. Be there. Pray there. Your presence lends support and affirmation, and your heart encourages theirs.

Many of the members of Houston's First lead support groups and Bible studies around town and early prayer breakfasts in various restaurants. Go to these groups and pray with them.

When there is a special need, call the people to prayer. Have a prayer line. Develop a prayer chain. Establish a prayer room. And, by all means, remove the lock from the prayer room door and throw it away.

There is really no such thing as public prayer, only prayer in public places. In form, a congregation may worship God, but the essence of prayer is in a relationship with God who sees in secret. It is a transaction no eye of man can see, even though heard by others. God has given us no higher privilege than communion with Himself.

The Scripture is replete with encouragement to pray. "The urgent request of a righteous person is very powerful in its effect" (James 5:16).

"If you ask Me anything in My name, I will do it" (John 14:14).

Virtually every Sunday morning we had a five- to ten-minute time of prayer. Circling the front of our platform is a long prayer rail with padded knee rests. Lights were dimmed, music played, and people poured down the aisles to pray and be prayed for. As pastor, it is important for you publicly to conclude the time of prayer.

One morning I felt strongly impressed to pray for physical healing. God's power was obviously present in an exceptional way. A young college student in my wife's Sunday school class brought her blind mother to the altar. As I finished the prayer time with, "Amen," her mother stood to her feet and shouted, "My God, I can see!"

Praying must be the priority of the church. God is just waiting for His people to pray.

Sir Walter Raleigh once asked a large favor of Queen Elizabeth. The Queen lost her patience and petulantly said, "Oh, Raleigh, when will you leave off begging?" In a flash Raleigh replied, "When Your Majesty leaves off giving."

Prayer moves the hand of God. No prayer means no power. Little prayer means little power. Much prayer means much power. Call on the Lord. Be a church of prayer.

Prayer makes the difference.

Part 2

THE PASTOR
AS GOD'S MAN

Chapter 12

THE PASTOR'S CALL

In 1959 I was in Belfast, Ireland, leading worship in a citywide evangelistic crusade for evangelist Hyman Appleman. Speaking engagements at civic clubs, radio stations, shipyards, street corners, church meetings, as well as the rigor of the evening services left us exhausted.

When we finished, God allowed us several days to rest. We retreated to an old castle that had been converted into a hotel on the Irish Sea in Colraine, Ireland.

It was just the right time for me before our next crusade. Not only did I need the rest, but I was struggling with the decision to leave the music ministry and become a preacher. I called Dr. Forbes Yarborough, beloved former professor at Oklahoma Baptist University, for counsel about my decision. He mailed me a chapter from a book by Charles Haddon Spurgeon.

The famed Spurgeon lectured to his students in chapel each week at the school that bears his name. Those lectures comprise a classic book called *Lectures to My Students.* One chapter, "How to Know the Call to the Ministry," was just right for me. The chapter gave five ways to know if you are called. I read the chapter in fifteen minutes, closed the book, and said, "*I have the call.*" That was more than fifty years ago, and I've never looked back. Here are the five ways:

Desire. Psalms 37:4 says, "Take delight in the Lord, and He will give you your heart's desires." If we truly do delight in the Lord, our desires will become the same as His. When our passion is to love Him and please Him, as two streams converge into one river, so will our desires become one with His. If Jesus is your passion, your desire to preach is His desire for you as well. If you truly love the Lord, are trying to know His will and have a burning desire to preach that will not let you go, you have a call from God.

There was a time when I was passionate about the music ministry. Simultaneously that passion began to fade, and a new passion to preach began to grow. I wanted it more than anything else, and I knew it to be the call of God. He will put the desire in the sincere heart to do what He wants done. It is not a fleeting thing. It is an impression, a passion that will not let you go.

I like to call it a *"holy hunch."* How do you know when you're in love? You just know. How do you know when God is calling you to preach? You just know. If you can do anything else except preach, by all means, don't preach. But if the passion is unrelenting, then you must preach. If it is your all-consuming, magnificent obsession, *just do it.*

There was a time when leading worship gave great fulfillment. But that fulfillment began to fade, and a passion to preach began to grow. With the increasing passion of the *new* always comes a lessening of the *old*.

Ability. This is not to say you will be the greatest public speaker in the history of mankind. It is to say that God gives us some natural abilities and gifts to do what He wants us to do. He doesn't call blind men to be truck drivers or deaf women to be music critics. If you have the ability to organize your thoughts and express them, let alone exceptional skill in communication, and a passion to proclaim the gospel, the call of God is indicated.

Opportunity. Where God leads us to serve and gifts us to serve, He provides opportunity to serve. Open and closed doors are important in reading the hand of God in our lives. The more I considered preaching, the more opportunities I had to preach. And I was faithful to every one of them—street corners, jails, retirement homes, Sunday morning Bible study classes—everything. God will open the door for you to do what He wants you to do. A closed door is an indication of a spiritual detour, wrong timing, or a clear "no."

Blessing. The confirmation of God comes upon a person who is walking in His will. Again, this does not mean you will have a hundred decisions every time you preach. Conversely, it does mean, if you preach a hundred times with no apparent results, you might need to rethink driving that truck.

Many a man has seen a burning sign in the sky that said "GPC," which he interpreted to mean "Go preach Christ," when it actually meant, "Go plow corn." There should be some degree of visible affirmation upon your ministry as you pursue what you think you're supposed to do.

A gift is best determined by what you do naturally, what you do well, and what God blesses. I have not been called to the counseling ministry because I don't particularly enjoy counseling, and I'm certainly not very good at it.

No one ever came back to say, "You changed my life," after I counseled with them. But many persons have greeted me at the door after I preached and said, "That really impacted my life."

Others' Opinions. Talk to the saints of God. Discuss your decision with those in whom you have great spiritual confidence. Ask their advice; seek their counsel. Let them hear your heart and listen to them.

"It's hard enough to preach when you know you're called without *trying* to preach if you're not sure."

But I think it's *also true* that God doesn't get upset with us for trying to do what we *think* we should do. But seek counsel and watch for the hand of God. He will make clear His will for your life. If these five tests add up to a yes, don't wait a minute more: start writing that sermon!

Chapter 13

VARIOUS KINDS OF MINISTRY

When we think of the call to the ministry, we normally think first of a preaching ministry as pastor of a church. Today, however, there are hundreds of opportunities to serve the Lord in full-time ministry other than being a preaching pastor of a local church.

Ministries abound—youth, music, education, counseling, missions—to name a few. On our church staff is an orchestra director, a program coordinator, an activities director, a prayer coordinator, a retreat ministry director, a full-time sound technician, a reprographics person, a missions director, a day care director, a school administrator, and many others. In Houston's First many dedicated men and women also serve in support roles as assistants and associates.

I am privileged to be part of a denomination that has the most expansive and effective worldwide missions ministry in history. To ensure minimizing turnover and maximizing longevity of service, we have a high standard. Frankly, the majority of people who apply to our International Mission Board are turned down for various reasons.

My counsel is always this: If you are turned down by our board and are firm in your call, then go some other way. Go with an independent board, raise your own support, move overseas and get a job, but somehow get to the field to which God has called you.

There are a thousand ways to serve the Lord in full-time ministry—architects, church planters, missionary aviation pilots, television producers, sports ministries, tent makers, etc. If you are called of God, somewhere in the world there's a place to use your gifts, somewhere a need that only you can fill. Don't give up because you might not fit the stereotype of a preacher. Find God's tailor-made will for you and do it.

My own son Timothy was called into full-time Christian service at age fourteen. He spent several years in frustration because he did not fit the mold of the traditional eight-to-five church staff member. Tim had a passion for his generation—not just those who happened to be age fifteen to thirty but particularly those with green hair and rings in their noses—the unreached, unloved untouchables, that "business as usual" ministries will never reach.

So Tim organized a Christian rock band because rock music is the language they speak. For four years he worked as a missionary with Youth with a Mission in Amsterdam, Holland, and Auckland, New Zealand. They traveled across two continents playing in nightclubs, concerts, brothels, street corners—anywhere anyone would listen.

And it wasn't contemporary praise and worship. It was "smash nose," "in your face," "you're going to hell," "you need to quit your drugs and get saved and do it right now" kind of music. Yes, they were cursed at, beat up, and thrown out, but they won hundreds of kids to Christ. Tim didn't do it the usual way but God's special, unique way, just for him. My grandson Jonathon didn't fit the mold of the standard student ministry he had considered. He is today extremely blessed as an agricultural missionary.

Don't be deterred. If God has called you, God will use you. If you can't find a ministry, create one. Don't just drift away from your call. Better to be on a side street in Calcutta in God's will than in the White House out of it. If you're called to be a servant of the King, don't stoop to be president.

The body of Christ has many parts, and the toes are just as important as the fingers. The most important parts of the body are the least glamorous. We can live without beautiful hair and pretty eyes but not without our kidneys and liver.

How can I preach a sermon unless someone operates the sound system or projects its illustrations on the video screen? My executive pastor ran the day-by-day operations of our church. My administrative assistant took care of every detail within that ministry. Both were priceless treasures to my ministry. Neither had their name in lights.

Nor can the importance of lay ministry or bi-vocational ministry be overstated. Some of the biggest work of the kingdom is done in some of the smallest places.

> But unto every one of us is given grace according to the measure of the gift of Christ. Wherefore he saith, When he ascended up on high, he led captivity captive, and gave gifts unto men. (Now that he ascended, what is it but that he also descended first into the lower parts of the earth? He that descended is the same also that ascended up far above all heavens, that he might fill all things.) And he gave some, apostles; and some, prophets; and some, evangelists; and some, pastors and teachers; For the perfecting of the saints, for the work of the ministry, for the edifying of the body of Christ: Till we all come in the unity of the faith, and of the knowledge of the Son of God, unto a perfect man, unto the measure of the stature of the fullness of Christ: That we henceforth be no more children, tossed to and fro, and carried about with every wind of doctrine, by the slight of men, and cunning craftiness, whereby they lie in wait to deceive. (Eph. 4:7–14)

Chapter 14

MINISTERING IN YOUR GIFTEDNESS

What God wants you to do, He has gifted you to do. If there's one thing you don't want to do, it's walk in Saul's armor. David grew up in the fields. He knew the ministry God wanted him to do by what He had given him to do it with. A stick, a sling, a rock—that was stuff of the earth, right on the ground, right in the field. Slingshots came naturally to David. Spears and shields did not.

It's nothing to be ashamed of to have the security to say of a ministry position, "This is not me; this is not who I am." Some of the most effective ministers and staffers I have known changed ministries. Not masters: ministries. Some of the best pitchers in the big leagues started out as first basemen.

There are many positions on God's team, lots of instruments in His orchestra. And the song is never as beautiful if even one member is playing the wrong instrument. Your gift is important to the body of Christ, both locally and universally. And often the most obscure gifts are the most important. I think you can do just fine without your "baby blues." Your liver? That's another matter.

The question then is, How do I know my spiritual gift? I know I'm called to play in the orchestra, now what chair? The answer is easy: you know your gift by what comes naturally and by what God blesses. Here is another way to say it: ease and effectiveness.

What comes naturally to you? What do you do really well when you're just being you? Are you a natural-born salesman? Maybe an evangelist. Is the guitar your first love? Maybe the praise band. An accountant? Perhaps a church administrator. Accountants have the ability to see the bottom line and make everything fit together.

Some are natural-born caregivers. Hospitals and shut-ins need just that from a caring minister of pastoral care. A high school coach can make a terrific activities minister for a church. First and foremost, you have to love what you do. If you're miserable, if you really hate your job, you're doing the wrong job.

The second indicator of your giftedness is God's blessing as you perform your ministry. People often say, "You really helped me," after I preach. No one ever said those words after a counseling session. Preaching? Want the truth? It's the easiest thing I do. Counseling? Well, how long do you have?

Whatever position you play, there will be a great deal of fulfillment and some measure of Divine approval. God's affirmation doesn't necessarily translate to a hundred converts after every sermon, nor does it translate to none—ever. There will always be some degree of tangible blessing on the man or woman who is ministering in God's perfect will.

And God doesn't want you to struggle to know what that is. He *wants* you to know His will more than *you* want to know it. And He's trying to make it obvious to you.

Naturalness and blessing—what you like, coupled with what God honors, is the key to ministering in your giftedness. If that's not what you're doing, make a change.

God's call to any ministry is always a call to go in faith. I've never gotten over the impact of Abraham's response to God's call to leave his home and go to a land, not knowing where he was going.

I could not name all the men and women I've met through the years who told me they were called into special service and never did it. They all deeply regret it.

Every great decision is made in faith. The visible affirmation comes after the commitment.

If you do it naturally, enjoy it, and it makes an impact, you should probably start doing it in faith, for Him, full time, right now. Serving the Lord is wonderful.

Chapter 15

SEMINARY EDUCATION

A call to preach is a call to prepare to preach. Unquestionably, Moses is the overpowering figure on the pages of the Old Testament. Moses earned two Ph.D.s. His first was in the culture of Egypt. He learned literature and history, law, warfare, leadership and the arts, and he learned them from the best. But these things do not a prophet make.

These experiences constituted the first forty years of his life, but Moses was not yet ready to serve. A forty-year Ph.D. in the arts and humanities must be followed by a forty-year Ph.D. in spiritual maturity.

Moses had to unlearn much of what he had learned. He had to learn to depend more on what God *would teach* him than what men *had taught* him. So it was off to the back side of the desert for another forty years. There he tended sheep, waited on God, and learned His ways.

Finally, toughened in the steel of his soul, Moses was ready to lead. But the Exodus from Egypt and the forty years in the wilderness that followed were only the last phase of his life. Leading two million people through the wilderness journey from Egypt to Canaan was but the tip of the iceberg of the eighty years that preceded it.

The apostle Paul was a master in Israel, a Hebrew of the Hebrews, a Pharisee of the Pharisees, but he too had a lot to learn. Only after the years in Arabia alone with God was he ready to confront the scholars at Athens and Rome with the message of the cross.

And what of our Lord? Jesus had the greatest earthly ministry the world would ever know, yet it lasted only three years. What was Jesus doing the first thirty years of His life? Preparing.

Though He was God, He laid aside all He inherently was and restricted Himself to the limitations of a man. He did not just study *as an example*; He studied because He *had* to. He did not confound the teachers of the law by accident.

Yes, God empowered Him; yes, God spoke through Him; and, yes, He was God in the flesh, but still He prepared. He searched the Scriptures and *grew* in stature and favor with God and man. He grew in every way for thirty years.

No, He was not, as some liberal scholars suggest, only coming to an awareness of His godhood. He *was* God and *knew* He was God. But He chose to lay aside what was inherently His for thirty years to study, pray, fast, and prepare Himself for His ministry as a man. The God-Man.

Think of it, thirty years of preparation, and a three-year ministry. But what a ministry He had! Today we go to seminary for three years and set out on a thirty-year ministry. I wonder if we've got it right.

I have often wondered whether Jesus was tempted to begin His ministry early. What a tremendous youth evangelist He would have made at age twenty-two. What a terrific *new media* pastor at twenty-five, even a *mega*-pastor at twenty-eight. But He wasn't in a hurry. He knew the value of preparation. The call to serve is always a call to *prepare to serve*.

The question, then, is the importance of a seminary education. To be sure, there are those whom God has greatly used who did not attend seminary. Billy Graham did not; Wendell Estep, longtime pastor of the great First Baptist Church of Columbia, South Carolina, did not; nor did Winfred Moore of the great First Baptist Church of Amarillo, Texas; and certainly numbers of others. But for every person like them—uniquely gifted to gain their education outside the traditional channels of seminary classrooms—there are many who are not.

By all means do everything possible to secure a seminary education. Opportunities abound. Extension campuses, online—to name a few. Southern Baptists operate six of the greatest seminaries in the world. And thanks to the contribution by thousands of Southern Baptist churches through the Cooperative Program, one can attend them comparatively inexpensively. And there are many others, such as Dallas Theological, Asbury, MidAmerica, and Regents, to name a few.

Pay the price and get the education. You'll be usable in a far greater way if you do. God can use a dull axe, but He can use a sharp one a whole lot better.

But if the opportunity eludes you, seek God with all your heart, serve Him in the beauty of holiness, be faithful to every opportunity, and He will still use you in a wonderful way.

Through the years I've had the joy of personal study with many gifted seminary professors. Personal study of the right books can also make accessible to you much of the information you will find in the classroom. And of course keep your eyes and ears open. Always be a learner.

Good preparation does not ensure great usability. But the chances of great usability are severely limited when formal education is lacking.

Looking back, there are three things I wish I had done differently.

- Prayed more.
- Remembered people's names better.
- Gone to seminary.

I've made the effort to compensate through books and personal mentoring. But I shall always regret not learning the languages, not being in the academic environment, and not having the opportunity to make lifetime friendships with seminary classmates.

My son-in-law and grandsons are graduates of Southwestern Seminary, Southern Seminary, and Regents Seminary. I love them a lot and envy them just a little.

Chapter 16

A TOUCH OF CHARISMA

Charisma. What a fascinating word. It is most often used in the secular sense with a gifted leader, movie star, or singer. What do we mean when we say, "This woman has charisma; that man has charisma"?

The dictionary defines *charisma* as "grace" or "favor," a special quality that captures the popular imagination and inspires allegiance and devotion.

Charisma makes people want to be in your presence and want to please you.

Let me go beyond that and attempt to define *charisma* as it relates to the ministry. Charisma is a God-given touch that attracts people to you and makes them want to do what you want them to.

In the life of a man of God, it is a special touch that makes the persuasion of the gospel easier when the anointing of the Holy Spirit rests upon a gifted and charismatic leader.

Any spiritual gift may be used or abused. A gifted leader can use his God-given gift to sing for the Lord or sing in a bar. A charismatic man can persuade a woman into the church house or into the bedroom.

He can use the gift of administration to run a Sunday school department or run a business. A good salesman can persuade you to buy a car or, sanctified by the Holy Spirit, to accept Jesus as your Savior. The temptation is to use the gift for selfish purposes, or perhaps even worse, use the gift in ministry while not depending on the power of the Holy Spirit.

Can a person develop charisma? Perhaps. But assuredly it is the anointing of the Holy Spirit on a person's life that enables them to be a most effective instrument through which the Spirit can convince people to follow Christ.

The ability to convince a person to accept Christ, live a holy life, join the church, give his money, develop a prayer life, or *do anything* is ultimately done only through the power of the Holy Spirit. But the wise minister will enhance every tangible faculty with which God has endowed him by that Spirit to maximize the effectiveness of his ministry.

Certainly we can prepare our best, educate ourselves, have a pleasing appearance, a heart filled with the love of Christ *and* the power of the Holy Spirit. Yet there are those whom God has endowed with an extra measure of charisma. The bad news is that it might be used for secular, even evil, purposes. The good news is: when all the faculties of one's personhood are honed to a fine edge and the Spirit of God anoints their ministry, that person to whom God has given special charisma has awesome potential for extraordinary usefulness in the kingdom of God.

Billy Graham had more charisma than any person I have ever known.

Listen to those old films and videos from the fifties and sixties. No one ever came close to Billy. Just look at him. Just watch him open the Bible, and you'll want to run down the aisle.

But Billy Graham never depended on his looks, authority, or charisma. He took God seriously, but he never took himself seriously. The recipient of uncountable honorary degrees, he never became Dr. B. Franklin Graham. He was always just Billy the kid. Billy, the guy who lived next door. He never went to seminary, but he moved the world. All that he was, was God's. Billy Graham lived on his knees and never lost his anointing.

I knew an evangelist in the fifties who stuttered and had no charisma. I know a pastor today who stutters. No charisma there. But what an awesome anointing of God's power rests on both!

If you have it, it's extraordinary, rare, special, and potentially dangerous. Be careful here: to whom much is given, much is required. And those who fail here will have a lot for which to be accountable.

If you have it, the devil will shoot at you extra hard. He really wants you. I know some of the guys he actually hit. And it's all over. Be careful. Walk in humility and holiness.

Chapter 17

THE PASTOR'S PERSONALITY

Preachers can be downright obnoxious people. Someone ought to write a book entitled *Games Preachers Play*. The first chapter could be entitled, "Don't Act like a Preacher."

Most ministers have a preconceived image of how a clergyman should act, dress, walk, talk, and live. Trying to fit the mold and fulfill the image often takes them completely out of their own personality and into something unnatural.

That, "I have never met a preacher I really felt comfortable around," has been said too many times. "Dr. Holy Joe," "Professor Bottletop," and "The Right Reverend Whistlebritches" can turn off more people than all the good gospel preaching in the world can turn on.

Preaching is "truth through a personality;" the proclamation of God's Word through a human instrumentality. But if that instrument turns off his hearers, they may never get beyond *him* to the *truth* he is attempting to communicate.

The likability factor is huge. If they don't like you, they're never going to get past *you* to *your message*.

Don't try to fit the image. Throw away the mold. Quit playing "Reverend Minister." Don't hide behind a clerical façade. Act natural. Be believable. Act like a normal human being. Relax and be yourself.

Lay off the high-sounding ecclesiological phrases. You are probably scaring away half of your potential hearers.

See this scene. It is repeated a thousand times every Sunday in the parking lots and the hallways of our churches. The preacher greets the people with a warm and sunny "Good morning, Joe." He is cheery and natural. He is himself. But when he walks out on the platform, he becomes someone else.

His voice gets a holy quiver, and his vocabulary is strictly high church. After church he is a normal human being again, with a natural style and everyday vocabulary. The people have seen him turn it *on* and turn it *off.*

The preacher tells the people their faith should be a part of their everyday lives. They should be a witness in the home, in the school, and on the job. But the old Sunday morning switcheroo belies that idea. He plays the religion game for an hour on Sunday and then steps back into the real world for the rest of the week. If the preacher separates the two worlds, how can the people not be expected to do the same?

Perhaps there is so little penetration of the gospel into the secular world where people really live, for this very reason. And is it really any wonder?

To emulate the preconceived universal image of the preacher is to frustrate God's unique plan for your ministry. Remember, He made you like you are, and probably put you where you are, when He put you there, because there are more people at that time and in that place who can relate to you than anywhere else in the world. When you try to become someone other than who you are, you thwart what God wants to do through you. Don't act like you think a preacher is supposed to act. Act like you.

Someone said, "So live that no one will ever suspect you're a preacher. But if they find out you are, *they won't be surprised.*"

Do you think there is no universal preacher image? Think again. No movie or television program ever shows a sharp, successful-looking businessman type in the role of a preacher. Never! He is always a Catholic priest; a phony; a hick from the sticks; or a Tweedle-dee, Tweedle-dum, Mr. Milquetoast. These are the world's images of a preacher.

As a pastor, it is most important to be approachable, and *approachable* means likable.

Shortly before that fatal trip to Dallas, Jackie Kennedy reminded her husband, President John F. Kennedy, to be warm and gracious with the throngs of people they expected to encounter.

"Dear," she said, "don't be in a hurry. Take plenty of time and give the people your undivided attention one at a time. *Walk slowly through the crowds.*" Good advice for a president or a preacher.

When you stand before a large group, or a long line, give each person your undivided attention until each one is through speaking to you. Better to let fifteen walk away, unwilling to wait because you were genuinely interested in one, than to give partial attention to fifteen.

Take time for individuals, classes, and small groups, as well as large groups. Arrive early. Be relaxed. Listen well. Don't talk to one person while staring over their shoulder to see who else is waiting. Be genuinely interested in the individual. Never make a grand entry. If you cannot arrive on time, get there *early* but *never late.*

Genuine humility and sincere Christian sweetness are a rare combination in the personality of far too few. Speak softly; look straight into people's eyes. Give them warmth and genuine attention.

Walk slowly through the crowds. Remember preaching is "truth through a personality." If people can't get past the personality, they'll never get to the truth. If they don't like you (and nobody likes a phony), they won't have a shot at liking what you have to say.

Lighten up. Cheer up and *be you.* After all you're what God had in mind when He made you.

Chapter 18

A TEACHABLE SPIRIT

The day you think you've arrived is the day your ministry will begin to leave. Few things are more important to know than that you *don't know much*. A teachable spirit is inseparably linked to humility, and humility is an absolute essential in usefulness. Don't ever think a teachable spirit is a side issue in the effectiveness of ministry; it may well be the heart of it.

Since Charles G. Finney began mass evangelism over two centuries ago, there has always been a world-class evangelist with an *heir apparent* on the scene. Through the Finneys, Moodys, Sundays, and Grahams, it's always been true. Until now!!

Let me put it bluntly. Where is the next Billy Graham? Dr. Graham is beyond ninety years of age. Why, at the most critical juncture in American history, has the cycle been broken? Why is there no heir apparent to Dr. Graham?

I believe the reason is that *someone missed it!* Moreover, I think I know *who* that someone was, or at least one of the two whom it *may* have been.

Years ago I had the privilege of organizing a great citywide evangelistic crusade in a large Midwestern city. In spite of ice storms, the arena was packed night after night. Hundreds made decisions for Christ as the Spirit of God moved in a tremendous way. We asked the local newspaper to cover the crusade, to no avail.

The evangelist said, "I'll get the coverage." We tried to talk him out of it. The next day he went to the editor and placed his scrapbooks on his desk.

"See the front-page coverage I've had in other crusades," he said. The editor, obviously agitated, said, "All right, we'll cover you."

That night a reporter attended the crusade and took pictures. The problem was, he took them from the back of the platform, showing only the evangelist's back, and the one empty spot in the balcony. The next afternoon, that picture was on the front page.

The evening the reporter and photographer were present, the evangelist had called down some teenagers for moving around. The headline of the article read, "Shut up and sit down, or we'll throw you out," Evangelist Tells Local Teens.

Rather than being broken, the poor man came to the pulpit that night, held up the front page, and said, "Look at the coverage we got. The preachers couldn't get it, but I got it."

I don't think he was smart enough to figure out that he had been insulted. I have grieved over this man. He knew it all.

One night after a service, we invited him to our home for dinner. He looked over the buffet as my wife said, "I hope you like it." He responded, "Lady, I don't like a thing you've got."

Although I never knew a man with more authority and power in his preaching, today he has only a limited ministry. The reason? No humility. No teachable spirit. No long-term ministry.

Let me tell you about another evangelist who may have been "the man who missed it."

Years ago I worked with an evangelist whose ministry I helped to birth. I wrote his first sermon, taught him to outline and to preach. I taught him how to set up a crusade and give an invitation. I never knew a young preacher who had the hand of God upon his life as did he.

When he walked to the pulpit, the entire auditorium was charged with spiritual electricity. I've seen him give an invitation without a sermon and watched people pour down the aisles. But he was a novice. It was too much, too fast, and he never learned the great lesson of humility. Before he was twenty-five years of age, he knew it all.

I've seen him fly across the country to spend an entire day with me, to seek my counsel about decisions in his ministry, only to argue with me the whole time, saying what I was telling him was wrong, go back and do what he wanted to do in the first place.

Today he also enjoys only a limited ministry.

One of these two men, I believe with all my heart, may well have been the next Billy Graham.

I don't intend to write a book on *My Humility and How I Obtained It*, but let me tell you with all candor that to this very day it is regularly my pleasure to seek counsel and advice, and not only to accept correction but to invite it.

A teachable spirit is an indispensable part of effective ministry.

> "Mankind, He has told you what is good and what it is the LORD requires of you: to act justly, to love faithfulness, and to walk humbly with your God." (Mic. 6:8)

Chapter 19

YOU AND YOUR PEOPLE SKILLS

S omeone once said, "The ministry would be a piece of cake if it weren't for
the people." Leaky roofs and broken pipes are more easily fixed than broken
relationships. The answer obviously lies in not letting the pipes get broken in
the first place. Nothing is more important in the ministry than the ability of
the pastor to get along with people.

Perhaps the best place to start in relating to others is to put yourself in their
shoes. I think I remember something about a Golden Rule.

Treating others as you want to be treated, caring enough to know where
they're coming from, and respecting it—this is the heart of getting along with
people.

Everyone is "coming from some place." Each person thinks as he does for
a reason. Take the time to know him. What's going on his world? What forces
have shaped his life? What was happening in the world around him when he
was about age twelve? We tend to get locked in to the attitudes and perspectives
that shaped our lives at that age.

As pastor, you don't always have to be Mr. Right, but you do have to be
Mr. Gracious. Surprise, surprise, dear pastor friend, you just could be wrong.
Someone else's opinion might be the right one. Listen more than you talk.
Be open to the other person's view, and when he differs, be gracious in your

response. "Mary, have you considered this?" "Joe, let's look at it from this perspective." "Sue, could it possibly be that . . ."

Montaigne, the French philosopher, said, "My life has been filled with terrible things: most of which never happened." May I add, "My ministry has been filled with terrible conflict: none of which ever happened."

That person who seems to be your enemy may just be a friend you haven't nurtured yet. As God's children and certainly as his spiritual leaders, we must be the initiators of reconciliation and the encouragers of friendship.

Within the membership of Houston's First was a highly regarded man who for years was a great encourager and supporter. The introduction of a style of music into our worship services to which he objected turned him into a critic, at best, if not an opponent.

One night I called to ask for an appointment. Visiting him in his home, I began by saying I had obviously offended him. I knew he was upset with me, and I wished not only to apologize but also to have the opportunity to share our views and see if we could make at least *some* progress toward a meeting of the minds. While we made only slight progress in our differences about music, we made great progress in our friendship.

The wise pastor will speak his mind with firm conviction but with gracious latitude for the opinions of those who disagree.

When people do a *poor* job, lovingly show them a better way and encourage their potential. When they do a *good* job, commend them personally and publicly. When they are down, encourage them; when they are wrong, teach them.

Years ago Billy Graham arrived in London, after an overnight flight, to preach a citywide crusade in Harringay Arena. Tired and caught by surprise, Dr. Graham was immediately whisked away to do an interview on national television. It was, in fact, not an interview but an ambush.

Four liberals were waiting to debate him. Dr. Graham did not pretend to be an intellect, but the kindness and humility of his spirit completely disarmed everyone.

The next morning *The London Times* carried an account of the debate. The closing line of the article said, "Dr. Graham lost the debate, but he won the hearts of England."

Even when you are wrong, and you will be; even when you lose, and you will lose, you must ingratiate yourself to your people and live to serve another day. Tenderness of spirit and genuine humility are always in order. When you are wrong, admit it. When you blow it, acknowledge it. When you lose, get over it. When you don't know, ask for help. When you are corrected, accept it.

Perhaps no element contributes more to developing good people skills than a true love for people. Ask yourself this question: Do I see people as objects, as prizes to be won, as statistics to be added, that my denominational paper might write an article about my growing church, enticing a larger church to call me as pastor? Or do I see people as sheep in need of a shepherd?

A real shepherd never sacrifices the feelings of his sheep for his own; a true shepherd *lays down his life for his sheep*. A self-serving shepherd *drives* his sheep; a true shepherd *leads* his sheep. A hired shepherd compromises for the sake of popularity; a God-called shepherd speaks the truth and defends his sheep at any cost.

Our heavenly Shepherd gave us the perfect example in every personal relationship. The successful undershepherd will learn to follow it.

> A thief comes only to steal and to kill and to destroy. I have come that they may have life and have it in abundance. "I am the good shepherd. The good shepherd lays down his life for the sheep. The hired man, since he is not the shepherd and doesn't own the sheep, leaves them and runs away when he sees a wolf coming. The wolf then snatches and scatters them. This happens because he is a hired man and doesn't care about the sheep. "I am the good shepherd. I know My own sheep, and they know Me. (John 10:10–14)

Chapter 20

THE PASTOR'S HOME

The pastor's relationship with his family is the essential part of his ministry. The pastor and his family are subject to the same trials and temptations as other families. Being in the ministry is no guarantee of rearing a perfect family. To the contrary, it can be a detriment. This, of course, in no way suggests a pastor should not have a family, although many single men are effective pastors. Our Lord and the apostle Paul, to name two, were incomparable shepherds of the flock. And certainly the qualification (the husband of one wife), addressed elsewhere, does not restrict the pastorate to those who are married.

There is, however, something special about a pastor with a good family. The love and care he receives *from* them and the nurture he gives *to* them can be important factors in his spiritual development as undershepherd to the family of God.

"If anyone does not know how to manage his own household, how will he take care of God's church?" (1 Tim. 3:5). And, of course, there is enhanced credibility when a happily married pastor speaks on matters of marriage and family life.

Perhaps no other factor has the negative influence on the family as does the feeling of "having to perform." The daily pressure of life in the spotlight brings added stress to family life—in addition to those already existing in the culture.

Dear pastor, be exceedingly clear with your family and your congregation that neither your spouse nor your children must ever feel any pressure to *do* or to *be* anything for any other reason than their love for the Lord Jesus.

When you deal with a pastor search committee and they ask if your wife will teach Sunday school or play the church piano, let them know lovingly but firmly that it will be her decision if she so chooses and senses God's leadership. The church must understand they are not calling two staff members. They are calling a pastor whose wife graciously serves at her pleasure and God's bidding.

The same applies to the pastor's children. They are all different, aren't they? Our daughter Ginger was exactly like her mother, happily serving the Lord with no sense of pressure because of who she was. Our sons, however, were quite different. Both felt a self-imposed sense of real pressure. They chose different routes to find their "way." But the Lord is gracious, and His promises are faithful.

Proverbs 22:6, "Teach a youth about the way he should go; even when he is old he will not depart from it," is not just a promise to parents that consistent spiritual nurturing assures our children will ultimately be godly. It is also a warning that leaving a child to his own willfulness is the path to destruction. Parenting involves a process of making disciples of our children. We teach obedience in the home as a pattern of authority in order to bring them to salvation and discipleship. Godly discipline provides an umbrella of protection under which a child learns to obey God during the days of greatest vulnerability.

Relate to your children the same way you relate to your wife. Let them be themselves. Train them, teach them, and guide them, and then let them make their choices, take their knocks, and learn to take responsibility for their own actions. They will usually test the boundaries. But when you have raised them in the things of God to the best of your ability, you have to release them to the Lord to find their own way.

As pastor you will have constant tension between the time required to meet the needs of your congregation and your family. The answer? Family first!

You can always find someone to help do the work of the church, but no one can love your wife and raise your children except you. Someone else can make a hospital visit for you, but no one else can go to the Little League game. That church committee can meet without you, but your daughter must never perform that piano recital without your being there.

Date nights with your spouse and family times with your kids must be scheduled as priorities in your week. Many are the times I have declined an engagement saying, "I am sorry, I have another appointment." That appointment was often with my family, and I still consider it most important of all.

God's people are gracious and forgiving, and I have even known a few instances where a pastor survived divorce during his pastorate; however, those situations are few and far between. Lose your family and you will likely lose your ministry.

And don't forget those family vacations. You are not a hero if you never take a vacation. In fact, you are not even smart. Take every day you have coming. Our Lord regularly drew apart from the pressures of ministry, and so must you. It is best not to take three or four short five-day mini-vacations through the year; take it all at once. Get away three or four weeks. Change locations, change pace, don't call back to the office, and don't preach on your vacation. You and your family need a real vacation, and your church will be better for it.

I couldn't count the times I have returned from vacation to hear my people say, "Preacher, you were really on fire today. You ought to go on vacation more often!" Surprise your family. Do fun things. Let your family know you are a regular dad, and they are first in your life.

Chapter 21

THE MINISTRY WIFE

My wife, Uldine, is the dearest Christian I know. She is an awesome example of how a ministry wife should view her role, and she was adored by our congregation. To their credit, our people never placed undue expectations on her simply because she was the pastor's wife. She graciously served the Lord because that was her heart.

For nearly thirty of my thirty-five years as a pastor, she taught a Bible class. Her scrapbook is filled with letters from young adults whose lives she touched when they were her students. There were seasons when she did not teach simply because she chose to serve in other ways. But never did she feel the pressure that she *must* serve in a particular area.

She was comfortably seated in the worship center with our beloved congregation 98 percent of the time. Other times she felt total freedom to rest. No legalistic formula for attendance, as it should be.

She was not the church fashion trendsetter. She neither underdressed nor overdressed. Sometimes casual, sometimes dressy. But she always looked like a million dollars and was an encouragement and inspiration to the women of our church. Uldine's father was a minister, and he and her mother did a terrific job training her. In a sentence they gave her the *freedom to be herself.*

I want you to hear the testimony of my beloved helpmate of fifty-seven years, written to the special women of God who stand by their husbands:

One of the verses that has given me great pleasure through the years is "The share of the one who goes into battle is to be the same as the share of the one who remains with the supplies. They will share equally" (1 Sam. 30:24).

I stayed with the supplies, like "keeping the homefront," while John went to battle—you know, deacons meeting, things like that. We both shared alike!

A thousand volumes could not contain my gratitude to God for choosing me to be a preacher's daughter and a ministry wife. Serving Jesus side by side has been my life from the beginning. My parents were totally committed to Christ and the work of His church. Dad pastored churches in ten states, seven while I was living at home. I had fun being a P.K. In fact, I always thought it was special. I even liked the silly jokes and sly remarks about preachers' kids and deacons' kids. It is, and has always been, good to be with God's wonderful people. And now being a ministry wife is like graduate school, a bigger challenge and greater blessing.

A ministry wife is not something I do; rather, it is someone I am. As I look back on my life, I have focused on Jesus and who I am in Him. I don't ever want to search for temporary significance in something in which I am presently involved, either at church or in the workplace. I find total satisfaction in Christ and the joy of becoming more like Him every day.

He fills my life with warmth and color. "The result of righteousness will be peace; the effect of righteousness will be quiet confidence forever" (Isa. 32:17).

The congregation is looking to us to lead the way to victory. I believe my relationship with my husband is a mirror of my relationship with Jesus. How can we lead God's people if things are not right at home? Communion with Jesus through reading His Word, through prayer, through rest and proper nutrition are basic. Our life's purpose, as seen in the life of Jesus, is to love one another, to be kind, to be forgiving, and to serve joyfully. Loving Jesus, my husband, and myself will be my foundation for loving His people and His work.

A few years ago, the wife of our student pastor and I were talking. The subject turned toward our husbands and prayer. She said, "I don't seem to know how to pray for my husband so I guess I don't pray for him at all. Do you ever pray for your husband?" "Darling," I said, "maybe 90 percent of my prayers are for my husband." I am so sorry to say, they are not married today. Pray! Pray for your husband and pray together.

Love the Lord with all your heart, soul, and mind. Love your man with all your strength and purpose and passion. And no matter what comes against you, stand strong!

Whatever your hands find to do, do with all your heart, and do it to the glory of God. Surrender your hands and lift them to His resurrection power. What you cannot do, He can and will.

I thank Jesus for coming to live in my heart early in life, for keeping me on "the way" instead of some pointless path. Thank You, Jesus, for the road of grace, and thank you for calling John and me to walk with You.

Let's tell everyone about His redeeming love!

Uldine Bisagno

Chapter 22

MANAGING YOUR TIME

No one but you can control your schedule! The increasing demands of a growing church consistently increase the pressure to choose priorities. As pastors, we are not first of all administrators, pulpiteers, or executives. We are first and foremost "shepherds of the flock." As such, nothing tears at our hearts more than to have to say no to even the smallest need of the least recognized member of our congregation.

Two or three times during my ministry, I have spot-checked the number of demands on my time, calls for attention, and decisions made in the course of an average day. That number is usually around 150.

In my only other pastorate, the First Southern Baptist Church of Del City, Oklahoma, I came to a crisis late in the second year of my five-year tenure. The church had grown from about six hundred to a thousand in attendance, and I was quickly coming to grips with the reality that I *couldn't do it all.*

I couldn't grant every request for an appointment. I couldn't visit every prospect. I couldn't see everyone in the hospital. I couldn't make every meeting, and I couldn't accept every speaking invitation. What to do, what to do? My heart was truly torn. How could I balance the passion in my soul to be a true shepherd to the flock, with the demands on my time for administration, study, prayer, family, and relaxation?

Most pastors go through the same battle as their churches approach eight hundred to a thousand in attendance. The answer is obvious. Like it or not, we must prioritize. Here are some things that have helped me.

1. *Find your security in Christ.* We all want the approval of our people and recoil from their criticism, but frankly, that's life in the fast lane. If you can't take the heat, stay out of the kitchen. You cannot pastor a growing church without going through crisis and criticism, as you begin to move from one-to-one ministry to the necessity of touching people with broader strokes and in larger groups.

People's commendations and approval are nice, but they're not essential. Our priority is pleasing the Master.

2. *Expand your efficiency by expanding your morning.* If you start at 8:00 a.m., it will take you until midnight to get finished. If you start at 5:00 a.m., you might be finished by 4:00 or 5:00 p.m. The principle is simple. The early morning hours are the best. Give them to God. That hour or two in the Word and in your prayer closet will facilitate God's going before you, smoothing the way and working in your behalf. What takes you twelve hours to do alone, God and you can do in six or eight.

3. *Determine your priorities.* Through the years I have been blessed with numerous invitations. I have come to realize that preaching at a seminary or conference of pastors multiplies my ministry and allows me to touch many more church members through them than I ever could by accepting every invitation to preach directly to their churches.

As you develop leaders within your church and learn to delegate authority to them, you will multiply yourself through those whom you empower. You can touch more people by doing so, less often, but in larger groups.

Our church had fifteen to twenty members in the hospital at any given time. Which of them should I visit? This might not be best for you, but it is the plan God gave me, and it served me well: I visited the leaders of our church and their families. I visited those who specifically requested me, and I visited the seriously ill.

A lady once asked, "Pastor, how sick do I have to be before you visit me in the hospital?" "Ma'am," I replied, "you don't want to be that sick."

4. *Learn to control your telephone.* Through the years my administrative assistants learned that for various reasons some people should be put through immediately. Then there are always those calls that need your attention, just not at that particular time.

If there was any question, my secretary would say, "Mrs. Jones, the pastor is unavailable right now. May I help you?" In the majority of cases, she could either answer the question or transfer the caller to a staff member who could. When the need still existed for a return call, she would say, "Thank you; we will call you back before long." Notice she said, *we* will call you back, not *he* will call you back. Within an hour, an associate pastor or assistant would return the call, saying, "The pastor is still busy and asked that I call you back." If the matter lingers, return the call as soon as you are able.

5. *Group your meetings.* You can't attend every class meeting, but you can attend gatherings when several classes are together. You might not visit each Sunday morning Bible study class, but you can attend joint social gatherings or retreats with several classes together. In other words, touch your people in large groups. Walk slowly among the people. Be casual. Don't hurry. Give them your time and attention. Don't rush into the services or rush out. Get there early and visit with your people. Stay until virtually everyone has left. In any gathering you're not going to be able to have a conversation with each individual. Better one meeting with ten classes than one each with ten different classes.

Managing your time is not simply important to your ministry; it is a spiritual discipline essential to your life. Time is God's gift to you. Your use of it is your gift to Him. Managing your time wisely speaks to boundaries, structure, and discipline. Self-control is a fruit of the Holy Spirit. And that goes to the issue of the lordship of Jesus Christ. So take control of your time. Better yet, let Him.

Chapter 23

HOW DO I DRESS?

I recently preached at a nationwide senior adult conference in the beautiful mountains of Glorieta, New Mexico. On the program were The Master's Men, a double quartet from First Baptist Silsbee, Texas. I was deeply impressed to see these men in matching suits, dress shirts, and ties in both evening and morning services—even in that remote, rural setting.

Just two days before, I had preached at a young singles retreat in Texas. Both staffers and young worshippers wore jeans, T-shirts and flip-flops throughout the retreat.

In many denominations, even some Baptists, pastors preach in robes and mantles. I honor them all.

The question is, What's right for me? That is a question to which you will have to find your own answer. Here are some things that will help.

Both "flip-floppers" and "double-breasters" feel it is important to dress in the style of their congregation and those they are trying to reach. I wore a barong each night in a citywide crusade in Manila, Philippines.

On the flip-flop side, there's something to be said for "I don't want anyone to stay home because they feel they don't have anything good enough to wear to our church."

On the "double breaster" side, there's something to be said for "I want to dress in a manner worthy of the dignity and majesty of the God I worship."

The Old Testament goes into great detail describing the elaborate robes worn by the priests who ministered in the temple. In the New, the common people were drawn to Jesus "just as they were." Our Lord always started with people where they were, and I think that may be the key to this puzzle.

If you are in doubt, lean to the side of being a bit too respectful in your dress rather than vice versa. If I'm the only one in the service with a tie, I'm not nearly as uncomfortable as if I'm the only one without. Placed in an unfamiliar setting, always better to be overdressed, than under.

When going to preach in a new church, I call ahead and ask four questions:

1. How does the pastor dress?
2. From which translation of the Bible does he preach?
3. How long do I have to preach?
4. What type of invitation does he extend?

Always follow the pastor's lead in these matters. However you dress, be clean and neat. "Cleanliness is next to godliness" is the most commonly quoted *non-Scripture* in all of Christianity, but it's important nonetheless.

"But the LORD said to Samuel, 'Do not look at his appearance or his stature, because I have rejected him. Man does not see what the LORD sees, for man sees what is visible, but the LORD sees the heart.'" (1 Sam. 16:7)

Chapter 24

MANAGING YOUR PERSONAL FINANCES

A well-known seminary president asked that I include this chapter. "John," he said, "many of our young pastors have no idea how to manage their own finances, let alone teach their people how to manage theirs."

The elephant in the living room is debt, and its mother may well have been an overdose of materialism.

Paul said, "I have learned to be content in whatever circumstances I am" (Phil. 4:11). The quality of your clothes, the size of your home, the model of your car are of no importance. The quality of your family, the size of your heart, the model of your peace—these are treasures.

Start with an evaluation of what's really important. Prepare a budget and stay with it. Cut down your lifestyle to fit the budget. Downsize, eliminate, and consolidate. You can save everywhere. Carpool when you can, cancel some subscriptions, eat out less, buy in bulk, but get your budget down to your income.

Bill Earle said, "If your outgo exceeds your income, your upkeep will be your downfall." Keep God first. And that starts with your tithe.

Everything Jesus said or did exceeded the law, and that includes giving. The New Testament believer, like his Lord, always exceeds the law, fulfills the law, goes beyond the law.

You can't have a prosperous, growing church without money to pay the bills. And if you're not giving biblically, neither will your people. Tithe. And do it *off the top*.

The heart of our faith is the cross, and like Jesus on that first Easter Sunday, when we die, we live. "Seek first the kingdom of God and His righteousness, and all these things will be provided for you" (Matt. 6:33).

Making God's priorities your priority makes you God's priority. You preach it; *now live it*.

Keep only one credit card for emergency and pay it off monthly. Never make only the minimum payment. The minimum monthly credit card payment on a $5,000 balance will take you thirty years to pay off.

That piece of plastic in your billfold is your biggest financial enemy. Every time you pull it out, something psychologically deceptive says, "I'm not really paying for this."

Next time you fill up your car, count out 40 or 50 one-dollar bills, and you'll understand how much you're really paying. And don't try to keep up with the Joneses. If you ever do, they'll just refinance.

Teach your kids to work. They can earn an allowance, better still have a little part-time job. I was throwing 120 newspapers in my neighborhood at age thirteen.

My senior year in college, Uldine and I lived in a 16 x 16-foot cubicle and worked hard. She had a full-time job at a bank. I was carrying twenty credit hours my last semester. I drove a delivery truck for a florist and drove an average of two hundred miles round-trip every night conducting youth revivals.

I have observed that pastors quit the ministry primarily for three reasons: discouragement, immorality, and financial stress. The temptation to make money on the side, which derailed their ministry, was the direct result of not managing their personal finances in an orderly, biblical manner. You can do better. Don't be a statistic.

> For an overseer, as God's administrator, must be blameless, not arrogant, not hot-tempered, not addicted to wine, not a bully, not greedy for money. (Titus 1:7)

> Shepherd God's flock among you, not overseeing out of compulsion but freely; not for money but eagerly. (1 Pet. 5:2)

> No one can be a slave of two masters, since either he will hate one and love the other, or else he will be devoted to one and despise the other. You cannot be slaves of God and of money. This is why I tell you: Don't worry

about your life, what you will eat or what you will drink; or about your body, what you will wear. Isn't life more than food and the body more than clothing? Look at the birds of the sky: They don't sow or reap or gather into barns, yet your heavenly Father feeds them. Aren't you worth more than they? Can any of you add a single cubit to his height by worrying? And why do you worry about clothes? Learn how the wildflowers of the field grow: they don't labor or spin thread. Yet I tell you that not even Solomon in all his splendor was adorned like one of these! If that's how God clothes the grass of the field, which is here today and thrown into the furnace tomorrow, won't He do much more for you—you of little faith? So don't worry, saying, "What will we eat?" or "What will we drink?" or "What will we wear?" For the idolaters eagerly seek all these things, and your heavenly Father knows that you need them. But seek first the kingdom of God and His righteousness, and all these things will be provided for you. (Matt. 6:24–33)

Chapter 25

ESTABLISHING PRIORITIES

So much to do. So little time. Think you're struggling now? Cheer up, it will get worse. As the size of your congregation grows, so will the size of the problem. Somewhere between six hundred and a thousand in attendance, everything changes, and you must come to grips with a new reality. "I can never again touch everyone personally. I have to make choices." For the executive it's no big deal. For a shepherd who's the genuine article, it's heartbreaking.

You have two choices: (1) Turn your back on the Great Commission, quit thinking outreach, stop reaching people; or (2) deal with it. For better or worse the reality is, it's a new day: you must choose your priorities.

Some people will not be seen. Some jobs will not get done. Some ministry will be designated to others.

This will help: Pastor those who pastor others. You must give primary attention to your leaders and their families. Most church members in the hospital may get *only a phone call* from the pastor. The chairman of deacons *gets a visit.*

Favoritism? No. Necessity. In a world of order, we see chains of command:

- Generals command colonels.
- Colonels direct majors.
- Majors lead captains.
- Captains give orders to sergeants.

You must pastor your leaders and their families.

Still feeling guilty about showing favoritism? Go ahead, counsel, visit, do everything. Work eighteen hours a day, and you'll burn out and soon won't be able to minister to anyone except the undertaker. Jesus poured His life into twelve men—and changed the world. He primarily touched people in groups and crowds, even multitudes, but He did it with such love, such humility and grace, they felt comfortable in approaching Him personally as well. It's *not* your job to do *everything*. It *is* your job to see that everything *gets done*. Good staffing, organizational meetings, accountability, structure, and planning that turns into ministry that touches lives—that's your job, your responsibility, and your ministry. The buck stops at your desk.

After years of frustration at this point, my eyes one day fell on a passage of Scripture that set me free.

> I exhort the elders among you: shepherd God's flock among you, not overseeing out of compulsion but freely, according to God's will; not for the money, but eagerly; not lording it over those entrusted to you, but being examples to the flock. And when the chief Shepherd appears, you will receive the unfading crown of glory. (1 Pet. 5:1–4)

Keep in mind the terms *elder, pastor, bishop, overseer,* and *shepherd* are interchangeable for the same person, the God-called leader of the congregation.

Note the pastor is to *be* six things, but he is to *do* only two things. Keep that clearly in view. *Six things to be. Two things to do.*

1. Feed the flock.
2. Take oversight.

I take that to mean, I clearly have only two biblical priorities.

1. Be prepared to teach and preach the Word of God every time I stand before the people. If I haven't prepared, really prepared, God will fill my mouth, but He'll fill it with hot air.
2. Take oversight. Give general direction to the work of the church, and assume ultimate responsibility.

I am to seek the heart of God, point the way, cast the vision, and take responsibility for the work accomplished in the church as we pursue the vision. What happens on my watch is my responsibility. I need to be able to go before the people and say, "Dear church, I have been with the Lord, and this is what I feel He would have us do." Someone has to lead and that someone is you.

Everything else in the life of the church can be done by someone else—a staffer, deacon, teacher, layperson, committee, etc. But no one can study for you, pray for you, and teach and preach for you *but you*. No one!

And no one can seek the heart of God for you *but you*. No one! You are to cast the vision and point the way. The function of leadership is to lead. The purpose of leadership is to get things done.

These two things are your priorities. Do them well. Do them thoroughly. And don't do anything else until you have. When you do, all the rest will fall naturally into place.

Fail here and you will grow a church that is only a caricature of the beautiful church God intended you to pastor when He called you there.

Let me put you at ease. People join a church because it has a whole lot of what they want. In all candor, most are willing to give up whatever it takes to be part of a church they really like. If that means driving farther, a longer walk across the parking lot, less accessibility to the pastor, they don't mind and generally don't expect it anyway.

People are smart, and they know pastors of larger congregations simply have more to do. Follow God's clearly stated prescription for pastoral priorities and be at peace. God can manage the fallout very well, thank you.

Chapter 26

YOUR WEEKLY SCHEDULE

E ven the best train goes nowhere without well-established tracks on which to
run. The minister's weekly schedule should be well thought out and tailor-
made just for him. To arrive at the Sunday terminal of a week well spent means
having run Monday through Saturday on a disciplined track.

There is no right way or wrong way to do this. You must seek God's
leadership and take into consideration your own unique personality.

Through the years you will experiment and make changes before finding
the best approach for you.

I cannot, however, overstate the importance of this: People never *interrupt*
our ministry; they *are* our ministry.

It is not necessarily a compliment for a church member to say, "Our pastor
is always available." One must wonder when he spends time with God, time
with his family, and time in sermon preparation.

On the other hand, nothing is so important as never to allow interruption.
Urgent needs must be met with urgency. Crises must be handled immediately.
What might seem like "just another interruption" to your day might be life and
death to the person on the other end of the line.

Jesus was never too busy for people, and the servant is not greater than his
Lord. When you talk to people, look at them. When you hear people, listen to
them, and don't just give the appearance of looking and listening. Really look.
Really listen. And really care.

The earliest part of the day is always the best, and, as with the tithe off the top, always belongs to God.

The psalmist said it beautifully and well, "Early will I seek thee" (Ps. 63:1 KJV). Before the phone rings, before the distractions of the day, before the morning television news, before the sunrise—these are God's special hours for you. Meet Him in the morning, and He will walk with you through the day.

Again, any schedule is a good schedule as long as it's God directed, works for you, and is subject to interruption. Generally speaking, I have found the following schedule to work for me:

5:00 a.m. Prayer

6:00 a.m. Personal devotional Bible reading

6:30 a.m. Breakfast

7:00 a.m. Exercise

7:30 a.m. Study

10:30 a.m. Dress

11:30 a.m. Arrive at the office for staff luncheons, meetings, office work, dictation, phone calls, etc.

4:00 p.m. Hospital visitation and other visits

6:00 p.m. Dinner

Try to save at least four nights in seven for home and family.

The question of evening priorities is not an easy one. There will always be tension between time for your family, time for yourself, time for meetings, and time for visitation of members and prospective members.

Interruptions will abound. The only thing of which you can be sure about your schedule is that it will not be sure. There will be interruptions: sickness, crises, speaking engagements, committee meetings, travel, etc. But the majority of the time, I have found it possible to maintain the above schedule.

Three of the special gifts God has given to facilitate our ministry are the cell phone, voice mail, and the Internet. Use those hours in your car to make and return phone calls, particularly on the way home from the office. And don't text and drive.

Once you enter your home, do everything possible to maintain the sanctity of family time. This is where you can use your telephone answering machine to great advantage. This is particularly important during mealtimes, which should be unhurried and relaxed. A return call a bit later will normally suffice.

Occasionally I am asked, "What if it's an emergency?" In my ministry I can recall few, if any, true emergencies. It is your responsibility to determine what is and what is not an emergency. If you do not stay in control of your schedule, no one else will do it for you.

Finding the balance between accessibility to your people and responsibility to your family and yourself can be difficult. Our Lord will help you hold the scales.

Chapter 27

SPEAKING ENGAGEMENTS

Which of us have not attended conferences and seminars, crusades and conventions and wished we were the person doing the speaking? At such times there may be a thin line between our pride and a true God-honoring desire to serve.

Early on the young pastor must learn to deal with the issue of outside speaking engagements. There is something heady about the wine of popularity, and it is not completely unlike Satan's subtle whisper, "Ye shall be as gods" (Gen. 3:5 KJV).

When I am invited for any type of preaching engagement, I am immediately flattered.

Newly introduced into this kind of opportunity, the young preacher will be tempted to take everything that comes along. These invitations normally come because your church is growing rapidly or because you're especially good in the pulpit. But if those engagements begin to take you away too often *from* your pulpit, your church will begin to suffer, and your time away will be counterproductive.

In my first pastorate I succumbed to the flattery of many such invitations. One day the Lord gently spoke to me, "John, if you spend all your time traveling and speaking about what is happening in your church; it will quit happening."

Ideally pastor and people will have a clear understanding about time away. For example, three weeks for vacation, two conferences, conventions, two evangelistic crusades, and eight one-night speaking engagements out of the city per year. Determine those numbers in advance, fill in the blanks, and make a serious effort to stay within the guidelines. Speaking engagements outside your church but within your city should not be part of the equation.

Few churches are legalistic at this point, and seldom will a personnel committee be looking over the shoulder of a pastor to monitor his time away. Flexibility on both sides is always appropriate, but the wise pastor will be sensitive to the church's needs and the leadership of the Holy Spirit in this regard.

In some cases a major stream of invitations for such things as marriage seminars or evangelistic crusades may indicate God's leadership into another type of full-time ministry. Be careful here. Be certain there is no ingredient of financial gain or personal popularity involved in your decision.

The lasting work of the kingdom is still centered in the local church.

Chapter 28

GIVING BACK TO YOUR COMMUNITY

"Sow a seed in this ministry and be blessed." "Plant a good faith seed and claim your birthright." That's TV preacher talk for "send me your money and you'll get rich." The secular public is on to it, and it hurts the cause of Christ. Too often we are perceived not as givers but as takers.

Seeker-friendly pastors often do their people a great disservice in going to the *opposite extreme* and not preaching biblical stewardship at all, even though it is the number two theme of the New Testament. Giving back to your community is one way to negate the image of the stereotypical preacher many people hold of pastors and churches.

"All they want is your money" is too often said of us. Other than the arena of the "capital campaign," which is far more a dollars-and-cents issue, I never agree in advance on a set honorarium amount. But like it or not, we are too often viewed as self-serving, just in it for ourselves.

Giving back to your community is not primarily to offset that image but to walk in the steps of the Master. We give, we serve, because we truly care. Pouring out your life for people who don't even know your name, or even that you did it, is filled with satisfaction and blessing.

Cutting the lawn of a neighbor on vacation. Shopping for an elderly person. Doing a favor for a shut-in. Serving on the school board or PTA.

Many things are at the tip of your finger. I was once president of the Southern Baptist Convention Pastor's Conference and once associational pianist. I look back with fond memories of my piano playing days *and smile*. (I only knew five songs.)

When the King of glory became the ultimate servant, He lived out the reality of the cross to which He would go. He who said, "The last will be first" (Matt. 20:16), and "The greatest among you will be your servant" (Matt. 23:11), who came not to a palace but to a manger, not on a white stallion but a donkey, is the One who changed the world.

Serving our fellowman lives out the reality of the Christian faith and impacts our world for the Master. It took awhile for people to recognize who He really was. But they did. We would be wise to do the same.

Don't do it for personal recognition or you lose your reward and impact for Christ. Do it because the love of Jesus has really made a difference in your life. Do it in love, and do it anonymously as much as possible. It not only blesses your heart and honors your Lord; it authenticates your ministry.

Chapter 29

GREENER PASTURES

ountry singer Johnny Lee said it well in his popular song "Looking for Love in All the Wrong Places." Perhaps Al Jolson had the answer for Mr. Lee's futile search: "The bird with feathers of blue is waiting for you back in your own backyard."[1]

The thesis of Mr. Lee's song applies to far too many pastors looking for personal and professional fulfillment in all the wrong places. The happiest, most fulfilling, most productive place for your ministry is potentially right where you are. Quit looking around. Stop glancing over your shoulder, and bloom where you're planted. God wants to bless you in a powerful way, and it is not in that greener pasture across the fence. I write of one of the most common pitfalls of the ministry.

I am told that through the years I have developed a reputation as a "friend of pastors." It is a reputation justly deserved. I do, indeed, love pastors—particularly pastors of small churches and pastors with big problems.

In these fifty-plus years of ministry, I have received hundreds of panic calls from young pastors. "When you hit solid rock," I tell them, "keep on drilling; there is probably a pool of oil just below."

Jesus did not enlist us as kings to sit on thrones but as warriors to fight battles. The hymn writer said it well:

> Must I be carried to the skies
> On flowery beds of ease?

> While others fought to gain the prize,
> And sailed through bloody seas?[2]

The call to ministry, particularly the pastorate, is not set to the strains of "At rest in Jesus, safe at last," but "Onward, Christian soldiers, marching as to war."[3]

For the young pastor, not yet battle hardened by the realities of life in ministry, the first reaction to problems may be *to run*. Opposition, criticism, misunderstanding, and conflict will be part of your daily fare. But that's what you signed on for. Our Lord spent His entire earthly ministry being misunderstood and subsequently opposed and even crucified.

The servant is not greater than his Lord. Jesus did not simply say, "I'm sending you forth as sheep," but, "I'm sending you out like sheep *among wolves*" (Matt. 10:16). It can be tough! Expect it. But know that God's grace is more than sufficient.

Your supporters will always outweigh your detractors, and your blessings will far surpass your heartaches. When you hit your first snag in that new pastorate, remember to slow down for the speed bump. Don't fight it. Don't run and don't try to go around it. Slow down, pray it through, and work it out. Drill that oil well!

With or without the problems, however, most of us live with the mirage of greener pastures. Let me assure you, that larger church down the road has the same problems as yours. Just add a few zeros to every equation, and you have the only real difference between a small church and a large church.

Some of my dearest friends through the years have constantly been consumed with the desire to move. Every time a large church becomes available, telephone calls begin, "Recommend me here, recommend me there."

I fear the secular world has placed an unreasonable pressure on young pastors to "succeed." Success is not measured by numbers. The size of your congregation and the percentage of growth, so important to the world and far too often to our peers, is not the measure of success in the eyes of the Father. Integrity. Holiness. Commitment. Faithfulness. These are the qualities dear to the heart of God in the lives of His servants.

Do you want to pastor a larger church? Let me tell you how to do it. Stop looking over your shoulder, put down deep roots, double your prayer life, and go to work building that great church right where you are.

Too many young men, consumed with a secular perspective of success, have driven themselves to reach people for numbers' sake, trying to move to a larger field. Every large church was once a small church that God built by the faithfulness of a godly pastor and people. And you can do that, *right where you are*!

Some of the world's greatest churches have been built in some of the least likely places. Who does not admire the incredible accomplishment of Pastor Jim Cymbala, who built the great Brooklyn Tabernacle Church in an extremely difficult part of inner-city Brooklyn. Pastor Cymbala's secret: Bloom where you're planted.

Plant your life and put down deep roots of prayer. Rome wasn't built in a day, and neither was any great church in history. If you are looking for God's best for you in those green pastures across the fence, you are likely looking in *all the wrong places*.

I'm constantly shocked at the number of pastor search committees who tell me they receive a large amount of self-recommendation letters from pastors.

Stay put. *Never promote yourself*. Let God be God. He's really good at being God.

Endnotes

1. Billy Rose, Al Jolson, Dave Dreyer, "Back in Your Own Backyard," © Bourne Company, Memory Lane Music Group.
2. Isaac Watts, "Am I a Soldier of the Cross."
3. Sabine Baring-Gould, "Onward, Christian Soldiers."

Chapter 30

FAITHFUL AT THE FIRST

Well done, good and faithful slave! You were faithful over a few things; I will put you in charge of many things" (Matt. 25:21).

Notice the connection: "*were* faithful," "*will* put." My faithfulness yesterday impacts my blessing tomorrow.

What more beautiful words did our Lord ever speak? While this precious promise is primarily for eternity, it certainly applies to the present.

The persons I know who have been greatly used in large places have this in common: They were faithful to the little opportunities.

Let me tell you a story. In 1952 I became a Christian and enrolled in Oklahoma Baptist University. Immediately I was faced with a conflict.

I had committed my life to serve the Lord and, because I was a former jazz band leader, had a small reputation among my classmates as well as the churches of Oklahoma. Instantly there were opportunities to play the trumpet and give my testimony, even leading the music and preaching in every conceivable kind of place.

My dilemma was the attractiveness of campus life. The girls were not only beautiful; they also were godly, Christian young women making them doubly attractive. There were parties, fraternities, sororities, movies, homecoming parades, basketball games, sock hops, and more.

I opted for the service of the Lord. I had met my bride to be and fallen in love, but for every date we could squeeze in, there were a dozen other engagements, off campus, serving the Lord. Uldine was so supportive. She agreed God's service should be my priority, and it remains that way today. God has blessed me with a wonderful wife. Her attitude is much like Ruth Graham's.

A reporter once asked Mrs. Billy Graham how she handled being married to a man who was gone virtually all the time. She responded, "I'd rather be married to Billy *part* of the time than any other man in the world *all* of the time."

I often reflect on those early years of marriage, serving the Lord together. One of my most blessed memories is God's amazing way of opening doors for ministry.

As a young evangelist, I was always booked solid for two years in advance. I never sought a place to preach, distributed a brochure, or recommended myself. God has been my booking agent and remains so today. Well into my twelfth year of retirement from the pastorate, I continue to receive more than two hundred invitations a year. The reward of these golden years is not unconnected to those early years.

Pastors often amaze me with the limitations they put on the Lord. "I want a church to pastor but only one right here." "Oh, no, I couldn't leave the Bible Belt for Nebraska or New York, let alone the foreign mission field. My family and relatives are here in the South."

Dear pastor, put neither size nor location restrictions on God.

"Wherever He leads I'll go," means, "*Wherever* He leads I'll go."[1]

Our churches are filled with unemployed pastors. There are lots of "almost" pastors, "used-to-be" pastors, "want-to-be" pastors and "gonna-be" pastors, but it is often surprisingly difficult to get them to take a Sunday morning Bible study class, speak at a nursing home, or work in a small mission.

During my first years of ministry, I was a full-time student in college. I conducted fourteen revival meetings out of every eighteen-week semester going through Oklahoma Baptist University. These were weekend revivals, week-long revivals, and two-week revivals in small towns and country churches across Oklahoma, Texas, Arkansas, and Louisiana.

In the average day we would get out of class at 2:00 p.m., drive until 6:00 or 7:00, conduct services, get back in the car at 9:00, and drive home, taking turns studying by flashlight in the backseat, arriving back at school at 1:00 or 2:00 a.m. We would get up at 7:00 the next morning, go to class, and repeat the process at 2:00 p.m.

Week after week we did this. Sometimes I didn't have a car. Sometimes I didn't have any money. Sometimes I hitchhiked to Alabama or Mississippi on

Thursday, skipping class on Friday to be at some small church for a weekend youth revival, only to spend most of the love offering for a bus ticket home, and ride all night to get back to class on Monday.

And it was a joy. It came naturally. And today I still love the small country churches.

God has given me the opportunity to expand my ministry in a greater way in my years beyond the pastorate. Somehow I think there must be a connection to Matthew 25:21.

Endnotes

1. B. B. McKinney, "Wherever He Leads I'll Go."

Chapter 31

FAITHFUL TO THE END

My father-in-law, Dr. Paul Beck, is in heaven. Dr. Beck was a special man. An ordained minister with three earned doctorates, he preached the gospel faithfully for sixty-five years. When I became engaged to his beautiful daughter Uldine, he gave me his blessing and admonished me to be faithful in the ministry to which God had called me.

"John," he said, "it has been my observation that only one in ten men who begin in the ministry at age twenty-one are still in it at age sixty-five." I didn't believe it at the time. I believe it today.

I made a list of the names of twenty-five of my peers and wrote them in the back of my Bible. Through the years I removed their names as they quit the ministry. Only four made it to the finish line: Ron Dunn, Charlie Graves, Freddy Gage, and Homer Martinez.

Some fell through discouragement. Some quit because of opposition within their own churches. Some had affairs. Some became obsessed with making money. Some became liberal in their theology, hence ineffective, and quit the ministry.

It is not important whether you have five hundred members or five thousand. It is important that you be true to the Lord, that you love the Lord and His people, live a clean life, do the best you can with what you have, where you are, and do it for the glory of God. "Faithful to the end!" What a testimony.

What more could you want as an epitaph across your life than these words, *"Well done, good and faithful slave"* (Matt. 25:21).

Guard against things that can trip you up. Never be suggestive or flirtatious. Tithe to your church. Don't live above your means. Be prudent in your investments for retirement but not obsessed with it. Tell the truth.

Do your best and leave the results to God. The single most important thing about your life will not be how many people you won to Christ, how much money you raised, the size of your church, the number of books you wrote, or the offices you held. The single most important factor of your life will be that you were "faithful to the end."

And don't feel compelled to retire at age sixty-six. Retire when God leads you to retire. The pressures of the pastorate are heavy and will need to be eased at some point in your life. But remember other ministries await you in your later years that can greatly profit from your experience. Always look forward to tomorrow. The best is yet to come.

One of the great dangers of the ministry is giving up about age fifty-five or sixty and just hanging on until retirement. We all begin with hopes and dreams and ambitions. We all want to be special! But somewhere about age fifty to fifty-five, reality begins to set in. "I'm not special." "I'm not being used in a great way." "I'm not going to have a big church." And it's easy to give up and *coast to the finish line.*

Ambition has no place in the ministry. God knows your phone number, and He has a wonderful plan for your life. Don't try to move and don't ask anyone to recommend you anywhere. Put down deep roots and just let it happen. It's a long way to the finish line, and faithfulness is its own reward.

Don't be caught up in the standards of the world or even your denomination. Success is not setting records. Success is not raising millions. Success is not baptizing thousands. Success is not preaching at conventions. Success is not writing best sellers, winning elections, having your name on buildings, or being applauded. Nor is it being handsome, wealthy, educated, winning awards, serving on boards, or having your name in lights. Success is being faithful to the Lord Jesus Christ with all that you have, in everything you do, to the glory of God.

"Well done." Just two words matter. Not a thousand, not a hundred, just two: "Well done."

> Therefore, fear the LORD and worship Him in sincerity and truth. Get rid of the gods your fathers worshiped beyond the Euphrates River and in Egypt, and worship Yahweh. But if it doesn't please you to worship Yahweh, choose for yourselves today the one you will worship: the gods

your fathers worshiped beyond the Euphrates River or the gods of the Amorites in whose land you are living. As for me and my family, we will worship Yahweh. (Josh 24:14–15)

I have fought the good fight, I have finished the race, I have kept the faith. There is reserved for me in the future the crown of righteousness, which the Lord, the righteous Judge, will give me on that day, and not only to me, but to all those who have loved His appearing. (2 Tim. 4:7–8)

Part 3

THE PASTOR
AS SPIRITUAL LEADER

Chapter 32

THE PASTOR AND HIS PEOPLE

On a recent trip to the Holy Land, we enjoyed observing that special relationship between a shepherd and his sheep. No more beautiful illustration exists of the relationship between God's pastor and God's people.

The shepherd is always in front of the sheep, and he is out there *alone*. He is the leader and enjoys the privilege of leadership. But he is always the first to lay down his life for his sheep, to fight and even die in their defense.

Far too often words like *authority* and *leadership* are criticized by those who do not understand the concept of "servant leadership." But leadership is deserved not demanded, granted by the people, earned by the pastor.

The ideal pastor is much like his people. In all great growing churches, there is the common denominator of a homogeneous mix between pastor and people. They are comfortable with him, he with them.

Houston's First is a good example of that. I have never been comfortable with just the rich or just the poor, with just the black or just the white. As such, the church was extremely eclectic, a good cross-section of our city—not racially, as much as I would like but certainly socially and professionally. We had bankers and homemakers, old and young, short hair and long hair. We became all things to all people that we might by all means *win many*.

It is important to be like your congregation. To be like them, you need to know them. To know them, you need to spend time with them. To spend the time you need to love them sincerely.

The highlight of my week was to enter the worship center early as the people gathered and linger as they left. I loved to walk up and down the aisles and greet our people. I loved it when little children came up and hugged me and the older children told me about their Little League baseball games.

I loved it when our folks invited us on a trip with them or when they asked us to come to their homes and play softball or cook hamburgers. It was not a game I played. I really did love it. I was comfortable with our people, and they were comfortable with me. You can't simply appear to love people; you *really* have to *love them*. You can't play the game on Sunday morning; you have to live the reality seven days a week.

Every wise minister will protect his time for personal devotions, study, sermon preparation, and prayer, but accessibility is always important. People don't want a pastor who is available twenty-four hours a day. They want their pastor to be alone with God and alone in his study. But that's not all day, every day. The rest of the time, take time for people. Remember these words: The people's needs are never an *interruption* to your ministry. They *are* your ministry.

I could name some Southern Baptist megachurch pastors I called several times across the years. They never returned my calls. I have often wondered if they return calls from their own congregants. If so, which? All of them? Or perhaps only the rich and famous.

With ever-increasing ministry, the larger the church becomes, the more difficult accessibility to the pastor becomes. But it can also *be easier* because large churches have more staff, and pastors are free to give more time to study and prayer, leaving others to do much of the ministry. All of which equates to at least *some* more time for accessibility to his people than if he had no staff.

It can be a difficult balance to establish. But the bottom line is this: Remember you are called to be a shepherd first—not a church growth guru, not an executive, not a ranch owner, but a shepherd. A faithful shepherd who works for the Owner takes *really good care of His sheep*.

Be honest with yourself. Do I really *love* the sheep? Or do I *use* the sheep to build my ministry and enhance *my* kingdom instead of *His*. You have to face this. Examine your heart. You can't truly love the Shepherd and not love His sheep and vice versa. And as His undershepherd, they will see Him in you and love Him the more. And isn't that what it's all about?

"I am the good shepherd. The good shepherd lays down his life for the sheep. The hired man, since he is not the shepherd and doesn't own the sheep, leaves them and runs away when he sees a wolf coming. The wolf then snatches and scatters them. This happens because he is a hired man and doesn't care about the sheep.

"I am the good shepherd. I know My own sheep, and they know Me." (John 10:11–14)

Be a good shepherd!

Chapter 33

THE PASTOR'S PRAYER LIFE

At age twenty-five I wrote a book on prayer that has enjoyed worldwide success: *The Power of Positive Praying.* Today there is *The New Power of Positive Praying.* Looking back, I think, "I didn't know I knew that much." Surely God had something to do with writing that little book.

I still have much to learn in the school of prayer. But let me share something new and exciting that God has been teaching me.

He doesn't necessarily respond in the areas about which I have been praying; He often moves in apparently unrelated areas. How is it that when I increase my prayer life, God starts to move in areas I wasn't even praying about or thinking about?

The answer is at once simple and beautiful. He is blessing me simply because I am trying to be a man of prayer. My whole world changes when I am serious about prayer. Everywhere there is blessing as I spend serious time with God. Many truths are still developing in my heart about prayer, but I can tell you this: *It's important to pray.* In fact, it's *most important* to pray. Above everything else, be a person of prayer.

Let me give you two simple principles about the preacher and his prayer life. First, when you pray, things happen. Second, you have to pray a lot. Yes, the Bible says we are not heard for our much speaking, but far too often that is simply an excuse not to pray very much. God-blessed prayer is time-drenched prayer.

Stay in an attitude of prayer. To think that our hearts can be silently praying to God while our lips are verbally addressing another in conversation is awesome. Practicing the presence of God is a constant attitude of communion with the Father and is both commanded and commendable, *but that doesn't let you off the hook in the matter of longevity in prayer.* Every pastor should spend at least an hour a day, seven days a week, on his knees before God in prayer. You will be amazed how easily that hour turns into an hour and a half and then two.

The time you spend in early morning prayer is time that shortens your time the rest of the day. You will find that you don't spend nearly as much time running around, solving problems, blowing whistles, and pushing buttons. When you spend that early morning time in prayer, you will have fewer problems and fewer obstacles. When you get to the problems you fear and the situations you dread, you will often find God has already been there before you, and your day is easier and shorter: "Even *before they call*, I will answer" (Isa. 65:24).

How much should we pray and when should we pray? Let me repeat: At least an hour, seven days a week, early in the morning. How often did Jesus arise a great while before dawn and go into the mountain place alone to pray? If the Creator of the universe, incarnate in a man, found prayer essential, how much more ought we?

I believe God has a special time to meet each of us in the quietness of the day. Your time might be 4:00 a.m. or 6:30 a.m. For me it is 5:00 a.m. No, I don't make it every time. Far too many evenings until midnight can make it most difficult, but 70 to 80 percent of the time, that's *my time* to meet God. Find yours. You will know it when you find it.

Early in the morning our world is quiet and our thoughts uncluttered. Early in the morning you can sense His voice, feel His touch, and know His mind.

Whatever you do, cultivate the habit of early morning prayer. This is not a time for sermon preparation, rambling thoughts, study, or idle daydreaming. It is a time to talk to God and listen as He talks to you.

Prioritize God's priorities. Pray about the things He is interested in, His glory, His body on earth, a lost world for whom He died. Pray for your family, pray for direction, and then listen.

When you wait upon God, He will speak to you in the quietness of your soul. His voice will come not with heavenly vocal cords or crashing thunder but in the still, small impression of the Holy Spirit deep in your heart—a voice without words: louder, clearer, more distinct than any you will hear from another person. The hymn writer said it so well:

> I come to the garden alone
>> While the dew is still on the roses.
> And the voice I hear falling on my ear,
>> The Son of God discloses.
> He speaks and the sound of His voice
>> Is so sweet, the birds hush their singing.
> And the melody that He gave to me
>> Within my heart is ringing.
> And He walks with me and He talks with me,
>> And He tells me I am His own.
> And the joy we share as we tarry there,
>> None other has ever known.[1]

He waits there for you in the garden of prayer, and He will be waiting every morning. Don't be late.

Endnotes

1. C. Austin Miles, "In the Garden."

Chapter 34

SABBATICALS

W e're talking about more than your vacation here. Many young pastors today are taking annual sabbaticals. I commend them for doing it and their churches for allowing it.

The sabbatical can be scheduled separately from your vacation or in one extended period following your vacation. I recommend the former. Both are "musts" if you are to be your best for the Lord and His people.

The object of the family vacation is *their* fun. The object of the sabbatical is spiritual enrichment for *your* soul. Vacations include lots of travel to theme parks, relatives, and friends. Sabbaticals are one trip to one place and stay there.

As always, our Lord is our example (Mark 1:35).

There's no way for the average church member to comprehend the spiritual, emotional, and mental drain of the pastorate. Multiple Sunday services leave you in a trance and for more than just Monday morning. But there is no possibility in the pastorate to take successive days off after an exhausting Sunday. And the cumulative effect of each successive week makes it more difficult to refill your tank each week than the one before. You'll never know how empty it is until you begin your sabbatical.

Discuss all this with your search committee before you begin your new pastorate. And be certain your church has been fully informed and is fully supportive.

I love what Pastor Gregg Matte tells our church, "You can have me just okay for fifty-two Sundays a year or really fired up for forty-two."

During my pastorate I took a full month of annual vacation, with three Sundays away, and three or four additional Sundays to preach in other places. I never took a sabbatical. Looking back, I wish I had done things differently.

Sabbaticals are not meant to be in fun places. That's for vacations. Follow Jesus' example. Go to a solitary place, a quiet place, alone, unhurried, and remote. I'm writing these words in a mountain cabin in northern New Mexico, and they're flowing easily.

1. Focus on the Lord.
2. Refresh your spirit.
3. Focus on your family.
4. Get a new vision.
5. Do some general calendaring for the next twelve months.
6. Plan your preaching for a year. I didn't say write fifty-two sermons.
7. Let the staff, pastors within your congregation, and outside guests fill the pulpit. Hearing a new voice can be refreshing to your people.

Chapter 35

INTEGRITY ABOVE ALL

Does it even need to be said that integrity is inseparable from Christian ministry? Unfortunately today I'm afraid the answer is yes.

An infinite number of things define this generation. One of the most prominent is this: They have been let down by virtually everything and have confidence in almost nothing.

There are three basic institutions of society: the home, the church, and government. In the home nearly 50 percent of those who once said, "I do," don't. The divorce rate is growing at an astronomical rate. In the government the Nixons, Harts, Kennedys, Clintons, and a myriad of others cause us to doubt. In the church an endless stream of leaders disappoint us. And the end is not yet. Continuing disappointment in leaders is inevitable.

We have a generation that hasn't seen integrity modeled, and we strongly need to encourage it in the young.

Integrity, and the lack thereof, might well be the most important issue in America today, certainly in the ministry. Few persons whom God has greatly used were greatly gifted, but they were persons of great integrity. Listen again to the words of the apostle Paul in his letter to the church at Corinth:

> Brothers, consider your calling: Not many are wise from a human per-
> spective, not many are powerful, not many of noble birth. Instead, God
> has chosen what is foolish in the world to shame the wise, and God has
> chosen what is weak in the world to shame the strong. God has chosen

what is insignificant and despised in the world—what is viewed as nothing—to bring to nothing what is viewed as something, so that no one can boast in His presence. (1 Cor. 1:26–29)

You don't have to be highly educated, talented, or attractive to be greatly used of God, but you have to have integrity. God can drive the ball a long way with a small club but not very far at all with a crooked one.

At no time in history has the world so justifiably questioned the integrity of ministers. Circumstances beyond your control have created a stage upon which we minister under tremendous scrutiny.

When new people come to your church, they are checking *you* out long before they check out your message. It is unspoken, often even unrealized, but virtually every unbeliever goes to church with a question about the credibility of the person speaking to the congregation.

Statistics gathered by Houston's First when I was pastor there indicated the average guest attended three to six weeks before joining. Today in virtually every church, that time is three to six months.

Your integrity relates to your finances, your moral life, your word—everything. People will love you and forgive you your faults if you admit them and are honest about them before your people. They can accept fellow strugglers who are still *on the way*, but they will reject the leader who pretends to *have arrived* when, in fact, they know he hasn't.

Integrity is honesty. Integrity is truthfulness. Integrity means *you do what people assume a man of God does when nobody's looking*. Integrity means you talk like people assume a man of God talks *when nobody hears*. Integrity means you're the same in *private* as you are in *public*.

Be real. Be authentic. Our world expects no less. Our people deserve no less. Our Lord requires no less.

You are the light of the world. You are the salt of the earth. What you *are* may impact the world for Christ more than anything you ever *say* or *do*.

Keep your word, keep pure, stay on your knees, and do what you say you'll do. If you don't, admit it, apologize, and ask forgiveness. Above all, be open, transparent, and honest. Integrity is the rudder that guides the ship of successful ministry.

Don't you know that the unjust will not inherit God's kingdom? Do not be deceived: No sexually immoral people, idolaters, adulterers, or any kind of homosexual, no thieves, greedy people, drunkards, verbally abusive people, or swindlers will inherit God's kingdom. And some of you used to be like this. But you were washed, you were sanctified, you were justified in the name of the Lord Jesus Christ and by the Spirit of our God.

"Everything is permissible for me," but not everything is helpful. "Everything is permissible for me," but I will not be brought under the control of anything. (1 Cor. 6:9–12)

Chapter 36

MAINTAINING MORAL PURITY

The most common reason for ministerial fallout is sexual impurity.

I could have no greater joy than helping you personally in this area. Whether you ever preach at a big convention or have fifty in worship or five thousand is not important. That you honor Christ, live a life of purity and integrity, preach His Word with fidelity, and are faithful to the end—that is everything.

I offer ten suggestions for strengthening your marriage and avoiding the pitfall of moral failure.

1. *Keep your love affair with Jesus passionate.* Falling *into* an affair, or into pornography, is only a symptom of falling *out* of love with your wife. And losing your passion for her is only a symptom of having lost your passion for the Lord Jesus.

If you don't fall in love again with your Savior, you won't fall in love with your wife. And if you don't fall in love with her, you're headed for big trouble.

2. *Give a new commitment to early morning prayer.* An hour or more in the Word and on your knees in prayer is the *key to it all*. A ruined ministry is a terrible thing, and it can last forty or fifty years. That hour each morning is not nearly as long, but one hundred times as important.

You may say, "I don't have the time to pray and read the Word in the morning." Dear pastor friend, you don't have time *not* to.

3. *Never be alone with another woman.* Don't get in the car with her. Don't be in your office with her alone, with the door shut. Counsel with the door open. Dictate with the door open. Meet with a lady with whom you counsel or with whom you serve in your office *with your door open.*

And spend $150 and have a window put in the door of the office where everyone can clearly see what's going on.

4. *Be accountable.* There are more than 400 million pornographic Web sites. It's virtually impossible to be on the Internet and not come across a link to a pornographic Web site. Many are traps.

Get a program such as Covenant Eyes, where you can make a pact with a friend and check each other's activity on the Internet. Spend the money, buy the program, and do it today! Be accountable.

5. *Learn to talk to your wife.* We are the only creatures on earth with the gift of intelligible verbal communication. That woman to whom you are married is a beautiful and wonderful person. Do you really know her? Take time to talk.

6. *Learn to turn your head.* Between your eyes and your heart, there's something called the neck. It can save your life. Job said, "I have made a covenant with my eyes. How then could I look at a young woman?" (Job 31:1). There are *looks* and then there are *looks.* You can *seldom* avoid the first look; you can *always* avoid the second.

7. *Prioritize family time.* Have a date night with your wife every week. Go to your kids' ball games. Don't miss a school play. Run errands together; go places together, and hold her hand as you do.

8. *Attend a marriage retreat once a year with your wife.*

9. *Keep a picture of you and your wife on your wedding day, along with a picture of your kids, on your desk.*

10. *Go to bed at the same time.* People who have a problem with pornography acknowledge that late-night television and the Internet are often the avenues through which it developed. You've got enough time during the day to get your work done. When it's time to go to bed, go to bed—together!

He who was tempted in all points like as are we fully understands and is able to succor those who rest on His gentle breast. Together you can win the battle for purity, and you must.

God loves you. Your family believes in you. Your church trusts you.

> The pure in heart are blessed, for they will see God. (Matt. 5:8)
>
> Finally brothers, whatever is true, whatever is honorable, whatever is just, whatever is pure, whatever is lovely, whatever is commendable—if there is any moral excellence and if there is any praise—dwell on these things. (Phil. 4:8)

Don't be quick to appoint anyone as an elder, and don't share in the sins of others. Keep yourself pure. (1 Tim. 5:22)

Search me, O God, and know my heart today.
Try me, O Savior, know my thoughts, I pray.
See if there be some wicked way in me;
Cleanse me from every sin, and set me free.[1]

Endnotes

1. James E. Orr, "Search Me, O God."

Chapter 37

CHARACTER COMES FIRST

When I read a book or hear a sermon, I consider my time well spent if I come away with one good idea. In 1996, Dan Webster, president of Authentic Leadership Inc., led the staff of Houston's First in a leadership retreat. It was a wonderful experience and really too much to absorb in just two days. However, out of every good thing he said, and there was much, one idea stayed with me and impacts my life virtually every day. Dan Webster said, "The first part of your ministry, you lead out of what you can do. The last part, you lead out of who you are."

What did Mr. Webster mean by "leading out of who you are"?

For one thing it means you have stayed long enough for your congregation to establish confidence in your leadership. It means personhood is more important than programs, truth more important than goals, spiritual confidence more important than spiritual plans.

Again, this takes time. When you have introduced several programs that have been successful, you gain a certain degree of credibility with your people.

But the time should come in the life of the pastor when the willingness of his people to follow has been created not out of a proven track record of successful programs but out of a quiet confidence that their pastor has been with God, heard His voice, and may be trusted not to lead them astray. It is leadership of *being* more than *doing*, of personhood more than programs.

In my ministry I found that the longer I stayed and the larger the church became, the easier it was to pastor. Houston's First grew to have many ministries—missions, schools, child development center, wellness program— more than 150 persons on the payroll. And yet the church was easier to pastor than when there were only fifteen.

There were, of course, layers of leadership and good generals who organized the captains and lieutenants who oversaw the sergeants. But though there was much more responsibility, there was a parallel increase of ease as I learned to trust the people and they learned to trust me.

Of course, neither my methods nor my leadership style remained stagnant. But it became much easier to lead because our people sensed at the helm of the ship was a leader not easily rattled, who stayed the course, and who had the composure of a Spirit-controlled life.

Don't sweat the small stuff. Don't lose your cool. Don't get rattled. Lead out of your quietness, your character, your spiritual maturity; and your leadership will become easier as the years go by.

My dear wife is a perfect example of this. She greatly influences my decisions, not because of what she says but because of who she is.

Her faithful devotion to Jesus Christ for more than fifty-five years has impacted my life every day of our marriage. I naturally and comfortably move into new things with Uldine because of the woman I know her to be.

Be yourself, love the Lord—really love Him. Love the people—really love them. If that's the foundation of your ministry, following your leadership will fall naturally into place.

Good words by Dan Webster, "The first part of your ministry, you lead out of what you can do; the second, out of who you are."

> How happy is the man who does not follow the advice of the wicked, or take the path of sinners, or join a group of mockers! Instead, his delight is in the LORD's instruction, and he meditates on it day and night. He is like a tree planted beside streams of water that bears its fruit in season and whose leaf does not wither. Whatever he does prospers. (Ps. 1:1–3)

> Surely You desire integrity in the inner self, and You teach me wisdom deep within. Purify me with hyssop, and I will be clean; wash me, and I will be whiter than snow. Let me hear joy and gladness; let the bones You have crushed rejoice. Turn Your face away from my sins and blot out all my guilt.

God, create a clean heart for me and renew a steadfast spirit within me. Do not banish me from Your presence or take Your Holy Spirit from me. Restore the joy of Your salvation to me and give me a willing spirit. Then I will teach the rebellious Your ways, and sinners will return to You.

Save me from the guilt of bloodshed, God, the God of my salvation, and my tongue will sing of Your righteousness. Lord, open my lips, and my mouth will declare Your praise. (Ps. 51:6–15)

Chapter 38

CASTING THE VISION

I t was business as usual. Prayer meeting night in a little suburban church. Five hundred seats, 475 empty. Twenty-five faithful souls. The organ began to play "Day Is Dying in the West." Sadly, that's not all that was dying in the West, and the East, and the North, and the South!

Regrettably, many churches are dead and don't know it or just won't admit it. Too many services are dead, dull, despondent, and depressing. Any ball game, concert, movie, or gang fight has more life than the average church. There are a hundred reasons people stay away in great droves. One reason is the absence of vision.

There is no life because there is no hope. And there is no hope because there is no expectancy. There is no expectancy because there is no vision.

There is no vision because the pastor has not instilled vision, and the result is always death. "Where there is no vision, the people perish" (Prov. 29:18 KJV).

Vision, like expectancy, always hopes for something better, always expects it, always believes it will happen. "Can do" is its motto; "The Impossible Dream," its theme song.

For five years at the First Southern Baptist Church of Del City, Oklahoma, people in large numbers came to Christ and joined the church every Sunday, but for several months during the first year at Houston, that intangible something I wanted, and to which I had become accustomed, was not there. I didn't know what it *was*, but I knew what it *wasn't*. Sunday after Sunday

I would go home from church and say to my wife, "It was a good service, but it's not the same. It's not right, but I can't put my finger on it." That elusive "something" was missing.

One Sunday morning fifty-seven people made decisions for Christ and joined the church. The next Sunday there were thirty-nine. The following Sunday it happened! That special "something," I had been missing was there. I didn't know it was what I was looking for until I reviewed that service over and over again in my mind. The thing that made the difference? Expectancy! An atmosphere of expectancy, optimism, and excitement filled the church. They truly expected it to happen again and again. And it did.

I knew that we would probably never win everyone in Houston to Christ, but I didn't want anyone telling my people that. They were almost convinced that they could! They were expecting to do it. They were expecting a packed worship center, souls saved, lives changed, and fire from heaven every Sunday.

Sunday after Sunday I told them that because we bore the name "First," it was our responsibility to lead the way, to set the pace in evangelism, in missions, in giving—in everything.

Four million people live in greater Houston. It is the crossroads of the nation, heart of the Americas, gateway to outer space. Revival here could impact the world.

Slowly it began to dawn on them that our church must be one of God's great bastions of the gospel. It must be a mighty lighthouse in the heart of a mighty city. He had placed us there for a purpose. We must set the pace. We must launch out. *Houston must be won for Christ. Now!*

They began to believe it could happen. The raindrops began to fall. Then the flood. Faith became sight. Dream became reality. Then there was even more expectancy. They prayed, worked, and expected it again and again.

As pastor you are to be the vision caster. You first must get alone with God and stay until you hear from heaven. Once your soul is stirred about the direction of your church, call your leaders together and share it with them. Listen to their response. Massage your dream, refine your focus, and then take it to the pulpit. It might not be popular, it might not be easy, but God will always bless the person who has His vision and follows it.

If you would lead people, you must get out in front of them. Deep in the heart of every child of God is a desire to follow an earthly shepherd they believe to be following the heavenly Shepherd. God has called you as the spiritual leader of His people, and the purpose of leadership is to lead.

The front of ancient sailing ships was called the "pulpit." That small protruding portion extending beyond the bough was where the lookout watched for rocks and other dangers. Standing there was called "riding the pulpit." In times of danger, a volunteer allowed the captain to tie him to it.

If he died, he died. But he pointed the way and gave the vision to the crew. Go to God, get the vision, ask your heavenly Captain to tie you to it, and lead His people by His grace. "Where there is no vision, the people perish" (Prov. 29:18 KJV).

> Like a mighty army moves the church of God;
>   Brothers, we are treading where the saints have trod.
> We are not divided, all one body we,
>   One in hope and doctrine, one in charity.
> Onward Christian Soldiers marching as to war.
>   With the cross of Jesus going on before.[1]

Endnotes

1. Sabine Baring-Gould, "Onward Christian Soldiers."

Chapter 39

HOSPITAL CALLS

Our Lord was the master at touching hurting people. How often have we watched "television healers" and said in our hearts, "If they are really doing what they claim, why don't they walk up and down the halls of the hospital and heal everyone?" While we readily admit that too few of our prayers for healing appear to be answered on the spot, a healing touch occurs just because you cared enough to come and to pray. How often the Gospel writers remind us, Jesus had great compassion upon the people.

I readily confess that hospital ministry was not easy for me.

Searching my soul, I think the reason is that I felt so inadequate. I wanted to do *so much* but was able to do *so little*. Though having made thousands of such calls through the years, I admit occasionally to having tried to find a reason *not to go*. But of this I have become confident after thirty-five years of pastoral ministry: Of most importance is not *what I said* but *that I came*.

Few will ever remember what *I said* at their bedside. Few will ever forget *I came*.

As your church grows larger, you must come to grips with the heart-wrenching decision of whom to visit, whom to see, which invitation to accept, etc. The struggle for priority of time in a day with only twenty-four hours is never easily resolved. In a larger church your staff can help visit the hospitals. Additionally, in Houston's First retired deacons did a wonderful job, often even visiting the same person three or four times in a week. But what of you as pastor? How are you to confront the reality of too many visits and too little time?

First, determine your priorities. I visited the critically ill first. Those who are in the hospital overnight for an operation on their finger would probably not get a visit from their pastor.

Second, you must pastor your leaders. All other things being equal, the staff member, Sunday morning Bible study teacher, deacon, or members of their families will get a visit from their pastor before another church member with the same need. This is simply a part of learning to pastor your leaders, who in turn pastor others. Remember the principle of leadership Jethro taught Moses, to let others lead.

Third, I visited those who specifically requested me.

When you are unable to go, send a card. Your assistant can help you here. But your handwritten note is best. Better yet, make a phone call. In a city the size of Houston, I spent many hours a week in my car. I was constantly on the phone calling shut-ins, calling hospitals, calling prospects, dictating letters, and returning telephone calls. This is an ideal time to call those in the hospital. They will be deeply appreciative that you remembered they were there, and remember you can pray over the phone.

Even if you have a staff member who regularly visits the hospitals, go see your leaders, those who ask for you, and the critically ill. And ask your staff and deacons always to say, "The pastor asked me to come see you, and he's praying for you."

As you enter the hospital, be certain you have the right person and the right room. Remember, bed A comes before bed B.

Knock gently before entering. Ask permission to come in. Be certain your presence is appropriate. If it is not, offer to wait a moment.

Upon entering the room, call the person by name and greet him or her with a smile. Let the person talk. Be encouraging. Assure patients that they are in a great hospital with wonderful doctors. People are in the hospital because they are sick, and sick people have neither the need, energy, nor time for small talk. Stay ten minutes or less, hold their hand, pray, and leave.

Assure them of your continuing prayer and interest and tell them to feel free to call if the need arises.

Remember, a warm smile, a friendly touch, and just that "you were there" will leave the lingering fragrance of our Lord, who said that in visiting those who were sick, we visited Him.

When the Son of Man comes in His glory, and all the angels with Him, then He will sit on the throne of His glory. All the nations will be gathered before Him, and He will separate them one from another, just as a shepherd separates the sheep from the goats. He will put the sheep on His right and the goats on the left. Then the King will say to those on His right, "Come, you who are blessed by My Father, inherit the kingdom prepared for you from the foundation of the world.

For I was hungry and you gave Me something to eat; I was thirsty and you gave Me something to drink; I was a stranger and you took Me in; I was naked, and you clothed Me; I was sick and you took care of Me; I was in prison and you visited Me."

Then the righteous will answer Him, "Lord, when did we see You hungry and feed You, or thirsty and give You something to drink? When did we see You a stranger and take You in, or without clothes and clothe You? When did we see You sick, or in prison, and visit You?"

And the King will answer them, "I assure you: Whatever you did for one of the least of these brothers of Mine, you did for Me." (Matt. 25:31–40)

Chapter 40

DEATH CALLS

The most difficult part of the ministry is ministering to a person whose loved one has just passed away. But it must remain number one on your priority list. The membership of Houston's First congregation was scattered across a wide area. The majority of our people drove at least ten miles to church, and hundreds drove twenty to thirty miles and farther.

The first reaction that usually came to mind upon receiving notice of the death of a member was, "Oh, but I'm so busy, and their home is so far away."

That thought came from Satan. That which most always immediately followed came from the Lord. "But think how many hundreds of times they've made the trip to church. Surely you can make this one trip to their home."

People, particularly in times of crisis, are never an *interruption* to your ministry; they *are* your ministry. As our churches grow larger, we must guard against becoming high-powered executives, cloistered in luxurious offices, barricaded by two or three secretaries and assistants. Your church might have fifty thousand members, but never forget that you are not first an executive but a pastor, and pastors care about people.

Even interrupting your important morning study time to make a death call is always appropriate. I cannot count the times I have received such a call on my cell phone on the way to another engagement. Immediately I turned the car around and went to the home of the bereaved.

If at all possible, I quickly picked up a staff member or friend and took them with me because I needed their support. It may be easy for you, but it never became easy for me.

When you arrive, go quickly to the door and ring the bell. Often the individual will fall into your arms weeping. What you say is relatively unimportant. Through the years they will remember little, if anything, you say, but they will never forget your love and your presence.

Once inside the home, ask all the members of the family to gather in the living room. Be seated next to the nearest relative, normally the parent or spouse. Put your arm around this person, allowing time for them to grieve and talk, and as they do, listen—really listen. Don't be thinking about what you're going to say or the questions you need to ask about the funeral arrangements, in order to hurry off to your next engagement. And don't just *act* as if you care. Care, really care.

As the family begins to allow you time to speak, ask them to tell you more about the deceased, about their childhood, or marriage and occupation. Ask them to share with you when and how this person came to know Christ and became a member of the church. This is not the appropriate time to discuss funeral arrangements. That will come later on in the day or, more likely, the next day.

All suggestions about the memorial service—when, where, pallbearers, music, etc.—should come at an appropriate time and only as tender suggestions from you. You must not try to manipulate the scheduling of the service for your convenience, but encourage the process of finding the best time for their schedule *and* your schedule.

I normally spent about forty-five minutes to an hour in the home. Encourage all members of the family to talk. When you feel the need has been satisfied, ask the family if you may read from Scripture. Appropriate passages are always John 14 and/or Psalm 23. Others will come to mind.

When you finish, bow your head and pray. Leave your home, office, and cell phone number with the family, suggesting they place it by the telephone. Assure them they may call you at any time.

Later that day or early the next, call to see if they need any assistance in making arrangements for the memorial service. Offer the services of your office to help contact pallbearers, florists, musicians, etc. There should never be any charge to the family of a church member for these services or for the use of the building.

Often the funeral director will offer you an honorarium in the fifty- to two-hundred-dollar range at the conclusion of the service. Remember this money was given to them by the family.

I have never been comfortable keeping this and have often given it back to another family member, particularly in the case of a family of low income.

Through the years, however, I have come to understand that while we don't need to receive this honorarium, the family feels the need to give it. Be tender and sensitive at this point. God will guide you in each situation.

Often there will be a "wake" or "viewing of the body" the evening before the day of the memorial service. The viewing is usually held in the evening. It is not essential that you attend the wake unless you choose to do so or the family specifically requests you to do so.

Another important call is made after the funeral. By telephone or preferably in person, contact the family within three days after the burial for additional ministry, comfort, and support. If you're unable to do so, be certain that a staff member, deacon, or elder does so in your behalf.

Encourage other church members to give ongoing support to the family. Nothing is more lonely than a home with an empty chair.

Your most tender and meaningful ministry can be done in touching those who have been touched deeply by death.

Chapter 41

BEFORE THE FUNERAL

When the time and place have been determined for the memorial service, contact the funeral director to be certain you are in agreement about every detail of the service and subsequent burial. Advance planning will save confusion and resultant embarrassment.

I say this kindly but firmly: Assume leadership in planning the service. You are in charge of the funeral, not the funeral director. He serves at your bidding, not you at his. Don't *ask* him what *he* wants. Tell *him* what *you* want. I have never found a funeral director to be uncooperative. Funeral homes conduct many types of funerals for various denominations and religions throughout the year. They expect to be adaptable, and they await your direction.

A call or visit to the home of the family, early on the day of the funeral, is a special, warm touch and will take only a few minutes of your time. Ask if they have any questions; tell them you are praying for them and that you will meet the entire family just a few minutes before the service begins. Be sure to pray with them whether in the home or over the telephone. The family will never forget that prayer.

In most cases the funeral home will pick up the family members of the deceased and transport them to the place the service is to be held. Normally the coach provided by the funeral home will arrive at the home about an hour before the service begins, depending on the distance to the church or other venue. Determine the approximate time the family will arrive for the service and coordinate your arrival at the funeral site with theirs.

Family members will have come from many places, and there will be those whom you have never met. As you enter the room, embrace the widow and other close family members whom you know and ask everyone to be seated. Address the entire family and relatives by first introducing yourself. Then express your sympathy and appreciation on behalf of your congregation for the loyalty and service this person has given your congregation through the years.

Assure the family the service will not be long, and see that it is not. Nothing is worse than an hour and a half funeral service. Thirty minutes is ideal, and forty-five is maximum.

Tell the funeral director that you and others assisting you—such as another person who might read the obituary, read Scripture, sing, or pray—are to be seated with you on the platform *before* the service begins. You must already be seated before the family procession into the chapel or worship center by the funeral director.

As they enter the room, rise from your seat and take a step forward. Gently lift both hands a few inches, palms upward, indicating that the congregation is to rise. An area will have been reserved for the family by the funeral director at the front of the room near the casket, which may or may not be opened at the family's discretion. This will, of course, have been determined in advance.

Remain standing with the congregation throughout the entire procession of the family into the room. Once they are seated, reverse the process, palms down, hands lowered, to indicate the congregants may be seated. Let the service immediately begin with brevity, grace, and dignity.

When you conduct the funeral, your spirit is of utmost importance. Nothing has helped me more than this: Imagine the person in the casket is your mom or dad, your husband or wife, your son or daughter. The deceased may be a virtual stranger to you, but to their family he or she is life's dearest treasure.

If the person was a believer, rejoice. If not, ignore it and comfort the family. If you are not certain, be vague about the spiritual condition of the deceased but clear about the gospel. Don't preach the deceased into hell or into heaven.

Don't hold back the tears, and never be rushed. Never will you minister in the tender footsteps of Jesus more than here. We are His hands and feet. Through us He touches broken hearts.

Chapter 42

CONDUCTING
THE FUNERAL

Fifteen minutes before the service is scheduled to begin, the organist or other instrumentalists should begin playing softly and continue until the service begins. Two solos or other specials are normally sung in a memorial service. They should, of course, be appropriate and, as with weddings, approved by you in advance. A good general order of service is as follows:

- Solo
- A welcome, including: (1) a simple statement of purpose, "We are gathered here today in memory of our loving friend, John Smith, etc." (2) An expression of thanks on behalf of the family for the many kindnesses shown to them.
- The reading of the obituary
- Scripture
- Prayer
- Solo
- Message
- Closing prayer
- Viewing of the body, if desired by the family
- Family recessional and exit

On occasion there will be a eulogy or testimony by a family member or friend about the deceased. These should be few and brief. A ten-minute eulogy is seven or eight minutes too long. If eulogies are given at all, there should be no more than two, one by a family member and one by a friend. Where the person was a member of the military, that portion of the service—folding of the flag, presenting it to the widow, and playing of "Taps"—should be done at the graveside.

Fifteen minutes is the maximum for your message; ten to twelve is better. Speak warmly and tenderly. Speak from your heart. Try to speak without notes so you may look compassionately into the eyes of the family as you speak. Every funeral, including the message and the entire service, should do three things:

- Honor the deceased.
- Comfort the family.
- Glorify the Lord.

When the service is complete, close your Bible, pray, and step to the head of the casket. If it is open and the people are going to file by, stay there until they are finished. Do not extend your hand to shake hands with each person who passes by, but respond in the manner they may initiate. Some will pause longer than others. Some will be weeping. Some will embrace you. Be tender and supportive in your response.

After the congregants have filed by, the family will come last, normally led by the nearest relative. As they approach the casket, move from the head of the casket to the side of the family, put your arm around them or take their hand, support them, and give them the time they need to weep.

Do not pull them away. They often will be leaning over, touching or even kissing the face of their loved one. When they are finished and have straightened up, take their elbow and walk gently with them, placing them in the loving care of other family members. Step a few feet down the aisle and pause, then lead the casket to the waiting funeral coach.

Walk slowly. Don't get more than six or eight steps ahead of the pallbearers. Once you have arrived at the coach and the casket has been placed inside, step, with the pallbearers, to the rear of the coach and await the instruction of the funeral director to the people to go to their cars. You may ride with the director or drive your own car. I choose to drive myself.

Once you arrive at the cemetery, return to the rear of the funeral coach, wait for the pallbearers to remove the casket, and again walk slowly ahead of it, and them, to the grave. *Do not* have a second service at the graveside. This should be no more than five minutes. One service is enough. You might wish to pour sand or perform some other rite customary to your denomination or church. I normally lead the people in one verse of "In the Garden," "What a Friend We Have in Jesus," or "The Old Rugged Cross," read 1 Thessalonians 4:13–18, and pray.

After the graveside service, it is not necessary for you to shake hands with every family member. Normally there will be two rows of chairs, four to five per row, seated in front of the casket, with everyone else standing. The nearest relative, such as a parent or a widow, will always be seated on that front row. Walk by slowly, grasp the hand of each person seated on the front row, tell them you love them, and assure them of your prayers.

Normally the funeral director will tell the people, "This concludes the service." Guests at the graveside will naturally move toward the family to express their condolences. It is not necessary to remain until everyone has left. Move among the people ten to fifteen minutes, and then you may leave. And don't forget that follow-up call or visit to the home.

It is acceptable to conduct the memorial service and allow someone else to conduct the graveside ceremony. If this is done, make arrangements in advance with family and funeral director as well as the person chosen to conduct the graveside service. Encourage them to be brief.

Chapter 43

THE COUNSELING MINISTRY

The gift of exhortation is one of the important gifts of the Holy Spirit given to edify the body of Christ. The gift of exhortation is not so much the ability to exhort people from your pulpit as to encourage them in your office. One cannot overstate the importance of good seminary and other professional training for those who would counsel, but few of us will ever have a Ph.D. or be licensed by the state as certified psychologists. Let me encourage you in two ways: Not only is the best counseling done from a listening ear and encouraging heart, but the only counseling that truly changes lives is biblical counseling.

Many persons who request a counseling appointment can be dealt with without an appointment. Often I call a person who has requested a counseling appointment and say, "Bill, my schedule is rather heavy for a couple of weeks, but go ahead and share your heart with me, and let's see if I can help you right now over the phone." Many needs can be met in this manner. Listen, understand, respond with Scripture-based suggestions, and pray. And assure them you'll continue to do so.

Counseling should always be done with an open door or with a large window in the door. Be cautious here. It is easy to listen compassionately to the personal details of a life and get emotionally involved. A word to the wise will suffice. I hope!

Pastors should not do ongoing counseling. The person whose needs cannot be met in one session should be referred to a professional. God-called and well-trained family counselors abound. Take every opportunity to refer.

When a counseling appointment is made, ask your assistant to inform the counselee that you have a thirty-minute slot available at a given time. If the time is running beyond that duration, the assistant should enter the room and say, "Pastor, your next appointment is here."

Gently control the conversation so the person is encouraged to get to the point. You really don't need a forty-five-minute family history to grasp the problem and give a biblical answer.

Some of the best counsel ever given is already in print. Books by John Trent, Gary Smalley, Chuck Swindoll, Robert McGee, to name a few, are an invaluable help. Recommend an appropriate book to the person you are trying to help. Needs are generally in a few predictable categories: marriage, family, guilt, depression, spiritual direction, financial, call to ministry, and broken relationships. There is always an appropriate book to be recommended and an appropriate Scripture passage to be read. Listen, offer biblically based suggestions, recommend a good book, and pray.

I do not wish to sound uncaring at this point, but pastors who spend hours a week in counseling should go into the full-time counseling ministry. Twenty hours a week invested in counseling will leave little time for your personal spiritual development, study, and family, let alone any time to meet the expanding needs of a growing church and a lost world.

Many experienced pastors will acknowledge, "I have spent over half my time trying to help the same five or ten people." When Jesus said, "You always have the poor with you" (John 12:7), He wasn't speaking contemptuously of the poor. He was simply saying that some things will never change.

And some will not be helped. I do not say they *cannot* be helped; I say they *will not* be helped. If some people didn't have a problem, they wouldn't have anything to talk about, and some create problems to have a purpose not only for their appointment but for their very existence.

As pastors, we will do some counseling, but that must not be the priority of our ministry. If it is, do it full-time. Better to help several people at once with a good sermon than to allow a few to dominate your available counseling time individually and repeatedly.

The counselor must always keep confidences. As pastors, we know things about people we must carry to the grave. Nothing is more despicable than a counselor who cannot be trusted to keep the confidence of the counselee.

Years ago a Christian psychiatrist in our church made an insightful statement. "Pastor," he said, "the problem with psychiatry is we are long on analysis but short on therapy. We can take them apart, but we can't put them together again."

Point them to the One who can take them apart *and* put them back together again. Urge the counselee to get in the Word of God and seek the Holy Spirit, who is the consummate Counselor. In the Word of God, that dear one will find the answer to their problem.

> For unto us a child is born, unto us a son is given: and the government shall be upon his shoulder: and his name shall be called *Wonderful Counselor*, The mighty God, The everlasting Father, The Prince of Peace. (Isa. 9:6)

> I will bless the LORD, who hath given me counsel: my reins also instruct me in the night seasons. (Ps. 16:7)

> Counsel is mine, and sound wisdom: I am understanding; I have strength. By me kings reign, and princes decree justice. By me princes rule, and nobles, even all the judges of the earth. I love them that love me; and those that seek me early shall find me. Riches and honour are with me; yea, durable riches and righteousness. My fruit is better than gold, yea, than fine gold; and my revenue than choice silver. (Prov. 8:14–19)

Chapter 44

WEDDINGS

There is no greater joy in the life of the pastor than being invited to participate in the marriage of a young couple who love the Lord and love each other. After an initial appointment to set the date on the church calendar and make preliminary plans for the wedding, direct the young couple to two different persons in the church.

The first is the wedding coordinator. This person may be a volunteer or a part-time or full-time employee of the church. He or she will assist the couple with music, decorations, candles, flowers, invitations, etc.

The second is the person who will lead them through the preparation-for-marriage course. This person may also be a volunteer.

You may or may not have time to attend the rehearsal dinner. If not, simply say so.

Be certain to find out whether it is appropriate for you to wear a dark suit, tuxedo, or robe. This will vary from wedding to wedding.

I do not normally conduct rehearsals. The wedding coordinator can do that very well. I don't need the practice: I know what I'm going to do.

You may use a wedding manual or other plan for the ceremony as prescribed by your church or selected by you and/or the couple. But I told each couple that I was going to be a bit spontaneous, trying to make each ceremony uniquely personal and individual. I always told the couple, "When you arrive at the altar, relax. I will tell you precisely what to do, when to hold hands, when

to look into each other's eyes, when to kiss, when to kneel, and what to say."
All my instructions were worked into the ceremony.

The wedding coordinator knew that while I was personalizing it as I went
along, I generally followed a predictable pattern in the order of service.

Before the wedding began, I asked her to inform me of anything out of
the ordinary, such as: Is there a unity candle? Will they kneel? Is there one
song or two?

Here's the drill:

1. Mothers and other family members are seated to music.
2. Pastor leads the groom and groomsmen in from the side.
3. Processional of bridesmaids down the aisle, each joined at the altar
   by a groomsman who escorts her to her place.
4. Flower girls and ring bearers enter.
5. Entrance of the bride, greeted by her fiancé.
6. Opening sentence "Dearly beloved," etc., with a short welcome.
7. Prayer.
8. "Who gives this woman to be married to this man?"
9. Step from floor up to the platform and stand behind the kneeling
   bench, followed by the couple.
10. Five-minute sermon on marriage.
11. Ask each person, "Do you take _____ to be your lawful
    wedded _____?"
12. Instruct them to turn to each other, join hands, and look
    into each other's eyes. Again ask each to repeat after me,
    "I _____ take you _____ to be my lawful wedded
    _____."
13. Ask them to turn and face you again.
14. "May I have the ring for the bride?" Say a few words about the
    ring, give it to the groom, and ask the bride to extend the third
    finger of her left hand to him. Instruct the groom to place the ring
    on her finger, look into her eyes, and repeat these vows, "With this
    ring, I thee wed, and with all my worldly goods I thee endow."
15. Ask the couple to kneel on the kneeling bench.
16. Normally I like to have someone sing "The Lord's Prayer" at this
    point. If they do, it is not necessary for you to upstage "The Lord's
    Prayer" with your own prayer. When the music is finished, simply
    say, "Amen." If a different song is sung while the couple kneels,
    pray your own prayer.

17. Ask the couple to stand. Say, "Now, by the authority vested in me by the laws of this state and this New Testament church, it is my pleasure to pronounce you husband and wife."

18. Say, "You may kiss the bride," at which time the groom will raise the bridal veil and do so.

19. Take each of them by the outside elbow, turning them all the way around to face the congregation and say, "Ladies and gentlemen, we present Mr. and Mrs. _____" (Groom's first and last name, i.e. Mr. & Mrs. John Smith).

20. They proceed out the middle aisle; the bride often stopping to give a flower to her mother and, perhaps, her new mother-in-law.

21. Observe the reverse order of processional of the bridal party—i.e., mother was seated last, mother exits first.

22. Step to the front of the platform and say, "This concludes our ceremony. _____ and _____ have asked me to invite you to the reception that follows in fifteen minutes in the parlor. Thank you, and you are dismissed."

A word of caution: Do not let the photographer control the ceremony. And don't ruin the reception by allowing more than fifteen minutes of posed pictures at the conclusion of the ceremony. Don't make the people wait. Let the photographer wait. The reception will be spoiled if the people have to wait forty-five minutes to an hour for the photographer to finish.

Someone asked, "What do you like best about the ministry?" That's easy, "The preaching, the kids, and the weddings."

Chapter 45

WHEN YOU LOSE YOUR CHURCH

I f you are struggling in your church, examine your heart, be transparent, be honest, and get help. What am I doing wrong? What am I not doing right? What should I drop? What should I add?

If your people are dissatisfied, you may be the right person in the wrong church. If you failed morally, repent, confess, get accountable, get renewed and restored. You can minister again. It will likely never be as good as it could have been, and certainly not at the *scene of the crime*. But you can serve again. Samson did. David did. You may land on the street, but you can still land on your feet.

1. Don't give the people a "piece of your mind" in your last sermon. You're bigger than that.
2. Don't blame God.
3. Don't become bitter.
4. Don't do anything for a while. Don't start calling your friends and constantly look for other places to preach.
5. Take off two or three months and do nothing. Reflect, pray, and meditate. What can I learn from what happened? How can it make me a better man? Don't burn your bridges to either the past or the

future. You've got some really great people in that church who still love you, and Romans 8:28 is still in the Bible.

6. Consider your options. With an open mind and a willing heart, pray, "Lord, did You close this door to open another?" The answer is likely yes. Here are some possibilities:

- Serve on a church staff.
- Be called to another pastorate. It may be smaller but have greater potential.
- Enter an entirely new type of ministry: teaching, chaplaincy, counseling, etc. I know very blessed pastors who after an unfortunate experience in the pastorate are doing these things and more.
- Start a church. A neighborhood Bible study with a few friends has been the nucleus of many great churches. Every large church was once a small church. A word of caution: Don't try to get even with the church you left by soliciting their members. If they leave their church and initiate the contact, that's another matter.
- Don't start your church in proximity to the one that terminated you. Such unethical moves just because you feel you were unjustifiably terminated are still unethical. *Seems I remember something about that other cheek.*

7. Get a job. You've got bills to pay and a family to feed. Go to work, work hard, and do it now. You can do any of the other six while you are doing number 7.

There are many options open to you.

Do you really believe Romans 8:28? You do.

Has He really called you into the ministry? He has.

Do you really believe God loves you and has a wonderful plan for your life? Absolutely!

Since your answer to all three questions is yes, rejoice. God is still on the throne, and the best is yet to come.

Chapter 46

SEARCH COMMITTEES

Few pastors spend their entire ministry serving one congregation. Virtually every undershepherd will be confronted at some point with responding to the opportunity to move to another field of service.

No more important decision will face the young pastor in particular than determining the will of God regarding the invitation to pastor a new congregation.

When God moves you from one place to another, two things will happen. There will be a *release* from the *old* and a *passion* for the *new*. These will not necessarily occur in any particular order, but *both will happen*.

1. *Don't try to move.* Don't recommend yourself. Don't ask your friends to recommend you anywhere. If you're that desperate, go drive that truck. Put down deep roots. Give your heart to the people you now serve, and let God move you to His new place at His own pace.

2. *Seek wisdom and counsel from mature believers.*

3. *Don't close the door on God.* Give Him the opportunity to do something new and unique in your ministry. When I moved from First Southern Baptist Church, Del City, Oklahoma, to Houston's First, the Del City church was four times as large. Though this is opposite the normal progression, I saw a vision of what Houston's First could become and sensed the tug of the Holy Spirit to try to fulfill it. Above all, look for "the tug," that deep abiding impression in your heart that, "This I must do."

4. *Don't get in a hurry.* Good decisions are made carefully.

5. *Don't try to sell yourself.* Be honest and transparent.

6. *Look for the potential.* At his inauguration President John Kennedy said, "Some people see things as they are and ask, 'Why?' I see things that never were and ask, 'Why not?'"

7. *Ask the hard questions.* The committee will want to know everything about you. Try to ascertain everything possible about them as well. When I was considering the church in Houston, I asked for the minutes of the last twelve months of deacons' meetings. Ninety percent of their meetings had been spent discussing whether to repair the roof garden in order to continue playing basketball on top of our nine-story downtown building. I knew immediately that the church needed to reexamine its priorities.

8. *Don't play games with the heartstrings of the committee or their church.* You should not agree to come for a trial sermon and preach in view of a call unless you have made up your mind to accept. Nor should the committee extend such an invitation unless they are confident you are the man and certain of the church's call.

9. *Remember the search committee has been selected as a cross section of the church and represents them to you.* Get a feel for who they are, and you will know who the church is.

10. *Have a meeting with the full deacon body of the new church as well as the staff before you agree to preach in view of a call.* This will prolong the process, but the relationship of a pastor and his people is like that of a man and his wife. There is a trusting and intimate relationship between two who will come to love each other more and more through the passing years. Take the time to have a sweet, open courtship, and sweet will be the marriage.

11. *Involve your family in the process.* The pastor's wife should be involved in every meeting with the committee and join the conversation. The couple should participate in all visits to the new church field with their children accompanying them at least once. Even though the children may be small, they should be made to feel it is a family decision and be comfortable with their new home.

12. *Be yourself with the church as you were with the committee.* Don't try to impress them with an old sugar-stick sermon. When I preached in view of a call in Houston that first Sunday in February 1970, I said to the church, "In my own pulpit in Del City, I am in the midst of a Sunday morning series on the Ten Commandments. Were I at home today, I would be preaching on the Fourth Commandment. I am going to preach that sermon today because

I want you to hear a good example of what you would hear on an average Sunday in my church in Oklahoma."

13. *At the conclusion of the service in which you preach in view of a call, you and your family should leave the sanctuary while the church votes on extending the call.* You should then be prepared to accept that call on the spot. Why wait? Once you have come that far, it's time to propose, accept, rejoice, and celebrate the future. The bonding you experience with your new church at that moment will assure a smooth beginning and set your pastorate forward by six months.

14. *It is customary for the church to pay all moving expenses and related costs, as well as a relocation allowance.*

15. *Have as clear an understanding as possible about every issue of the church.* Study the bylaws and constitution. And think twice about an advance agreement to bring certain staffers from your former church. A few months on your new church field may reveal they have the right staff after all.

The committee should arrange a reception for the pastor and his family and be as diligent in helping them settle into their new home and new church as they were in bringing them to it. When the process is completed, invite the committee to your home for an appreciation dinner. They have been God's special instrument in your life, and they will be deeply grateful for this expression of appreciation from you and your family. Pray for yourself and pray for the committee. The time spent in the marriage can and should be as sweet as was the courtship.

Chapter 47

PREPARING THE CHURCH FOR A NEW PASTOR

In some churches a new pastor is appointed by a bishop or appropriate denominational governing body. In a Baptist or Nazarene church, and others, a pulpit committee or pastor search committee seeks out a new pastor.

Once the committee is elected by the church, their responsibility is to seek the heart of God in finding the person they will recommend to the entire congregation for ultimate approval. Let's walk through that process.

To begin with, whether retiring or moving to a new ministry, the exiting pastor has a responsibility to help prepare both the church and the search committee for the interim. A wise pastor will not attempt subtly or overtly to be involved in selecting his successor. But he will give every help possible to the committee in facilitating the process.

The search committee should be instructed in the following ways:

1. *Prayer must be the priority.* God will direct the hearts of sensitive, sincere men and women who hunger to know His will.

2. *Personal preferences and agendas should be laid aside.* To say, "I want a pastor who has been to seminary" will create a problem with a fellow committee member who says, "I want one who hasn't."

For a committee member to have an agenda such as, "I want a man who likes this kind of music or that kind of music" is a mistake. The committee should gently but firmly confront the member with an obvious agenda.

3. *No restrictions should be established.* The committee that begins with the restriction, "We are not calling a man who has not been to seminary," has just excluded the possibility of Billy Graham being their next pastor. It is equally wrong to say he must be under fifty, over thirty, or have X number of years in his present church. Let God be God, and you will get God's pastor for your church.

4. *Solicit names of potential candidates from your congregation, friends, and fellow churches.*

5. *Be wary of one name recommended from many sources.* There is a strong possibility he is calling his friends, asking them to "recommend me to this church." Occasionally, multiple recommendations come because God is indeed spontaneously putting one name on the hearts of many persons. But far too often it is a personal campaign orchestrated by an unhappy or ambitious pastor trying to move, and that's the very one you *don't* want.

6. *Don't get in a hurry. Take ample time for names to be submitted.* Houston's First waited four and a half years for Gregg Matte. He was worth the wait.

7. *Eliminate, eliminate, eliminate.* Feel no obligation to run all over the country hearing thirty or forty prospects just because someone recommended them. This can easily be done by the use of God's great gift to the pastor search committee: *the video.*

8. *Don't ask the pastor to send you a video.* He will send you his sugar stick. Find a way to get several videos without his knowledge. Many pastors may also be heard online.

9. *Once you have "zeroed in," call the church to find out when the pastor will be preaching, but don't identify yourself.* Visit the church two or three times. Don't walk in as a group. Go in as individuals at different times, sit in different places, don't identify yourself, and don't tell the candidate you're coming.

Meet with him in his city, on his church field, before you invite him to yours. And don't make public with either his church or yours that you are talking about his possible candidacy.

10. *When you have determined to invite this person to be your pastor, inform the church of the date on which he will come in view of a call.* Follow his wishes in coordinating the release of information in his church that he will be preaching in view of a call at yours or has actually accepted your call.

11. *Remember, you do not want a person who is anxious to move.* The pastor who is not happy where he is, looking for greener pastures, or anxious to move will not long be happy with you.

12. *If a pastor recommends himself, cross him off your list.*

Lead your church to call an interim pastor. Select a great leader who has the time and ability to help you abound. Retired pastors, men temporarily out of the pastorate, seminary and Christian university professors, denominational workers, to name a few, can provide excellent leadership during an interim.

An interim can be a profitable time. An experienced interim pastor can help a church work through some issues and smooth the runway for the new pastor.

And be sure the interim pastor and the church have a clear understanding about what each means by *interim*.

1. Sunday morning only?
2. Conducting staff meetings?
3. Visiting the sick?

Variations abound.

And *if you* accept a position as an interim pastor, know two things:

1. You must have a clear understanding of what you will and will not do.
2. Regardless how much authority you are granted, the staff will never fully accept your leadership. And that is understandable. An attitude of, "Yes, but we were here before you came, and we'll be here after you're gone," is to be expected.

Chapter 48

WHEN YOU CHANGE CHURCHES

S eldom will you be pressured out of your church. The earlier chapter, "When You Lose Your Church" addresses that subject. But most of the time moving from one church to another will be a time of great joy and optimism. Of course you will give your people plenty of notice that you are moving, but tell your leaders in advance. Making the farewell a positive experience makes the coming of your successor even smoother. Remember that Golden Rule.

The first priority of timing the move is the consideration and calendar of the church you are leaving, not the one to which you are going. I know two pastors who left their church in the middle of a building campaign. They shouldn't have. If God led you to start it, He led you to finish it. Don't abandon your people in the middle of the Red Sea.

Take your time. Make sure your schedule and your church's are smoothly coordinated as you leave. Your new church is excitedly wishing you would come tomorrow, but you will have many happy years with them. You owe them nothing today. They can wait. Your priority is a beautiful exit from the old, *not a hurried entrance to the new.*

Don't announce you will leave one Sunday and leave the next. There is much to wrap up: calendar, future plans now on hold, an interim to prepare for, dinners with special friends, receptions, etc. Then of course there is always a bit of fixing up of your home before you put it on the market, a real estate company to select, accounts to be closed, graduations, and other special dates to consider, to name a few. And it'll take time to find a new house in that new town.

Churches normally pay the house payment for the pastor's old home, doubling up a while with the new house allowance until his old house is sold. It is customary as well that all moving expenses are paid, including a relocation allowance for those new things such as utility deposits, etc.

Love your people. Thank them. Brag on them as you leave. Don't bring up any troublesome issues. Exit gracefully. Say loving good-byes, take your time, and if you have been living in a parsonage, *leave it looking like a million bucks.*

Take your children tenderly through the entire process, and if at all possible, try not to move during the school year. If you move in the summer, be sure you're settled in for your first Sunday before the fall term begins.

Give the new church plenty of time to get used to their new pastor before you ask them to get used to your new ideas. Change slowly. Get to know your staff. Don't start hiring and firing, and remember to think twice about going with the understanding that you can bring certain staff members from your old church. Take adequate time to get acquainted with your new staff. You may find the people already in the position are better qualified to stay there than the ones you intended to bring. God led them there, and *your* coming does not necessarily equate to His leading *them* away.

Learn the system. How do things work? Who are the legitimizers? Which traditions and customs are important to them? And respect them.

You're the pastor and you're the one with the vision. *Vision* means "new," and *new* means "change," and *change* can be painful. So slow down and take time to learn your church. They don't have the vision—yet. And they're not there—yet.

Sheep are led, not pushed. Place a string on the table and try to push it rather than pull it. You get the point. Most of all, trust the Lord and trust the people. God led you to be their new shepherd, and they're glad you're there. Try hard to keep it that way.

Part 4

THE PASTOR AS
ORGANIZATIONAL LEADER

Chapter 49

BEING A LEADER

Our world is dying for lack of moral and spiritual leadership. Deep in the heart of every pastor lies a God-given desire to be the true spiritual leader of his people.

But beyond the bounds of your own congregation, both your denomination and the secular world yearn for respected, authentic leadership that only you can provide. Someone is going to provide it, and our Lord has chosen you to be that person. The apostle Peter lays down some marvelous principles of leadership. "I exhort the elders among you: shepherd God's flock among you, not overseeing out of compulsion but freely, according to God's will; not for the money but eagerly; not lording it over those entrusted to you, but being examples to the flock" (1 Pet. 5:1–3).

Let's talk about five principles of pastoral leadership.

1. *Don't even think about being a leader unless you are certain God has called you.* You're not the chief elder because you called yourself. When it really gets tough, the only thing that will sustain you is a deep conviction: "*This I must do* because God has called me."

The people of God will ultimately turn to you and say, "Pastor, what do you feel the Lord would have us to do?" Dear pastor friend, you had better have been with God and have a deep conviction that you are doing what He wants.

If your plan is God's plan, a deep affirmation will develop within the hearts of His people. First and foremost, be certain of God's call to lead.

2. *It is better to do a few things well than many, not too well at all.* "Shepherd God's flock among you, not overseeing out of compulsion but freely" (1 Pet. 5:2).

Peter begins chapter 5, "I exhort the elders among you." When I saw those words, I could not wait to read what followed. How would Peter instruct me as a pastor to go about leading my congregation? To my amazement and delight, Peter stated only two things for the pastors to do: *feed the flock of God* and *take oversight.* I take this to mean the primary responsibilities of my ministry are: (1) be prepared to preach and teach the Word of God every time I stand in the pulpit, and (2) give general direction to the work of the church and take ultimate responsibility.

You can hire someone to do everything in the church for you except study for your sermons and seek God's direction for your church.

3. *What you do may not be as important as how you do it.* Peter says only two things the pastor is to do, but several about how he is to do them. Humility, integrity, godliness, motivation, character, attitude—these are the qualities that make for great leadership. Style is never a substitute for substance, and style apart from this kind of substance is not authentic biblical leadership.

He who would inspire others to serve must demonstrate an eagerness to serve. The shepherd must be like his sheep, not lording it over others, but humbly serving alongside them as an example to the flock. A hundred books could not contain the names of Christian leaders who have disqualified themselves from service because of their lack of these qualities.

4. *Leadership holds sacred the trust of another.* Verse 3 tells us it is *God's* flock, *God's* heritage. We have nothing in the way of leadership and influence that is not given us by God and granted us by His people. How many times have we said, "Let me tell you about *my* church"? It is not *your* church but *His* church.

5. *The rewards of leadership are later and greater than the price you pay.* When you pass through deep waters in your leadership, you will probably want to untie yourself from the "pulpit."

Verse 4 says, "*When* the chief Shepherd appears, you will receive the unfading crown of glory."

Dear pastor, I cannot promise you that you will have an easy time. In fact, I can promise you won't. The road will be filled with potholes and detours, but great will be the rewards.

The ministry can be a tough job, but the retirement plan is out of this world! A special crown is promised to the faithful undershepherd.

Your greatest joy will not be receiving that crown but seeing His joy as you lay it at His feet.

Chapter 50

WHO MAKES
THE DECISIONS?

U ncounted decisions made in the life of a church are not covered in the New Testament. Certainly someone must decide these things. The question is, who decides what in a church?

Some years ago one of our deacons questioned my authority to make a certain decision. I said to our deacons, "Brothers, probably more than a hundred decisions are made around our church every day. We have seven major ministries, a school, and more than one hundred on staff. And every decision we make relates to some committee.

"If you wish, I can call a hundred committee meetings a day, and none of you will ever get anything done at your job. Or we can assume that we have a competent staff, men and women called of God, who are skilled in their field, who know how to make decisions. We also have a pastor who is not a novice and knows how to make good decisions.

"Obviously certain things need to be voted on by the church. And things of that importance will always be brought to you for counsel and support.

"The question then becomes, at what level are decisions made? The pastor makes decisions, the staff makes decisions, committees make decisions, deacons make decisions, and the church collectively makes some decisions.

"What we have here is a nightmare of trying to unscramble *who does what.* So I want to ask you to give me the authority for one year to be the man who makes the decision as to who makes the decisions. After a year we'll review it, and you can tell me how it's working."

Six years later no one had said anything. The church was operating smoothly so I again brought up the issue and asked how they thought the system was working with the pastor making the decision as to *who makes the decisions*. "Pastor," they said, "it's working just fine. Keep it up."

No set of bylaws could anticipate every type decision. Giving the pastor the authority to decide who decides what is the best and only workable way.

Committees or teams are of great value. As you use committees, you train leaders. During our four-and-one-half-year interim, Houston's First Baptist Church continued to grow. The reason? Great leadership. The leaders had been developed by giving them the opportunity to lead. It was not uncommon for me to go to a committee and say, "Here's an issue we're considering. I want you to discuss it and let me know what you decide."

But some things rise to a level of significance such that the deacons need to be consulted and their wisdom and support enlisted. These kinds of decisions can normally be made at a monthly deacon's meeting, without having to call a special meeting.

In Baptist life, deacons usually perform the function of participating with their pastor, provided by elders or trustees in some churches, in offering counsel to and participating with the pastor in the decision making process.

And it's a system that works and works well. I've never talked with my deacons about an important issue that we did not refine it and come out with a little better decision, and we did so together. Together we can do a better job than any of us can do alone, and it's biblical. At that juncture you then decide whether the issue rises to a level of significance such that the church should approve it.

The curse of little churches is voting on everything. And just as bad, if not worse, big churches far too often vote on nothing. *Both systems are unwise and unbiblical.*

In a smoothly functioning New Testament church, people must learn to trust one another and allow pastor, staff, and committees to make decisions, understanding that anything of major significance will be brought to the deacons or elders and ultimately to the church.

The great heartache I have observed in small churches is everyone wanting to know everything *about* everything and *vote* on everything.

The more you vote and discuss matters publicly, the more you open the door to controversy, division, and loss of testimony due to declining unity in your church. Vote on as little as possible. Only the big things should be discussed publicly.

> Love must be without hypocrisy. Detest evil; cling to what is good. Show family affection to one another with brotherly love. Outdo one another in showing honor. Do not lack diligence; be fervent in spirit; serve the Lord. Rejoice in hope; be patient in affliction; be persistent in prayer. Share with the saints in their needs; pursue hospitality. Bless those who persecute you; bless and do not curse. Rejoice with those who rejoice; weep with those who weep. Be in agreement with one another. Do not be proud; instead, associate with the humble. Do not be wise in your own estimation. (Rom. 12:9–16)

Chapter 51

THE BELIEVER
AND HIS BALLOT

Where God speaks clearly on stated issues in Scripture, no further action is needed than obedience. But many issues are not addressed in Scripture. In the New Testament the whole church made decisions but only the biggest decisions. The major issues always included the multitude. Don't go to the extreme of never deciding on anything collectively.

In the upper room the 120 were involved in the process of determining Judas's replacement as the twelfth disciple. "And the lot fell to Matthias" (Acts 1:26). The church also selected servant leaders, the deacons. In Acts 6, they congregationally expressed their will. They were not appointed by the apostles; they were chosen by the multitude. Clearly in Acts 1 and Acts 6, the whole church acted collectively in making a big decision in determining their leadership, the twelfth apostle and the deacons.

In Acts 10, several people received the Savior, were born of the Spirit, and the question was asked, "Can anyone withhold water and prevent these people from being baptized, who have received the Holy Spirit just as we have?" Others expressed affirmation and approval of their baptism. Clearly in Acts 10, the people determined who would be part of the fellowship. "Can anyone forbid water . . . ?"

In Matthew 18, another kind of church vote may be seen. Jesus tells the simplest form of a local church, "Where two or three are gathered together"

(Matt. 18:20), how to discipline a sinning brother. If he ultimately refuses to repent, he is to be dismissed from the fellowship. Clearly in Acts 10, the church decided who would be *part of* the fellowship and, in Matthew 18, who would be *dismissed from* the fellowship.

In Acts 15, at least one other time the church *acted congregationally*. Again, it was a major issue. The controversy over the circumcision of Gentile believers was so sharp, it was referred to the Jerusalem Council where all the elders and all the apostles gathered together to discuss it and make a decision. Please note it was made by the whole church. Let's examine Acts 15.

In verse 3, Paul and Barnabas make their journey to Jerusalem to discuss the issue with the larger group, and they were sent by the church. In verse 4, when they arrived in Jerusalem, they were received by the church, the whole church, and the apostles and elders.

In verse 7, Peter arose and said, "Brothers," addressing the larger congregation. It is apparently a public gathering, well beyond the meeting between a few disciples and elders, a meeting with the whole church.

In verse 12, all the multitude kept silent as Barnabas and Paul began to speak. In verse 13, James stood and addressed the same men and brethren. Clearly the discussion is going on within the larger group. In verse 22, "Then the apostles and the elders, with the whole church" decided to send Paul, Barnabas, Judas Barsabas, and Silas on to the rest of the churches in Asia Minor to tell them the decision that had been made.

Verse 23 says they wrote a letter and sent it by the hand of the apostles, but not only the apostles. It was sent by "the apostles, the elders, and the brethren."

To whom did they send it? Also in verse 23, "to the brothers." That is, to "the brothers . . . in Antioch, Syria, and Cilicia." Listen carefully to verse 30: "Then, being sent off, they went down to Antioch, and after gathering the assembly, they delivered the letter."

As I earlier mentioned, the heartache of small churches is often voting on *everything*. The tragedy of large churches is often voting on *nothing*. The biblical way is congregationally determining *some* things. The sensible thing is to follow the New Testament pattern and let the church be the ultimate authority in the decision-making process *but only on major issues*. At least three categories are suggested in the New Testament: electing leadership, receiving and dismissing members, and deciding a major issue.

Today many of our larger churches are appointing bylaw study committees; reviewing whether to have business meetings monthly, quarterly, or annually; and identifying what they *will* vote on as a congregation. Most have developed a list similar to this:

1. Who will be their leaders—pastor, major staff, Sunday morning Bible study teachers, committee members, and deacons
2. The annual church budget
3. Changes to the bylaws
4. Changing the name or relocating the church
5. Borrowing a substantial amount of money
6. A building program

Chapter 52

CONSTITUTION
AND BYLAWS

The Bible is our sole authority on who we are, what we believe, and how we function. A document called the "Constitution and Bylaws" is intended to give a brief summary of the truths and how they are fleshed out in the community of the church.

The church constitution (representing the official "constituting," or formation or founding of the church) usually includes the church's name, timeless objectives (perhaps), statement of faith, covenant, and a brief description of its polity (church government). The *bylaws* usually include details about church membership (how to join, general expectations of members, church discipline, termination of membership, etc.); church officers and committees (including pastor, staff, deacons, clerk, treasurer, etc.); job descriptions and expectations of pastor, staff, deacons, and certain committees; church program organizations and services (basic, permanent ones, e.g., Sunday school, mission organizations, worship, music, etc.); the church council; the ordinances; church meetings; church finances, and how to amend the document. This varies from church to church.

Many churches either don't have bylaws, never look at them, or don't know whether they have them.

Technically most states and certainly the IRS require church bylaws on file as part of the requirements for tax exempt status as a 501-C3 nonprofit charitable organization. If you have no such documents, borrow samples from other churches as a starting point to begin drawing up your own. There are no guidelines as to their length, but shorter is better.

The constitution, or statement of faith, sums up the church's position on basic scriptural doctrines of the church, what we believe and who we are as baptized believers bound together to advance the kingdom of God in our world. The SBC statement of faith is a great place to begin.

Some statements of faith or church covenants go so far as to include the church's position on such things as drinking alcohol, gambling, homosexuality, and other issues. If so, your statement of faith should be fleshed out not in legalism but in love.

This document will be studied, researched, and recommended by a study committee. That is not to say it may not be amended by the church in the future. It is to say the train runs better if it runs on its tracks.

The bylaws define how we operate: including how decisions are made. Be cautious here. The bottom line in a Baptist church in this area is *who* makes *what* decisions. There is no way to answer that fully, but remember that obvious pastoral authority in the decision-making arena must be balanced by tender, spiritual leadership that is at once exemplary and earned.

At Houston's First, I had the right to hire and fire. Looking back, I did so primarily in conjunction with the church's personnel committee. Try to vote on as little as possible and make the bylaws at once clear and redemptive. They would include the manner in which they themselves may be changed.

The mission statement should be so clear and brief it could be reduced to a simple PR slogan for your church. Mission statements or vision statements may be two separate documents or one document with two ingredients. The mission statement should be from Scripture and demonstrate and state what we are doing with the people we reach and what is supposed to happen in their lives when we do. *That's our purpose.*

The vision statement is what it's going to look like when we accomplish the mission and how we are going to do it. *That's our strategy.*

All documents should be approved by the entire assembly in a thorough, open, unhurried manner, in more than one business meeting. Take your time. These are huge issues.

Constitution: Who we are and what we believe.

Bylaws: How we operate.

Vision Statement: Our purpose and what it will look like when we accomplish it.

"Everything must be done decently and in order." (1 Cor. 14:40)

> We are one in the Spirit,
> We are one in the Lord,
> We are one in the Spirit,
> We are one in the Lord.
> And we pray that all unity
> May one day be restored.
>> And they'll know we are Christians
>> By our love, by our love.
>> Yes they'll know we are Christians,
>> By our love.
> We will walk with each other,
> We will walk hand in hand.
> We will walk with each other,
> We will walk hand in hand.
> And together we'll spread the news
> That God is in our land.[1]

Endnotes

1. Peter Scholte, "We Are One in the Spirit," ©1966 Peter Scholte, F.E.L. Publications. Assigned 1991 Lorenz Publishing Company.

Chapter 53

DIFFERENT AGENDAS

To ensure the growth and health of the church, we must maintain balance between three New Testament paradigms.

1. Biblically, we must accept *cause, community,* and *corporation* as valid views of who we are.
2. Typically each church member will lean heavily toward one, accept another, and minimize the third.

Cause. Many New Testament passages describe the church in distinctly military terms (2 Tim. 2:3). The core value is winning (Phil. 3:14). Here the emphasis is on commitment and sacrifice (2 Cor. 11:22–28). The person who sees the church primarily as cause is looking to be involved in a world-changing endeavor.

Community. We rightfully think of the church as family (Eph. 3:15). Seen in this light, our core values are love and care (1 John 3:11). We give priority to helping those who are physically weak: infants, members in the hospital, the elderly, etc. (1 Tim. 5:8). People expect the church to provide love, security, and a sense of belonging (1 John 3:1). Most people think of the church primarily in these terms.

Corporation. God's work is also described in business terms (Luke 2:49; 1 Cor. 14:40). Great emphasis must be placed on accuracy and efficiency. We've got to "do it right."

Sunday morning Bible study is a great example of corporation. Bible classes have directors, teachers, secretaries, in-reach leaders, outreach leaders, organized groups, and record keeping.

Churches are also corporations in that they have budgets, employees, health insurance, facilities, calendars, and programs. The "corporate view" person tends to see the church primarily in terms of the bottom line.

Consider the Church as Cause

The *cause* component is often called "being purpose driven." The biggest difference between growing and declining churches is often the presence or absence of a sense of cause. Cause-driven churches focus on the Great Commission; they produce cause-driven leaders who reach people, equip the saints, and instill the vision to start new classes, plant new churches, win the lost, and change the world.

The greatest barrier to church growth may be resistance to change and reluctance to get outside our comfort zone. *Community* is comfortable; *corporation* is necessary. And to our great loss, *cause* is often nowhere to be found.

Consider the Church as Community

Perhaps the most significant contribution of the Sunday morning Bible study to the life of the church is the sense of belonging that accompanies the small, cell-group experience. Even in large classes, the more effective organizations assign members to smaller care groups. Identity within the small group includes social networking, ministry, support, and significance. A prime characteristic of community is its tendency to rally to the support of the weakest family member.

Lifelong friendships in a church most often begin in a Sunday morning Bible study class. The larger the church and/or the larger the urban setting from which it draws its membership, the fewer the opportunities for good fellowship. Sunday morning Bible study must then become the "meeting place" where church members feel part of a community of faith. Sunday morning Bible study is the place where people know your name and miss you when you are absent. Sunday morning Bible study membership provides both accountability and security.

Consider the Church as Corporation

Few members like to think of their church primarily as a business. We much prefer the warm fuzzy of community or the challenge of cause.

But the church must also be viewed as corporation. Records must be kept, calendars coordinated, meetings scheduled, policies observed, bylaws followed, budgets balanced, and bills paid. In every church three kinds of persons may be found:

- Cause people—win the world.
- Community people—minister to me.
- Corporation people—balance the budget.

Every member in your congregation is coming from one of these three places. Understand that. Respect that. Celebrate that and balance it. It's what healthy churches do.

Chapter 54

THE LEGITIMIZERS

The *church boss* gains his position by self-assertion, arrogance, and pride. The *church legitimizers* gain their influence by years of loving service to Christ and His church. Diotrophes was the church boss (3 John 9). Demetrius was the church legitimizer (3 John 12).

Within any congregation are a few really special saints of God. The people recognize them. They love them and honor them and they follow them. "The last shall be first and the greatest among you is the one who is servant of all."

These wonderful people have sought nothing but the good of the church and the advancement of the kingdom of God. The wise pastor will know and respect these people. Their wisdom is proven. Their opinions have been right in the past, and the people, justifiably, value them today.

An insecure pastor may find them a threat. A secure pastor will find them a blessing and source of counsel, encouragement, wisdom, support, and influence.

Early in the new pastorate, you may find their influence greater than yours. No surprise—they've been there longer than you and likely will be there long years after you're gone.

As you must earn your leadership, they have *already* earned theirs. And remember, they are in a position of influence not because they are self-serving, pushy, and controlling but precisely because *they are not.* Befriend and appreciate them.

In any process of idea development toward a major decision, it is essential to *bring along those legitimizers*. They're the ones of whom people silently say in their heart, "If Joe's for it, it's OK."

It will not be spoken or even inferred, *but it will always be there*. It is an indication of your wisdom and your strength, not your immaturity or weakness, that you visit with them early in the major decision-making process.

There is much wisdom in many counselors, and that includes *the legitimizers*. They have never demanded leadership and influence. The people look to them precisely because they have not. They have earned their position as you are earning yours.

Any wise pastor will recognize the value of these people. Love them, seek their wisdom and enlist their support early on in the process of any important decision.

Chapter 55

MAKING TOUGH DECISIONS

I n the vernacular of the business world, "It's windy at the top." Leadership is a risky, dangerous, and lonely business. You have to go before God and stay in your prayer closet until you can come out with a firm and settled peace that you know the way God would have you lead your church. Then do it.

Talk to your people, explain the options, solicit input, and take them with you. Sometimes that process brings you to the point where not everyone is on board but you know you must go forward.

In 1993, in Houston's First, I came to the crossroads of three years of discussion, deliberation, conferences, think tanks, and prayer about the issue of starting a new contemporary worship service in our traditional church. After all that time I came to three convictions:

1. It was the right thing to do.
2. It would not be supported by everyone and would therefore be controversial and costly.
3. I had to do it.

I was not prepared for what would follow. Yes, the new service grew to eighteen hundred in attendance in just a few years and many thousands today.

But some of my best people strongly opposed it. Change comes hard in 170-year-old churches. And yes, I would do it again, but it was not done *without a price.*

Years later our young singles and married young adults are booming. Hundreds of new young couples are attending the church, and the preschool and nursery division recently enrolled thirty-seven new babies in one month.

When you come to the end of the road and have to make a decision, both the result and the fallout are in the hands of God. Remember, every great decision is made with an element of risk. We do not claim infallibility. We may be wrong, and perhaps often are, but we go forward in faith, doing the best we can to follow the will of God as we understand it. Great progress is accomplished at great cost.

Change is always difficult, and the only thing that will see you through is a deep, settled conviction that you have been with God, heard His voice, and know His will. Take your time. Everything must be done on God's schedule. Sometimes God's answer is, "Yes, but not now." Timing is everything, and "the battle is the LORD's" (1 Sam. 17:47).

The overreaching factor in tough decisions is the unwavering conviction in your soul that it is what God wants you to do. That takes total surrender and ample time.

Never forget it's God's church, not yours, and not even the people's. Nothing else matters in decisions about His church except His will. Nothing.

Once you know that you know that you know, move forward in confidence and faith. And don't let your confidence translate into obtrusiveness or arrogance. Humility and confidence are not mutually exclusive.

Patiently begin conversation with your leaders. Bring along those legitimizers and leaders. And don't forget the importance of full disclosure. God's people, given the facts, will normally do the right thing.

No surprises and lots of time to explain and re-explain. The *what* and *why* are essential. In a major decision let the people vote and move forward.

Never forget three important things:

1. Don't ever change deeply entrenched traditions quickly. That new wine will burst the old wineskin every time.
2. Change means life and life means growth. Healthy things grow.
3. The blessing of the new will linger long after the trauma of changing the old if it's God's change, not yours. If it's His, go for it. The prize is worth the price.

You, therefore, my son, be strong in the grace that is in Christ Jesus. And what you have heard from me in the presence of many witnesses, commit to faithful men who will be able to teach others also.

Share in suffering as a good soldier of Christ Jesus. No one serving as a soldier gets entangled in the concerns of civilian life; he seeks to please the recruiter. Also, if anyone competes as an athlete, he is not crowned unless he competes according to the rules. (2 Tim. 2:1–5)

Chapter 56

THE CHURCH BOSS

I wrote unto the church: but Diotrephes, who loves to have the preeminence among them, received us not. Wherefore, if I come, I will remember his deeds which he does; prating against us with malicious words: and not content with that, neither does he himself receive the brethren, and forbids them who would, and casts them out of the church" (3 John 1:9–10).

The Church Boss

Sad to say, virtually every church has one. John knew one and described him well in his third general epistle.

1. *He is self-appointed.* Think about that. How diametrically opposed to the teachings of Christ. "The last shall be first." "He that is greatest amongst you must be servant of all." In all things Christian the way up is down. The way to resurrection and ascension is the cross.

The clear pattern of the church in Acts is church governance by the church's will, not the church's boss. In Acts 1, the church determined the twelfth apostle. In Acts 6, the church determined the deacons. In Acts 15, the church collectively made the most important decision of the New Testament regarding Gentile circumcision.

2. *Diotrephes had a major problem with pride.* He loved to have preeminence. Perhaps he was emulating what he had seen some pastor have:

a king-type persona. First Peter 5:3 warns those who would "lord it" over the flock. I always see such people and ask, "Have they really been to the cross?"

3. *He speaks with malicious words.* Malice of forethought is fatal in a court of law. Malicious thought precedes malicious words. Words spoken from the arrogant drip with the bitterness of contempt, "Only I am the authority here."

4. *Church bosses are presumptive.* They presume to run the church by going so far as saying who and what goes on in the church and who gets booted out of the church. Unbelievable!

What to Do?

1. *Pray for them.*

2. *Understand these are insecure people.* Power grabbing is for little people who feel inadequate. Big people are secure enough to lay down their life for others. Pride, arrogance, and self are *spiritual problems.* Lost people are insecure. Believers are secure. They know *who* they are because they know *whose* they are "in Christ." I was commonly approached by one church boss. Every opening remark was the same, "Everybody's saying." One day I challenged him and asked him to name "everybody" that I might call them and discuss the problem. He could name none. "Everybody's saying" usually means me and my brother-in-law. The insecure invent support that doesn't exist.

3. *They are often living completely out of God's will.* Listen carefully. Let the church boss talk long enough, and you will often hear something about a call to the ministry he refused to obey. Not having the humility, courage, and faith to become a pastor, he's going to spend his life scratching the itch by telling *you* how *you* should pastor. Such people have no credibility in matters ecclesiastical. Ignore their opinion.

4. *Vow: I will make a friend of this person.*

5. *Don't make obvious reference and don't call them by name, but deal with it objectively in context of an expository series through 1, 2 and 3 John.*

6. *If all the above fails, consider church discipline.*

Chapter 57

THE LEGALIST

The legalist will always be "a thorn in the flesh" to those who minister in grace. Unfortunately, some churches have more than their fair share of them.

The classic example of legalism and how to handle it is the story of the Pharisees who brought a woman caught in the act of adultery to the feet of Jesus. The wise pastor will learn much of Satan's wily ways and Jesus' masterful response through this insightful story.

> And early in the morning he came again into the temple, and all the people came unto him; and he sat down, and taught them. And the scribes and Pharisees brought unto him a woman taken in adultery; and when they had set her in the midst, They say unto him, "Master, this woman was taken in adultery, in the very act. Now Moses in the law commanded us, that such should be stoned: but what sayest thou?" This they said, tempting him, that they might have to accuse him. But Jesus stooped down, and with his finger wrote on the ground, as though he heard them not. So when they continued asking him, he lifted up himself, and said unto them, "He that is without sin among you, let him first cast a stone at her." And again he stooped down, and wrote on the ground. And they which heard it, being convicted by their own conscience, went out one by one, beginning at the eldest, even unto the last: and Jesus was left alone, and the woman standing in the midst. When Jesus had lifted up himself, and saw none but the woman, he

said unto her, "Woman, where are those thine accusers? Hath no man condemned thee?" She said, "No man, Lord." And Jesus said unto her, "Neither do I condemn thee: go, and sin no more." (John 8:2–11)

Legalism is of course connected to the law and is by definition specific, precise, structured, restrictive, and tough. Legalism is everything grace is not.

Legalism is a mind-set. It's the policeman who tickets you for driving fifty-six in a fifty-five miles-per-hour zone. It's the diner who pulls out his Blackberry and calculates the 15 percent tip to the penny and not a penny more.

And in a Church It's Deadly

Legalism never asks how much can I give, only how little. Legalism makes God more restrictive than He is. Eve said, "God said, 'Don't eat of the tree or touch it.'" No He didn't. He said, "Don't eat of it." Grace wants to believe the best. Legalism wants to believe the worst. Grace sees the cup half full; legalism sees it half empty. Let's look at our story.

1. *Legalism looks for what's wrong; grace looks for what's right.* Notice the Pharisees got up *early in the morning.* Legalism does that. It's on the prowl, in the hunt, looking for something to exploit. The King James says the Pharisees reported this woman was taken in adultery, in the very act. They started the chase, pursued their prey, set the trap, and said, "Gotcha!" Legalism always *gets up early in the morning.* It's always wily, aggressive, and out to catch someone doing wrong.

2. *Legalism sets standards for others it seldom meets itself.* How did the Pharisees know where she was? Think about it. She was *caught in the act.* These things are committed behind closed doors, locked doors.

Perhaps they knew where *she* was because *he* was one of theirs. Likely *they* had frequented her chambers as well. Perhaps that's why, convicted, they left one by one, beginning with the eldest. Longer lives equate to more sin. More sin equates to more guilt and an early exit from the presence of holiness.

3. *The legalist is an insecure person.* Note the *Pharisees* brought her, not "*a Pharisee*" brought her. That was a lot of Pharisees! How many grown men does it take to drag one frail woman to the feet of Jesus? But the legalist needs support. *Insecurity always does.* The security and support of the crowd is the only way the insecurity of the legalist can operate. My official church legalist began every conversation with, "Everybody's saying."

4. *Legalism looks at what's been; grace looks at what can be.* They said, "Look what she did." Jesus said, "Let's look at what she can be." "Neither do I condemn you—go your way and sin no more."

5. *Legalists normally have good theology but a bad spirit.* She was *indeed* guilty, and they did *correctly* quote the law of Moses regarding her punishment. The Pharisees looked through the eyes of law; Jesus looked through the eyes of love. They cared nothing for the poor humiliated woman. She was only a tool to set a theological trap for Jesus by *using* the law. But Jesus came to *fulfill* the law with love. Liberals often have *bad theology* but a *good spirit*. Fundamentalists often have a *good theology* but a *bad spirit*. Why not both good theology *and* a good spirit.

6. *Jesus has the cure for legalism.* Across all the Old Testament law, Jesus stamped one word, *love*, and summed it all up like this, "You shall love the Lord your God with all your heart, mind and soul and your neighbor as yourself."

The legalist is totally out of place in a fellowship of grace and should never be given respect, credence, or positions of leadership.

Chapter 58

DEALING WITH OPPOSITION

The bad news is that some people will oppose you. The good news is, it's never as bad as you think. The great majority of the time, if a situation becomes serious enough to go to the floor of the church in a special-called Sunday morning business meeting, the people of God will stand with you.

Frankly some churches can be difficult to pastor. Houston's First was not. I know several churches with a long history of "running off the pastor" every year or two. Often the reason is three or four people in places of leadership who are frustrated preachers. Deacons and committee chairmen who heard the voice of God as youth, disobeyed it, and live in a state of rebellion against God are hard people to shepherd.

This does not mean that everyone who opposes you is such a person. It does mean that many times the church with a pattern of pastoral opposition is a church with a history of frustrated, disobedient people in places of leadership.

Things are seldom as bad or as widespread as you are led to believe. Adrian Rogers used to say, "*The devil can make one sound like a thousand.*"

As pastor of one of the more recognizable churches in our city, I received letters each month about people's opinions. Ninety percent were most encouraging and supportive, but ten in a hundred were negative and critical.

The first thing to do when you receive such a letter is absolutely nothing. Whatever you do, don't react and don't immediately answer the letter. Put it aside a week or ten days, settle down, cool off, and wait. At first your emotional response will be as great from those ten letters as from the positive ninety. But after a while it will subside.

Several days later read the letter again. Read it objectively and fairly. The writer has not only the right to their opinion but also the right to express it. And they think as they do *for a reason*.

Circumstances have shaped people. Their parents have affected them. Life has formed them. Everybody's *coming from someplace*.

Older people don't like change. They don't like new music; they don't like to sit in a new place in the worship center.

Continuity is closely connected to security, and rare is the person who can easily accept change in their older years.

Perhaps they lived through the Great Depression. The things that were happening in our world at age nine to twelve tend to lock us in attitudinally. Was there a divorce, a world war, a tornado, a family death, a depression?

Estimate the age of your critics. Backdate to what was happening in their lives when they were between nine and twelve, and you'll get an idea of the frame of reference from which they are coming. People who were that age at the time of the Great Depression are extremely cautious. They don't like to borrow money; they don't like debt. Something deep inside them says, "It can happen again."

Understand the person, take your time, and be gracious in your response. Carefully write the letter, set it aside a few days, pray over it again, think about it some more, rewrite it, and send it. Your response should be kind, gracious, and conciliatory.

I always thanked people for writing, told them I was glad they felt the freedom to express their views, and assured them that I would respectfully consider their opinions. Finish the letter with a word of appreciation for who they are and what they mean to the kingdom. And ask them to pray as together you seek the Lord in the matter under consideration.

Take seriously what your critic says. He just might be right. There is almost always at least *something* valid in the opinion of a critic.

You will also face difficult times when critics go beyond differences of opinion to outright anger. Years ago I received a letter from a former church member. He mistakenly said I had made the statement, "If God doesn't financially prosper you when you begin tithing, I will personally give you your money back." He demanded the return of some $7,000 in tithes.

My response did not address his demand and was rather an outpouring of genuine concern for his needs and those of his family. Today he is a happy and faithful member of our church.

God's people are good people, and some are certainly easier to pastor than others. But if we respond in love, our Lord will always help us find a way to deal with them in grace.

"A gentle answer turns away anger." (Prov. 15:1)

Chapter 59

SAVE YOUR LEADERSHIP

I f you get involved in every brush fire, worry about every problem, and fight every battle, you will use up your leadership and won't have it when you need it. Whatever you do, don't use up your leadership. Don't go to war over small issues. Don't even get involved. Let your leaders deal with the small stuff.

In my ministry I have had only one or two serious problems. By God's grace I was able to address both with complete success. The secret? I saved the authority and influence of the position of pastor until something major was on the line. But just because you don't sweat the small stuff doesn't mean you don't have to sweat.

Let me tell you a story. In the late 1970s, a plethora of strange doctrine began to invade our church from certain sources. I talked to all the people—church members, deacons, and teachers—who were caught up in and perpetuating it in our membership. It was a serious issue, and no one could address it but the pastor. I went straight to the pulpit on a Sunday morning and confronted the issue head-on. The sermon was comprised of ten aberrant doctrines being taught in our church and the biblical answers that refuted each.

Then I finished the message by saying, "Henceforth, the teaching of this doctrine will no longer be tolerated in the Sunday morning Bible study classes or other meetings of this church.

"It is the responsibility of the pastor to articulate the historic doctrines of the church. If it's not, then tell me whose responsibility it is. Is it the custodian's? Is it the minister of music's? I think not. It is mine, and I will accept it."

Pointing to our brick walls, I said, "See those bricks. See that mortar between those bricks. That's not concrete. That's blood. That's Baptist blood. When I came here ten years ago, I came to a Baptist church that had been built by the blood, sweat, tears, and sacrifice of Baptist people for more than a century; and when I leave, it will, by God's grace, still be a Baptist church. And if that's not acceptable to you, the door swings both ways."

You can't stand up on your haunches and talk that way and know the people will support you if you've dissipated your leadership in a battle over what color to paint the nurseries.

As a friend so insightfully says, "I'm going to choose the hill I die on." That afternoon I walked into the deacons meeting, and our men gave me a standing ovation.

Another incident happened in the early 1980s. A man in our church began following the teachings of Herbert W. Armstrong. During one morning service he put literature under all the windshield wipers in our parking lot, attempting to refute the deity of Jesus.

I called him on Monday morning and said, "You have until Wednesday night to give me your answer. You have three choices: You can stand before our church next Sunday morning and apologize and refute this doctrine; we can vote you out of our membership at the conclusion of the morning service; or you can leave the church and never come back." He chose the latter.

I am willing to die on the hill of the historic doctrines of the faith. Jesus Christ is God in the flesh. Salvation is by grace through faith. By His blood we are saved. I am willing to die on those hills.

The inerrancy battle in the Southern Baptist Convention was hard on all of us. As it began to peak, the Lord put in my spirit to wait until the time was right to take my stand. That time came at the watershed convention in New Orleans 1992. I enlisted four prominent pastors who had also been awaiting the right time. Together we stepped into the gap, put it all on the line, and the rest is history.

Some things are nonnegotiable. Don't use up your leadership on small issues. One day you will have a major battle to fight. And you will need everything you have saved up in your leadership bank.

Chapter 60

THE ART OF
EFFECTING CHANGE

A stagnant organization is a dying organization. Change means growth and growth means change.

Our criteria for change is never the latest "church growth" fad or the newest innovation of that church down the street. Change must be from the prompting of the Holy Spirit. Change for the sake of change is never appropriate. "This isn't working; let's try something different" is a blueprint for failure.

How does the wise pastor facilitate change? The Lord will normally give you the vision and direction He would have your people go before He gives it to them. This is not to say only you hear the voice of God. It's not to say that good ideas never come up "through the ranks." It *is to say* that the job of leaders is to lead, and that means getting out in front.

The key elements of change are *information* and *patience*. When the Lord gives you a vision for a new ministry or a new direction for your church, gather your leaders and begin to discuss it. Remember to bring along those legitimizers whose support you will need because of their influence with large numbers of your people.

Slowly begin to explain the issue, listing possible solutions, and share with your people what you sense the Lord is leading you to do. Every vision needs refining. The people will offer good suggestions, some of which may never have occurred to you.

Don't call for a decision on the spot. Lay it before your leaders, discuss it, ask them to pray about it and meet with you at a later date.

The next step is to speak to the appropriate committee, then your leadership team: deacons or elders, and then the church. At each level lay it before the people as something in which you sense the leadership of the Lord.

If a person says to me, "God told me," I am going to walk away. If they say, "God told me to tell you," I am going to run. If they say, "I sense the Lord is leading me," I will listen.

Before introducing a bold new program to win the world, spend some Sundays preaching about Jesus' compassion for the lost. Before you introduce that million-dollar building program for a new youth recreation building, preach about the needs of a dying generation of teenagers and the responsibility of the church to reach them.

Remind your people that *the message never changes, but the means must be ever changing.* The telegraph has been outdated by radio, radio by television, television by the Internet, and the end is not yet. Take your time, give adequate information, instill the vision, and try to get everyone on board.

Provide a forum in which to allow questions. What will happen if we do this? What will we lose if we don't? What are the risks? What is the cost? Are there other options? Will there be a committee? Will this be done at the sacrifice of other programs in the church? God's people are good people, and they can handle the truth.

When you begin a new ministry, don't be afraid to experiment. Everything doesn't have to be forever. While this is true, make every effort to see it through. Give new ministries time. Even the best will often struggle at first. The most common things that tear up Baptist churches are deacon-pastor conflict, worship wars, and changing too fast.

In a new pastorate members have enough of an adjustment to look up every Sunday and see a new face in the pulpit. It takes time to adjust to you before they're ready to adjust to your changes. Reverse the order and you are doomed to failure. Don't change anything quickly!

I could write a book on modern-day churches that lost hundreds, even thousands of members, in a few months. All were good churches with good pastors who had good ideas but bad timing. Too much too fast. Don't!

> Then John's disciples came to Him, saying, "Why do we and the Pharisees fast often, but Your disciples do not fast?"

Jesus said to them, "Can the wedding guests be sad while the groom is with them? The days will come when the groom will be taken from them, and then they will fast. No one patches an old garment with unshrunk cloth, because the patch pulls away from the garment and makes the tear worse. And no one puts new wine into old wineskins. Otherwise, the skins burst, the wine spills out, and the skins are ruined. But they put new wine into fresh wineskins, and both are preserved." (Matt. 9:14–17)

Chapter 61

PRINCIPLES OF
MOTIVATION

Information plus motivation equals action. Is there action in your church? Is there growth, purpose, and direction? Are there results? Is there progress and conquest? If not, and you are a man of prayer, if you live among prospects, and if you are preaching the truth, one of two things is likely true: there is either inadequate information or insufficient motivation. In other words, people must *know what* to do and *want* to do it.

The problem is that most of us *know* to do more than we *want* to do! We are the best-informed believers in history. We have more education, information, conferences, conventions, clinics, and colleges than our forefathers. Multitudes of us have covered our walls with seals representing completed courses of study. We learn, but we do not accomplish. We comprehend, but we do not do. We are hearers of the Word but not doers. Too many have *won a seal* but have never *won a soul*!

While we continue to use new methods, new witnessing ideas, and new ways to teach our people how to be soul winners, the truth is that most of them simply don't want to be soul winners. They have *information* but not sufficient *motivation*. If they had to, most Christians could probably tell a person how to accept Christ as their personal Savior. Few actually do.

The reason we do so little is that information—knowing what to do—is not being coupled with motivation—the desire *to do* what we know. To *know* what to do is human. To *do* what we know to do is divine.

The first ingredient in motivation is *enthusiasm.* Years ago I flew to Florida. On the plane I chatted with Darryl Royal, legendary University of Texas head football coach. I asked him to choose one word that was the major contributing factor to his unparalleled success as a coach. That word? *Attitude!* Solomon said it this way, "As [a man] thinketh in his heart, so is he" (Prov. 23:7 KJV).

A mediocre football team can beat a better team if it thinks it can. If you approach a situation with failure in mind, you will fail. Expect, plan, hope, and dream. Attitude is all-important. If *you* want to do it, and believe *God* wants you to do it, get your people excited about it, and you can do it. Motivation begins with *enthusiasm.*

Enthusiasm builds empires. Enthusiasm makes successes of common men. Enthusiasm does the impossible. Enthusiasm is half the battle. He who would excite must be excited.

The word *enthuse* comes from two Greek words *en* and *theos.* That means simply, "in God" or "God in you." It is the picture of the lesser containing the greater. It is like two wildcats in a gunnysack. The result: enthusiasm, excitement, and action!

Second, motivation is *repetition.* Wrigley built an empire on five-cent chewing gum. But he sold an awful lot of those packages. His advertising philosophy was simply "repetition."

Keep before your people the urgency of outreach, the imperative of evangelism. At every gathering, every committee meeting, and every assembly, talk about winning the world to Christ. Make it the driving, burning, consuming passion of your people.

Years ago I walked into a drugstore in Ohio to buy some razor blades. The store was having a sale on peach sundaes. Hundreds of flyers hung from the ceiling. They were everywhere: "Peach Sundae, 19 cents, Peach Sundae 19 cents." I went to the counter and took out a dollar to buy razor blades. The clerk said, "What will you have?" I said, "Give me a peach sundae!" I didn't want a peach sundae. I wanted razor blades! Repetition had won the day!

For years the First Baptist Church of Amarillo, Texas, led the entire Southern Baptist Convention in mission giving. I asked the pastor at the time, Dr. Carl Bates, for his secret. He said, "I have never preached a sermon on Sunday morning, Sunday night, or Wednesday night without at least mentioning tithing." Repetition. Repetition. Repetition.

Third, motivation is *illustration*. Every time I preach, I try to mention the name of one of our people who has done what I am asking my people to do. When a new convert is introduced and you know one of your people has led them to Christ, call that person to the front to stand by the new convert when he is introduced. Illustrate soul winning to the people. Show them what others are doing. Suggest they can do the same.

Fourth, motivation is *example*. Do it yourself. People are not naïve. If you go Sunday after Sunday without one conversion, people will justifiably begin to wonder why you as pastor can't win someone once in a while yourself. Lead the way. Set the pace. Show them how.

We motivate others when they see us do it, and only you know in your heart whether what they see is for God's glory or yours. If you know it and He knows it, that's all that really matters.

Chapter 62

SIMPLIFY THE ORGANIZATION

Without exception the great churches of America have established priorities and eliminated less important activity. Busyness is often the death knell of the modern church. While it is good to be organized and active, it is possible to relegate the primary to the secondary and organize yourself out of business.[1]

Wednesday night must be centered in preparation and outreach for Sunday's day of harvest. Any week that has a special activity—such as an extra one-night service, banquet, or fellowship—may negatively impact attendance at other regularly scheduled activities. People have only so many hours in a week, and they have more to do than go to church.

Christian families must have time to be a family. Home life, recreation, and other outside interests are important, too. Parents should attend their son's debate contest or their daughter's volleyball game. It is imperative that parents take interest in their children's activities. A well-rounded life is important. A family involved in church activities four or five nights a week may well become a family with burnout.

Because a particular church activity has met on a particular night at a particular time for a long time does not make it hallowed. That one hour meeting could be cut to forty minutes. With preparation and planning, that thirty-minute meeting could be cut to twenty. Consolidate Wednesday night activities. Go over every activity with a fine-tooth comb. Streamline and reorganize, plan, add, and eliminate.

In the best-case scenario, everything churchwide is accomplished in two nights per week—Wednesday and Sunday. It is possible to schedule all auxiliary meetings, including officers and teachers meetings, prayer and Bible study, and a Wednesday night meal from 5:30 to 7:00, with churchwide visitation from 7:00 to 8:00—on the way home from church!

Give people the opportunity to visit prospects on nights when they will already be at church by making a prospect visit on their way home. It's better for two hundred people to visit one prospect each on Wednesday night than for the faithful fifteen to visit three each on Monday night. Final score: two hundred to forty-five. By all means, find a way to streamline the organization.

Take one-fourth or one-third of the time off each activity and try to consolidate it all into a streamlined, swiftly moving Wednesday night program. Don't drag your people to church four or five times a week. They will be better for it, the kingdom of God will prosper, and you will have time to be a better husband and father, as well as pastor.

Doing less and doing it better is always wise. No church can be a "jack of all trades," and certainly not every pastor can meet every need. Busier and bigger are not always better. Great buildings and great numbers of people do not necessarily equate to great success in God's eyes.

Your people will not witness and attend, or bring their friends and talk up the church, if a negative attitude of despair and pessimism permeates your church because of exhausting, overloaded church programming.

It is important to instill pride in your people. Clean up the buildings. Paint that old sign. Mow the grass. Shine your shoes. Sharpen the service. Make your people proud to be Christians, proud of the church, and proud of their pastor. They will relate, they will want to come, and they will bring their friends whether you offer one hundred ministries or five.

Yours may be a small church, but in the heart of your people it should be the greatest little church in the world. Forget your problems and major on the majors. Do a *few* things and do them well and do *some* things better than anybody else in town. *And that may mean doing less.*

Reexamine your vision statement. What has God's uniquely directed your church to do and be?

Doing a few things well greatly exceeds doing a lot just for the sake of busyness and activity.

I know a great women's ministry that offers twenty-five special Bible studies each spring and fall. Perhaps ten or fifteen would suffice. The great apostle made clear the value of bringing all your spiritual, mental, and emotional faculties to bear on one main thing in making spiritual progress.

> "Brethren, I count not myself to have apprehended to these: but this one thing I do, forgetting those things which are behind reaching forth unto those things which are before, I press toward the mark for the prize of the high calling of God in Christ Jesus." (Phil. 3:13–14)

One thing.

Endnotes

1. See Thom Rainer and Eric Geiger's great book, *Simple Church: Returning to God's Process for Making Disciples* (Nashville: B&H, 2006).

Chapter 63

THINGS TO CONTROL

The pastor of a church, large or small, is not a dictator but a shepherd. There is a special combination of leadership and servanthood combined in the office of pastor, to which we often refer as "undershepherd."

On one hand, we are leading the people. On the other hand, we ourselves are being led by God and are servants of His people.

Leadership is never demanded; it is always deserved. It must be granted by the congregation but earned by the pastor. Jesus taught this concept when He said, "The greatest among you will be your servant."

One day a centurion, the commander of a hundred Roman soldiers, came to Jesus. His request to Jesus to heal his servant was met with a warm response: "I will come and heal him" (Matt. 8:7).

The centurion said, "Only say the word [right here], and my servant will be cured" (v. 8).

Then the centurion made an insightful statement. "For I too am a man under authority. . . . I say to this one, 'Go!' and he goes; and to another, 'Come!' and he comes" (v. 9).

The centurion was saying, "I understand how authority works. I have authority over my soldiers, because I am under the authority of the Roman government."

He recognized that Jesus had authority to heal his servant with a simple command because He was under the authority of His Father. Jesus responded,

"I have not found so great faith, no, not in Israel" (Matt. 8:10), and the servant was healed at Jesus' command.

Pastor, you have the responsibility and authority to lead your congregation only because you stay under the authority of God. And there is a sense in which you are, as well, under the authority of your people. The apostle Paul said, "Consider others as more important than yourselves" (Phil. 2:3). Yes, your congregation is accountable to you as you speak for the Father on the authority of His Word. You, in turn, are accountable to them. It is a system that is virtually impossible for the secular world to understand, but it is how the body of Christ functions.

When I came to the pastorate of Houston's First, I assured the pastor search committee that it would be my joy to work with the deacons and other leaders in making major decisions. But I also told them five things were not negotiable—five areas in which I must have absolute control—to which they agreed:

1. It was my responsibility and mine alone to articulate the doctrines of the church. I will speak from the pulpit and say, "This is what this church believes." If not the pastor, who?
2. New deacons, teachers, and committee members would be recommended to the church only with the advance approval of the pastor.
3. I must have control over who preaches in our pulpit and when.
4. I must have control over what special offerings are received, when, and for what purpose.
5. I must have the right to hire and fire staff.

In the higher levels of staff positions, I always made those decisions in concert with the personnel committee. To the glory of God, in thirty years we always agreed on the personnel decisions that had to be made. But I reserved the right to make the final decision.

Again, there is a delicate balance between leading the people and being their servant. Don't make a big deal out of small issues. Save your influence and authority until major issues are on the line. Some things are worth fighting for. Some are not.

The best time to come to agreement about these issues is when you begin to get serious with the pastor search committee about the possibility of accepting the pastorate of their church. Talk them through in advance. Be certain the committee is articulating the position of the church in these matters, and be sure they are fully conveying your positions back to the congregation.

Let there be no surprises three or four months into your new pastorate. Good marriages are in part the result of good courtships. And good courtships take time. Take your time and work these things through in advance. You must control some areas, and they must be clearly defined before your installation as pastor. No church wants a puppet preacher. People respect leadership, and the function of leadership is *to lead*. The smoothness of a leader's path can be greatly enhanced by clearly drawing up the map before the trip begins.

Chapter 64

ESSENTIAL UNITY

F ive times in John 17, Jesus prays for unity.
"That they may be one as we are" (v. 11).
"That they all may be one" (v. 21).
"That they all may be one in us" (v. 21).
"That they may be one just as we are one" (v. 22).
"That they may be made perfect in one" (v. 23).
Why? In order that "the world may believe you sent me" (v. 22).

The unity of the body of Christ is important to our witness to a lost world. The world doesn't read the Bible, but they do read us. Nothing makes Jesus the laughingstock of the world like perpetual fighting and division among His people. Unity *attracts.* Disunity *repulses.*

And after the fight *it can take twenty years* until another generation grows up that never heard about the fight, before you regain your witness in the community.

Many analogies are used in Scripture to illustrate the relationship between Jesus and His people. He is the Groom, we the bride. He is the Captain, we the soldiers. He is the Lord, we the servants. But there is none more meaningful than this: *He is the Head, we are the body.*

As the Head in heaven, Jesus flows His very being through His body on earth—His people. When that happens, a kind of perpetual ongoing incarnation of Jesus occurs every time His people get together. Jesus now reveals Himself in a new body, a *bigger* body, a *greater* body.

The church is *Christ's body on earth*. When Jesus was in one body in this world, He had tremendous magnetism and charisma. Women adored Him. Little children crawled all over Him. Men would die for Him. Everyone wanted to be close to Jesus.

In His earthly body Jesus was limited to one place at one time. But now, because He has come back invisibly in the person of the Holy Spirit, He lives incarnate in a bigger body, His people, the church. And the immediate expression of that is *the local church*, your church!

That is why we must absolutely protect the unity of the body of Christ, and it is best lived out in the spirit of Romans 12:10: "Show family affection to one another with brotherly love. Outdo one another in showing honor."

Here's what I think that means for your next business meeting; "I may not agree with you, but in love I'm going to fight harder for your opinion to be heard with respect than for my own opinion to be accepted."

There will always be issues to resolve. Everything is not addressed in the New Testament: What time your services should begin? Who should be the new pastor? Should the church relocate?

And how are those decisions made? The Head speaks through His body. We meet and pray; we express our views in honor, love, and respect; and then we vote.

Once the people have voted, we must assume Christ, as Head in heaven, has expressed His will through His body on earth. And once the congregation has expressed the mind of Christ through His body, case closed.

The person in opposition to the majority vote has two options:

- Support the majority and be quiet.
- Move on and get happy somewhere else.

No disgruntled believer has the right to disrupt the sweet fellowship of Christ's church. He has an obligation not to.

Preach unity. Teach unity. Pray for unity. Confront disunity. And consistently remind your deacons that they are the guardians of the fellowship.

> Now I urge you, brothers, in the name of our Lord Jesus Christ, that all of you agree in what you say, that there be no divisions among you; and that you be united with the same understanding and the same conviction. (1 Cor. 1:10)

> How good and pleasant it is when brothers live together in harmony! (Ps. 133:1)

> Diligently keeping the unity of the Spirit with the peace that binds us. (Eph. 4:3)

Part 5

THE PASTOR AS PREACHER

Chapter 65

FEED THE SHEEP

When they had eaten breakfast, Jesus asked Simon Peter, "Simon, son of John, do you love Me more than these?"

"Yes, Lord," he said to Him, "You know that I love You."

"Feed My lambs," He told him.

A second time He asked him, "Simon, son of John, do you love Me?"

"Yes, Lord," he said to Him, "You know that I love You."

"Shepherd My sheep." (John 21:15–16)

You can strike out almost anywhere else and survive. But fail here and you'll lose the game. Twelve years into retirement, we still get letters of encouragement and thanks from our sweet congregation. The number one theme of them all is "thanks for feeding us the Word of God." After it's all over, here's the test of your ministry: Did I build mature believers? Strong in the Word. Sound in doctrine.

After my retirement our church waited four and one-half years before calling our new pastor, Gregg Matte. The church grew during the interim for four reasons:

1. The leadership of our executive pastor
2. Strong Bible study units
3. Well-trained leaders
4. Sound doctrine

Pastor Russ Barksdale of The Church on Rush Creek in Arlington, Texas, once a college student in our church, wrote his thesis on my preaching. Carefully categorizing and analyzing 660 sermons over two years, he wrote, "Bro. John, you probably don't realize this about yourself, but you are an apologist for the faith. You defended every great doctrine, and that's why we're strong."

I can't think of a major problem in thirty years that wasn't fended off with strong doctrinal teaching. And you don't start after the problem arises.

Heresy and false teaching don't have a chance in a church fed on strong biblical teaching. An ounce of prevention is indeed worth a pound of cure.

Someone said, "The difference in teaching and preaching is I yell a lot more when I preach." Funny but not too accurate.

If teaching is exegesis, explaining what Scripture says and means, then preaching is application, how it applies to our lives, with inspiration and encouragement to do it. Good teaching contains preaching. Good preaching contains teaching. The meat of the Word is the depth of Scripture. Jesus didn't say, "Entertain my sheep or inspire my sheep." He said, "Feed them." Teaching God's Word is at once our privilege and our responsibility.

Preach thin sermons and you'll spend all week counseling weak sheep. Preach thick sermons and you'll raise healthy sheep who can take care of themselves.

Either way, it'll cost you time. Spend fifteen hours a week in study and preparation, feed the sheep on Sunday, and spend an hour the following week counseling. Spend an hour in study and preparation, preach on Sunday, and you'll spend fifteen hours the following week counseling weak sheep.

Healthy things grow. There are a hundred ways to create and promote attendance at your church. And your congregation might be a mile wide and an inch deep. Artificial growth, crowds, and numbers are easy to come by and costly. Rich expository exegesis of God's Word doesn't cost anything financially. The price is blood, sweat, and tears on your part, but the result is a church a mile wide *and* a mile deep. And remember the mile deep comes first.

Want to grow a church? Feed the sheep. Want to enlarge a ministry? Feed the sheep. The Word makes them strong. Strong makes them healthy. Healthy sheep reproduce. Healthy things grow.

> But the word of the Lord endures forever. And this is the word that was preached as the gospel to you. (1 Pet. 1:25)

> Hold firmly to the message of life. Then I can boast in the day of Christ that I didn't run or labor for nothing. (Phil. 2:16)

Let the message about the Messiah dwell richly among you, teaching and admonishing one another in all wisdom, and singing psalms, hymns, and spiritual songs, with gratitude in your hearts to God. (Col. 3:16)

Proclaim the message; persist in it whether convenient or not; rebuke, correct, and encourage with great patience and teaching. (2 Tim. 4:2)

Chapter 66

PREPARING THE SERMON

Jesus' priority was preaching. So is ours.

"Let us go into the next towns that I may preach there also: for this is why I came" (Mark 1:38).

Early in the week determine your subject and begin to read yourself full, watching for illustrations from life, from the media, from every source, praying, mulling over, and meditating about the subject for the following Sunday. By Wednesday go to work.

I urge you not to spend your time plowing through a plethora of commentaries. Let an Old Testament or New Testament seminary professor recommend the best two or three commentaries on the book you're preaching. A good concordance and a good word-study source, such as Pink, Robertson, or Wuest, are essential.

And remember, you don't have to *make* the Scripture relevant. *It is* relevant. When you explain it to people and apply it to their lives, the Holy Spirit produces the needed transformation.

What's the best way to prepare a sermon? It is *your way* and *God's way* for you. Don't try to walk in Saul's armor at this point. Be yourself. Find what fits you and go with it.

Do narrative as well as doctrinal preaching. Those great Old Testament stories, as well as the Gospels and Acts, are unbelievably powerful and rich.

We instantly relate to the characters and find our hearts open to the truths their lives teach us. Don't discount the Old Testament, and don't discount preaching from narrative. They are wonderful vehicles on which to hang the truths of the great doctrines of the New Testament. All the truth of God's Word relates to the human experience. When you can teach it from the vantage point of those who actually experienced it, you are miles ahead in the all-important ministry of communication.

What, for example, could be more relevant than a series on the life of Samson, the product of a dysfunctional home? Samson had relationships with three different women in his life. Each was bad news. Why did Samson never learn to relate appropriately to members of the opposite sex?

Twice at the beginning of the story of Samson, the angel bypasses Manoah, Samson's father, and goes to his mother. This is not the correct biblical order. The man is to be the spiritual leader of the home. The passive Manoah apparently gave no leadership. Looking to his mother as the spiritual leader, Samson developed a distorted view of womanhood, and the result was disastrous. This is relevant, biblical preaching.

Consider alternating preaching through a Bible book and a topical series.

As I begin to preach through a book in the Bible, particularly a book that is primarily narrative, as with the great stories of Abraham, Moses, David, Samson, Elijah, Daniel, etc., I first spend several long minutes in prayer, clearing my mind and opening my innermost self to God.

Then I turn to the passage at hand and begin slowly and meditatively to read word by word through the account. I read until the subject changes, and there I stop. Usually a particular portion of the story will cover somewhere from five to twelve or fifteen verses. Within the boundaries of those beginning and closing verses, I write the sermon.

The next step is to determine the central idea and condense it down to a single propositional statement. You are not ready to begin developing the passage into a sermon until you can answer the basic question your hearers will be asking.

Here's the question: If I do everything you want me to do, if I buy everything you're selling, if I say yes to everything you're trying to persuade me to do, tell me in one short, simple sentence, *what do you want me to do?*

You must answer the question in one concise sentence:

You should tithe to your church.

You should be true to your word.

You should develop an early morning prayer life.

You should get out of that immoral relationship.

Once you have determined the central idea and reduced it to a simple propositional statement, go back and find three or four things in the passage that support it. Why is that true? How did that happen? Why did it happen? What will happen if I do? What are the consequences if I don't? Is there any help? Every sermon must answer the grand *so what?* How does this apply to me? What are you trying to get me to do?

If you can't answer that, you're not ready to start the sermon. Determine the central idea; support it three or four ways from the text. Write your outline.

Chapter 67

THE APOLOGETIC ARGUMENT AND APPLICATION

Believe it or not, some people in your congregation don't believe a thing you have to say, and they are sitting there with their spiritual arms folded saying, "Convince me."

Give serious attention to the apologetic. Argue your case and defend your proposition.

Simply quoting Scripture anointed by the Holy Spirit has a powerful effect on the hearer. But when that Word is presented with apologetic argument and logic, it is even more effective. Think like a prosecuting attorney. Argue your case. Don't forget the importance of the apologetics argument.

Equally important, don't minimize the application.

I hear far too little application in today's preaching. Many sermons leave me with what I call "the grand so what?" A preacher gives me a lot of information, a lot of Scriptures, exegiting his meaning and says, "Let us pray." And I'm sitting there, saying, "Therefore what?"

Consider a new way of outlining in which you simply take the application, which is a life-relevant, biblical principle, and *make it the outline*.

In principle preaching,[1] you do no less exposition.

We are to be Bible expositors. Every passage of Scripture has only one correct interpretation, but it may have a thousand life-application principles.

In principle preaching, you simply make the *principles* the *outline.* Surely we are not preaching sermons with no application.

In most sermons the application is usually *buried in the exposition.* In principle preaching, expository preaching is still supreme.

All principle preaching does is to take great expository preaching, draw out the three or four *life application principles,* and make them the three- or four-word outline.

Read Joshua 1:1–6. The average sermon outline for this passage by most preachers would be:

  I.   The Call of Joshua
  II.   The Commission of Joshua
  III. The Conquest of Joshua
  IV.   The Courage of Joshua
  V.   Ho-hum.

If you preach that same text with the same exposition but simply *change the points to principles* at the beginning of each section of the sermon, listen to how it comes to life (remember these are not points but principles—the point *is* now the principle):

Principle 1. Don't get stuck in the past. Most people spend their lives stuck in the hallway between two great rooms: where they failed yesterday and what they're always *going to do tomorrow—but never get around to.*

God came to Joshua and said, "Moses My servant is dead. Now you and all the people prepare to cross over the Jordan" (Josh. 1:2). Stand up and move on with your life. When David's baby died, he immediately arose, went to the house of God to worship, changed clothes, ate dinner, and moved on with his life.

Principle 2. God's already in your tomorrow. In verse 3 He says, "I have given you every place where the sole of your foot treads." Not, "I *will* give to you." Don't be afraid of tomorrow; God's already there.

Principle 3. God has a wonderful blueprint for your life. Verse 4 clearly outlines the boundaries of the land. "Your territory will be from the wilderness and Lebanon to the great Euphrates River—all the land of the Hittites—and west to the Mediterranean Sea" (Josh. 1:4).

Principle 4: Yesterday's faithfulness ensures tomorrow's victory. Read again verses 5–6. "I will be with you just as I was with Moses. I will not leave you or forsake you. Be strong and courageous."

Each sermon should do four things: State the principle. Explain the principle. (That's when you do 10 or 12 minutes of expository preaching on each point.) Apply the principle. Illustrate the principle.

The exposition of the Scripture is still 95 percent of the sermon; nothing changes there. Expository preaching is still our priority. Principle preaching simply *rearranges* the expository sermon and rather than *hiding* the application *moves* it to the front and makes it the outline.

A simple *adjustment* in the *placement* of your application will make you a more effective preacher.

These principles make the sermon more translatable into the everyday lives of people. Everyone understands principles. Everyone relates to principles. And that greatly increases the likelihood that they will *actually practice them* in their daily lives.

A person needs to be able to hear you preach, write out your outline, put it on the refrigerator with a magnet, and say, "Now I can do that when I get to work tomorrow."

And isn't that what it's all about?

Endnotes

1. John Bisagno, *Principle Preaching* (Nashville: B&H, 2002).

Chapter 68

DELIVERING
THE MESSAGE

A baseball is the same from the minors to the majors. The way it's delivered to the plate separates the bush leaguers from the big leaguers.

1. *Don't overdo the outline.* Every point doesn't have to be alliteration, double alliteration, and constantly restated throughout the sermon. It's not only predictable; it's somewhat boring. And remember, principles as the outline are the best.

2. *Freshen your illustrations and use plenty of them.* The next time you tell a story in a sermon, read your audience. Immediately—though some may have been winding their watch, yawning, or texting friends—everything will become dead still, and every eye will be focused on you.

Use *up-to-date* stories. Don't tell me about Lord Fauntleroy, Victor of Aldersgate, or King What-His-Name in the Battle of Someplace three hundred years ago.

Tell a story everyone read in yesterday's newspaper or heard on last night's newscast, and you'll grab every listener by the heart.

3. *Don't use so many notes.* When you use other people's material, and primarily parrot their words, it can be difficult to memorize a sermon. But when the material is yours, birthed by the Holy Spirit in your heart and written by you, the fact is, you already know it.

Condense your sermon into a few key words and memorize them. You will find it much easier than you think. And the effectiveness of your communication will increase exponentially.

1. *It increases your sense of authority and confidence.* You're the master of the material, not vice versa.

2. *Your eye contact is 100 percent.* Look at the people. Move your eyes from person to person. Read the congregation and sense their response. This is essential in effective communication.

3. *Preaching without notes allows more freedom and spontaneity.* The Holy Spirit may bring something to your mind you hadn't planned to say or block out something you had planned to say.

4. *Don't shout at me.* In television, radio, and the Internet, people are accustomed to receiving verbal information conversationally.

Don't yell at me; talk to me. Oratory is out. Conversational preaching is in. Really in.

5. *Shorter is better.* Television, the overwhelming influence in our society, has dictated the thirty-minute medium of communication. People are accustomed to listening and thinking in thirty-minute segments. With commercials and station breaks, that's about twenty to twenty-two minutes of content at a time. I made the decision to go from forty-five-minute sermons to twenty-five to twenty-eight-minute sermons and immediately became a more effective preacher.

Preaching shorter is harder. You have to say it sharper, better, more quickly, and more effectively. *Condensing* a sermon is more difficult than *expanding* one.

Filler is easy; quality and class are difficult. The best sermon I ever heard was Chuck Swindoll's inaugural address as president of Dallas Theological Seminary. *It was only sixteen minutes long.*

6. *Be yourself.* Be natural. The best style for you is the person God made when He created you in your mother's womb. Affected preaching is phony preaching. And that's a downright shame.

> For the message of the cross is foolishness to those who are perishing, but it is God's power to us who are being saved.
>
> I will destroy the wisdom of the wise, and I will set aside the understanding of the experts.
>
> Where is the philosopher? Where is the scholar? Where is the disputer of this age? Hasn't God made the world's wisdom foolish? For since, in God's wisdom, the world did not know God through wisdom, God was pleased to save those who believe through the foolishness of the message preached. For the Jews ask for signs and the Greeks seek

wisdom, but we preach Christ crucified, a stumbling block to the Jews and foolishness to the Gentiles. Yet to those who are called, both Jews and Greeks, Christ is God's power and God's wisdom, because God's foolishness is wiser than human wisdom, and God's weakness is stronger than human strength.

Brothers, consider your calling. Not many are wise from a human perspective, not many powerful, not many of noble birth. Instead, God has chosen what is foolish in the world to shame the wise, and God has chosen what is weak in the world to shame the strong. God has chosen what is insignificant and despised in the world—what is viewed as nothing—to bring to nothing what is viewed as something, so that no one can boast in His presence. (1 Cor. 1:18–29)

Chapter 69

DEALING WITH HERESY AND ABERRANT THEOLOGY

You are the guardian of sound doctrine in your church. Some things are negotiable. Aberrant theology is not one of them. It can slowly infiltrate your church through many avenues. Perhaps the most consistent is the "health and wealth" theology and the misleading teaching on the Holy Spirit that pours into the homes of your people hours a day on Christian television networks.

While we respect those who hold different views, it is imperative that we teach what Baptists have historically believed to be biblical doctrine. The same is true of other denominations. I would respect an Assemblies of God pastor who would not allow the teaching of eternal security in his church. If members of your church believe other doctrine, they should go to a church in keeping with their beliefs. Unfortunately, that usually doesn't happen.

Your members will also be influenced by outside Bible studies, home fellowship groups, businessmen's luncheons, and other such nonchurch-connected gatherings. These may be entry points of unsound doctrine into the minds of your people. If you have home groups in your church:

1. Don't substitute them for Sunday morning Bible study.
2. Be certain your leaders are sound in the faith and committed to your church and its historical doctrines.

When it comes to dealing with unsound doctrine, even heresy, never forget, *prevention is easier than cure.*

I have repeatedly written of my support for seeker-friendly churches, young pastors, and the new paradigm for "doing church." But young pastors in particular must be ever on guard to "contend for the faith that was delivered to the saints" (Jude 3).

It's important not to neglect systematic theology. During my thirty-year pastorate in Houston, I preached apologetically, exhaustively and often on every great doctrine of the Word. Our people were strong in sound doctrine before the heresy invaded, and whatever it was, it didn't stand a chance at Houston's First.

Error dissolves before truth. Building the wall of sound doctrine is better than picking up the pieces after it hits your church. The best defense is a good offense. Topical sermon series on needed subjects are important. Marriage and family, current issues, and other topics should be addressed. But then get back to that systematic theology series. Six weeks topical sermons, alternating with six months exposition of a Bible book is a good way.

Chapter 70

REVIVING A CHURCH

M y friend Bill Eustis of Oklahoma had an unusual ministry of reviving churches. He's gone now, and I wish there were more like him. I served on his staff right out of college at First Baptist Church, Sallisaw, Oklahoma. Bill pastored twenty-five churches in fifty years. That's right, two years each. All twenty-five had two things in common: they were asleep and plateaued when Bill arrived, and they were vibrantly awake and growing when he left. And he did it just one way; by his preaching.

Bill was a big man, a powerful man, persuasive, and passionate. Once you heard Bill, you couldn't wait to hear him again. He could preach the stars down and inspire you to do anything. Bill didn't scold his people; he blessed them. It was never "What's wrong?" but "What we can become that's right?" Bill's cup was never half empty, always half full. He impacted me greatly.

In 1969, Houston's First had twenty-three hundred seats in an old downtown auditorium. Two thousand were empty. It was a tad discouraging. In 1970, things began to turn around. We ultimately outgrew our facilities, relocated, and became the church we are today. Unquestionably the recipe was the same I saw in Bill Eustis. Preach, brother, preach.

Vision is everything. No matter where or what they are, every church has potential. Impact your city, and you can also impact the nation and the world. An alive, vibrant church can send waves of influence and encouragement across hundreds of other churches. My scrapbook is filled with letters from small, discouraged congregations in our city saying, "Because First Baptist did it this way or that, it gave legitimacy to the fact that we could do it, and we did."

Jesus promised to build your church, and it's His job to do it, not yours. It is yours to pray it and preach it into reality. Bloom where you're planted. The deepest oil well in West Texas was capped three different times. After each, someone new came, removed the cap, and said, "Let's go deeper." Get on your knees. Get the vision and get the power. And whatever you do, preach, brother, preach. With enthusiasm. With love. With excitement. With passion. The world has yet to see what God can do with one man and one church, completely surrendered to His purpose.

Chapter 71

EXTENDING THE
INVITATION

Our Lord entrusts to us no greater honor than extending His invitation for people to come to Him. His last words were an invitation: "Both the Spirit and the bride say, 'Come!' Anyone who hears should say, 'Come!' And the one who is thirsty should come. Whoever desires should take the living water as a gift" (Rev. 22:17).

While many forms of invitation may be extended, every sermon should be marked by an appeal to persuade the hearer to make a response to what he has just heard. The physical expression of that response is important. It might be filling out a card, raising a hand, moving to an inquiry room, coming forward, or some other means, but it is important that the hearers be afforded the opportunity to make a tangible expression of their response.

Everyone our Lord called to follow Him, He called publicly. He called Zacchaeus to come down *out* of the tree; He called Matthew to get *up* from his revenue table; He called Peter and Andrew to *leave* their fishing boats. A physical expression of the intent of the heart was always called for.

Indeed, our Lord warned, "Whosoever therefore shall confess Me before men, him will I confess also before My Father which is in heaven. But whosoever shall deny Me before men, him will I also deny before My Father which is in heaven" (Matt. 10:32–33).

It's not that He needs our public stand as much as we need it. And the world needs the testimony and encouragement of our public profession of faith. For that reason I am most comfortable with extending a public invitation that calls for respondents to come to the front of the church and stand before the pulpit, although there are other acceptable ways. *More in the next chapter.*

The invitation of our Lord must never be extended in the flesh without the powerful touch of the Holy Spirit. It must never be manipulative, high pressure, overly extended, embarrassing, or confusing.

One of the most important ingredients in the public invitation is the manner in which it is begun. A smooth transition from sermon to invitation is best accomplished with the help of background music and prayer. I finished every sermon by asking the people to pray. Immediately the praise band, organ, choir, or ensemble began to play or sing. A soloist should never sing during the invitation. It draws attention from the pulpit, the focal point of the invitation.

The one who has delivered the message should extend the invitation. To give an invitation after someone else's message is awkward at best. As heads are bowed and music plays, pray a simple prayer that encapsulates the message.

Few things are more important in the invitation than specific instruction and clear information. Exactly what are you asking your hearers to do?

I once heard a stirring patriotic sermon with an invitation so confusing and so general I wasn't sure whether the speaker wanted me to join the church or the marines! Directing people to raise their hands, look up, stand up, and then come forward approaches the borderline of manipulation.

It is extremely important to be honest in your invitation. If you tell the people, "We're going to sing three verses," sing three verses. If you tell them, "This is the last verse," let it be the last.

We should be cautious at the extremes of both an invitation too long and one too short. Don't be afraid to sing more than two or three verses. If God is moving, let it go on. And above all, don't limit God by saying, "We'll stand and sing three verses, and if no one comes forward, we'll close." In fact, never suggest that "no one might come forward." Plant no negative seed thoughts at all. Satan's doing enough of that without any help from you.

Conversely, don't extend the invitation beyond the movement of the Spirit of God. Don't preach during the invitation, and do little, if any, ongoing exhortation. Let the Holy Spirit do His job; you've already done yours. When you sense He is finished, close the invitation.

Don't underestimate the power of a militant invitation. Songs like "Stand Up for Jesus" or "Onward Christian Soldiers" can stir the heart to respond. Plan a simple system of communication between you and the person leading the invitation music. You and you alone must determine what songs are sung and when.

If, for example, after three verses of "Come Just As You Are," the invitation music is changed to "Change My Heart, Oh God," it is the preacher, *not the worship leader*, who should determine it is time to change and signal the worship leader to do so.

Unless the attendance is rather large, as in a crusade where the people need to see the evangelist in the pulpit extending the invitation, leave the platform and greet the people at ground level, welcoming them, shaking their hands, even embracing them as they come forward.

Chapter 72

VARIATIONS ON THE INVITATION

The traditional "come forward" invitation is powerful. Who could ever forget seeing hundreds and thousands stream down the aisle in a Billy Graham crusade? I want to be clear that I think it is still the best way. There's a certain power and inspiration, a sense that "I am doing the right thing," as others come to Christ, that makes it more conducive to come forward.

But today many other forms of invitation are being effectively used. Before we look at some, let's address the obvious. Do you have to walk forward to be saved? The answer is no.

You can receive Christ in the bleachers or in the living room, the front of the church or the lobby.

When Jesus said, "Acknowledge Me before men," I do not believe He was qualifying salvation to a verbal pronouncement of one's faith. A church can provide many ways for people to acknowledge "Jesus is my Lord and Savior." If a verbal profession in front of a congregation is essential to salvation, millions of us are in a *world of hurt*. I don't remember when I've heard one person come forward, face the congregation, *and say anything*.

Baptism is the ultimate public profession of people's identity with Jesus Christ. Making an initial profession of faith through baptism is a powerful beginning of our faith walk with the Master.

Visiting Grace Church one weekend, I observed John McArthur giving an entire evening service to baptism. Each of the sixty individuals in the water turned to the congregation and articulated their personal testimony. The specialness of that service and the individual testimonies were an experience I shall never forget. But remember, *verbalizing* one's faith is not tantamount to its *validity*. The real test is more what we *are* than what we *say*.

An effective invitation may also be given by following the "come forward" appeal with the opportunity to fill out a card and place it in a plate or special exit box, whereupon one will be contacted by a minister of the church.

Sugar Creek Church in Houston has a "membership kiosk" in the lobby, as well as a first class membership room just off the lobby. Seekers are invited to go for a personal discussion after the public invitation, and as many make decisions for Christ there as at the front of the church. Do what works for you and remember the geographical location of one's conversion is not tantamount to its reality.

Throughout Southern Baptist history, more conversions and baptisms have come through traditional invitations in the church than marketplace evangelism. From 1998 to 2010, baptisms in Southern Baptist churches consistently spiraled downward.

Three critical invitation factors are at least part of the problem.

1. *Lack of clarity* in articulating the terms of the gospel such that no one can misunderstand.

2. *No sense of urgency.* Don't hide it. Stand up on your feet, look people in the eye, and urge them to be saved *now*.

3. *No music.* I repeatedly hear it and it's too sad for words: invitation music sung by only one person with one guitar singing an unfamiliar song that says nothing about coming to Jesus *right now*. Always use a praise band or choir, never a soloist. And sing something that is recognizable and conducive to *everyone joining in*. The power of surrounding music contributes to the ease of the "come forward" invitation. Even the most sincere soloist cannot help but draw attention to himself. And the better the soloist is, the worse it is. *No solo* should be sung during the invitation.

Find new ways to get the impact of "Softly and Tenderly," "Only Trust Him," "Oh Why Not Tonight," or "Just as I Am" before your people in a musically contemporary manner.

I recommend that you always begin with a "come forward" invitation. Other options are fine but only *following* the "come forward" invitation, not *instead* of it.

Preaching the gospel without a specific, public, immediate opportunity to respond to it is unthinkable. Jesus never did. How can we?

Chapter 73

DOING GOOD FOLLOW-UP

To take new members in the front door is one thing. To keep them from going out the back is another. That they "dip 'em and drop 'em" ought never to be said of your church.

The process of evangelism is never complete until the evangelized themselves become evangelists. The conservation and development of your converts is of utmost importance.

Building a great church means building great people. It involves making disciples of new believers and witnesses of new disciples. A good basic follow-up program consists of several things:

1. *The new converts must be well born into the kingdom.* It is impossible to make disciples of unbelievers. For many years at Houston's First, we followed the traditional Southern Baptist method of counseling with those who came to make decisions, on the front row of the church as the invitation music continued. They were then immediately introduced to the congregation with an explanation of their decision.

Through the years I came to believe that not enough time was being given to counseling. We began taking the people to a decision counseling room, followed by presentation to the church at a later date. This can be done in the following Sunday service, with pictures in the church paper, or from the baptistry at the time of their baptism. The counseling room might best be referred to as the *prayer* room, the *decision* room, or the *inquiry* room. The word *counseling* has implications you might not want to project.

2. *In the decision room a trained decision counselor should greet each individual, couple, or family.* The chair of the decision counselor should face those making the decisions and be separated from other groupings around the room. One individual might welcome a couple or a family, but it's important that one other person or more be brought over that you might counsel with each family member individually.

Whether persons are coming to join your church from another church or to receive Christ as Savior, begin with the assumption that none are believers and lead them through the process of giving their testimony in order to validate their conversion. If they are believers, they will not be offended. If they are not, they may be filtered through the process at the time and led to Christ.

3. *Counselors should be well trained, friendly, mature believers, willing to spend extra time after the service is over.* Their families may have to wait for them. The person making the decision should *never* be asked to fill out a decision card *at the beginning* of the conversation. Only after a person has been led to Christ, or adequate assurance given that he or she already *knows* Christ, should the record of their decision be made. Give the person time to ask questions. Share literature about the church. Get full and complete information on your decision card. Pray, and introduce the person as a new Christian or a new church member to someone immediately.

4. *Good follow-up begins in the follow-up room.* Decisions must not be allowed to abort at this delicate moment. Counseling new members should be done in a room located near the auditorium. This should include introduction of staff, get-acquainted time, and explanation of the contents of the new members' packet.

5. *All new members should be told they are being automatically enrolled in a Sunday morning Bible study class.* Their names should be entered into the Sunday school register on Monday morning and immediately mailed to their new teacher and director. They are now someone's personal responsibility. Those persons are the "teacher" and "in-reach leader" of their new class, who should also contact them immediately.

6. *Follow-up should be done as quickly as possible.* Every new family should be assigned to a deacon or other responsible person for follow-up. Ideally, they should be visited in the home the week they join, with a second visit a week later, a third visit a month later, and a fourth visit six months later.

7. A biannual membership survey should be conducted to check up on new members to find out where they are and how they are doing.

8. A new members' class taught by the pastor, associate pastor, or qualified layman should be conducted on a revolving basis for four to six weeks before the Sunday morning or evening service. Membership is automatic and attendance is expected.

Don't be a ninety and nine church. Don't lose even one new lamb.

Good spiritual food, good fellowship, and good follow up are essential.

Chapter 74

BAPTISM

Baptism is for a believer, not an unbeliever. If a person goes through a baptismal ceremony and subsequently becomes a Christian, he should be baptized again. Baptism pictures something. And if that something has not happened, it is not New Testament baptism.

That something is twofold. First, baptism is a picture of our identity with Christ and what He did for us in His death and resurrection. Our immersion under the water pictures His death. Rising from the water pictures His resurrection.

Further symbolism in immersion baptism pictures the death of our old rebellious nature and the beginning of a resurrected new life, yielded to Christ. These two beautiful symbolisms have no *saving* power, but they do have great *persuasive* power. They visualize to the world what Jesus did for us and the transformation of life that has occurred because we have embraced it.

The word *baptism* is a Greek word *baptizo,* meaning "to cover." As with the Lord's Supper, immersion has no saving grace but is a beautiful picture of what has happened in our life.

The question arises, "Who can baptize?" Whether in a swimming pool, a church, or a river in Africa, individuals should baptize on the authority of their church.

In Acts 2:41, those who were baptized were added unto *them.* The *them* to which the verse refers, is the church birthed on that day. The New Testament knows nothing of baptism apart from the authority of the church. But the human instrumentality the church authorizes to baptize can be anyone. I love to see a father baptize his own children.

At the conclusion of Simon Peter's sermon on the day of Pentecost, the people in Acts 2:37 were convicted in their hearts and asked, "What must we do?"

The question was not "What must I do to be saved?" but simply "What shall we do?" They had heard the Word, believed it, and received it with yielded hearts of faith. Verse 41 says it this way: "They . . . gladly received his word" (KJV).

Believing and receiving the gospel of Christ's death and resurrection brings salvation. These humble hearts simply asked, "What's next?" The answer in Acts 2:38 was, "Repent . . . and be baptized." If a person says to me, "I have heard the gospel and believe. What do I do next?" My response is, "Repent and be baptized. Change the way you live and join the church."

This story is different from the one in Acts 16 where the Philippian jailer had not heard the word of God but was under conviction because of the faith and praise of Paul and Silas.

The Acts 16:30 question of the Philippian jailer was not, "Sirs, what must I do?" It was, "Sirs, what must I do *to be saved?*" The only answer the Bible ever gives to *that* question is, "Believe on the Lord Jesus, and you will be saved" (v. 31).

In Acts 2, the people received the word and were already saved. The question was simply, "What do we do next?" The answer was, "Change the way you live and join the church."

Acts 2:38 further states, "Repent, . . . and be baptized . . . *for* the forgiveness of your sins."

The word *for* has many different meanings in English. In verse 38, the Greek word is *eis,* meaning "in response to." Repentance and baptism are not the *cause* of forgiveness but the *effect.* The people were told to change their lives and be baptized not *in order* to be saved but in response to *having been* saved when they believed the gospel.

Imagine you are seated next to me on a train going from Houston to Dallas. In your pocket is a gun, and you intend to go to Dallas to kill a man.

If I ask you, "Why are you going to Dallas?" you would say, "For murder." You mean, "In order to obtain or commit a murder."

If the following week I see you on the same train, handcuffed to a sheriff and ask, "Why are you going to Dallas?" you will again reply, "For murder." But this time you're not going to *commit* murder; you're going because you have *already committed* murder. The first *for* is a cause, in order to. The second *for* is an effect, because of.

For decades Southern Baptists accepted baptism only at the hands of other Southern Baptist churches as valid. Such a position essentially says the Southern Baptist Convention is the New Testament church. I don't think so. Fortunately, this position has virtually disappeared from the Southern Baptist landscape.

Baptists, Pentecostals, CMA (Christian and Missionary Alliance), Assemblies, Presbyterians, Methodists, Lutherans, and many others agree on the basic doctrines of the faith. If their baptism was as a believer, as a testimony of salvation, not in order to procure it, and by immersion, it should be accepted as authentic New Testament baptism, and the individual should not be required to be rebaptized.

Ask baptismal candidates to place their feet under the bar on the floor of the baptistery and not to bend at the waist. They are portraying a dead body. Lower and raise them gently. And try to be certain the "death to self" they portray has actually occurred.

Chapter 75

THE LORD'S SUPPER

The Lord's Supper is also called "the table of the Lord," "the sacraments," and "Communion." There are as many views and methods of observing this wonderful ordinance of our Lord as there are names.

The frequency of the Lord's Supper is optional. Jesus did not say whether to observe it weekly, monthly, or quarterly. *He did* say, "As often as you do it, do so in remembrance of Me" (see Luke 22:19; 1 Cor. 11:24–26). In Houston's First we chose to do so approximately once a quarter, four times a year. If I had it to do again, I would do it more often.

The quarterly tradition has primarily developed in Baptist life as a reaction to those who take it every Sunday and view it as an instrument of saving grace. All churches, of course, that receive the bread and cup weekly do not believe it plays a role in a person's salvation, *but many do.*

We believe it is a memorial that reminds us of the broken body and spilled blood of Jesus on the cross for our sins but is not a medium through which we receive His grace.

We also reject the doctrine of transubstantiation held by Roman Catholicism that the bread and wine *literally* become the body and blood of Christ.

Certainly, Jesus said, "This is My body, which is given for you, and this is my blood shed for you" (see Luke 22:19–20). But time-honored principles of hermeneutics require the question, "Did Jesus mean what He *said,* or did He mean what He *meant?*" When He said, "If your right hand causes you to sin cut it off" (Matt. 5:30), did He mean take an ax and sever it from your arm, or did He mean remove those things that are an impediment to your spiritual growth? Clearly Jesus spoke metaphorically when He said, "This is My body; this is My blood."

Serving the Lord's Supper should emphasize four things.

1. *An Inward Look.* The people should be challenged to look within their hearts, confess and repent of their sins, and be forgiven and cleansed before receiving the cup. "Whoever eats the bread or drinks the cup of the Lord in an unworthy way will be guilty of sin against the body and blood of the Lord" (1 Cor. 11:27). I'm not sure I know all that means, but I *am* sure I don't want to find out.

Some in the New Testament church drank the Lord's Supper wine to the point of drunkenness. For this reason some became sick; some even died.

2. *A Backward Look.* "When you drink this, ye do show the Lord's death till He come" (1 Cor. 11:26). The preeminent purpose of the cup and the bread is to visualize the cross. For this cause it should be taken with solemnity and seriousness.

3. *An Outward Look.* Jesus said if our brother has anything against us, we are to leave our offering at the altar and make peace with him (Matt. 18:15–21). We are not to receive the Lord's Supper with bitterness and unforgiveness toward our fellowman in our heart.

4. *A Forward Look.* In the Lord's Supper, we "show forth the Lord's death till He comes" (1 Cor. 11:26).

An inward look, a backward look, an outward look, and a forward look. Taking the Lord's Supper is a serious matter and should be taken as such.

At Houston's First a Lord's Supper table covered with a white linen cloth and covered trays was placed before the pulpit. I stood on the floor behind the middle of the table with our chairman of deacons at one end of the table and the vice-chairman at the other.

The two men removed the cloth, folding it carefully. They then gave each of our deacons on the front row a plate, who in turn passed it to an assigned section of worshippers throughout the worship center.

When everyone had been served, I read a Scripture passage about the breaking of bread and prayed God's blessing upon it. Then I said, "Let us all partake of the bread." The process was then repeated with the cup. After the prayer a hymn was sung, and a retiring offering for the poor was received.

By the way, when Jesus said, "Drink ye all of it" (Matt. 26:27), He was not saying, "Don't leave any; drink it all." He was saying, "All of you are to drink it."

Here is an essential link to an honored past. Videos and pictures of Christ's death are most appropriate during the serving of the Lord's Supper. Background music and soft lights greatly enhance the special time that is the breaking of the bread and the serving of the cup.

I fully support contemporary music and the manner of worship practiced by our young generation of pastors. The observance of the Lord's Supper generally, however, should not be made modern and relevant; it already is.

> For I received from the Lord what I also passed on to you: On the night when He was betrayed, the Lord Jesus took bread, gave thanks, broke it, and said, "This is My body, which is for you. Do this in remembrance of Me."
>
> In the same way He also took the cup, after supper, and said, "This cup is the new covenant established by My blood. Do this as often as you drink it, in remembrance of Me." For as often as you eat this bread and drink the cup, you proclaim the Lord's death until He comes.
>
> Therefore whoever eats the bread or drinks the cup of the Lord in an unworthy way will be guilty of sin against the body and blood of the Lord. So a man should examine himself; in this way he should eat the bread and drink from the cup. For whoever eats and drinks without recognizing the body, eats and drinks judgment on himself. (1 Cor. 11:23–29)

Chapter 76

CALLING OUT THE CALLED

Few contributions you will make to the kingdom of God exceed the importance of encouraging and developing ministers and mentoring them. A regular challenge to your people to use their gifts in the service of the Lord is a high priority; training and actually using them are even more important.

The wise leader will do this on a regular basis and, with the education pastor, develop an ongoing program of training workers. But I speak primarily here of extending the challenge and call of our Lord to those whom He would call into full-time Christian ministry.

Francis Schaeffer was right when he taught that every Christian is in full-time ministry. I refer, however, to the vocational minister whose salary is paid by a church or Christian organization and who devotes their time to nothing else.

The beauty of the work of the Lord is that no matter how a person may be gifted or employed, there is somewhere in the world both the need and the opportunity to use his talents in full-time Christian ministry. Agricultural missionaries, for example, are doing a marvelous work in teaching people better methods of providing for the physical needs of their families, all the while witnessing to them about Jesus Christ, the Bread of life.

Often we report the visible results of an outreach event, "Twenty accepted Christ, ten joined the church, plus a few rededications and one for special service." The obvious inference is that the rededications and special-service decisions were somehow less important than the others. Next Sunday morning, ask your congregation, "How many of you accepted Christ as your Savior at some point in your life and subsequently recommitted your life to Him? And, as far as changing the direction of your life, your recommitment was more significant than your conversion?" You will be amazed to find the latter number may be greater than the first.

Additionally, too little emphasis is placed on inviting people to give their lives to full-time Christian ministry. In fact, I seldom see it done at all.

In my ministry in Houston, I never recall preaching a stirring message on missions and thrusting the sickle into the harvest without reaping a large response of those who were ready and willing to go into full-time ministry. Admittedly, not all actually got there, but over eight hundred did.

When extending an invitation to full-time Christian ministry, several things should be emphasized.

First, be clear. Few people who respond will be able to say, "God is calling me to a particular ministry in a specific place." The invitation should be clearly given for response by men and women who feel a stirring in their soul that *ministry is the will of God for me. Now!* Only after we respond in obedience today does He shed light on the specifics of tomorrow. His direction in our lives is an unfolding revelation.

Emphasize to the congregation that you will help them come to understand and refine God's call on their lives. Little did Saul of Tarsus dream what lay before him when he answered the call of Jesus, "Lord, what wilt thou have me to do?" (Acts 9:6 KJV).

Help your people understand that if they can be happy doing anything else, they should do it. A life of full-time Christian ministry is filled with peril and discouragement as well as blessing and joy. There will be times of loneliness, rejection, failure, and despair, but blessed will be the journey. And we don't need any more dropouts.

Help them understand that a call to serve is a call to prepare. God's great servants have always spent long years in preparation. Whether in the classroom setting or the backside of the desert, they have much to learn.

Sermons that "call out the called" should contain two things. First, they should include the need. A lost world is waiting for Christian workers.

Second, the sermon should contain an appeal to listen to your heart. The tug to "respond" and the pull to "go" is not from Satan; it is from the Lord. How do you know when God is calling you? You just know. And if you know, say yes. Take the first step of willingness. God will take it from there.

Chapter 77

PREACHERS OR PASTORS

Two obvious functions are required in the ministry of the pastor. The first is to shepherd the people of God. The second, to deliver God's Word to them. While many other responsibilities also demand our time, these are the most important.

In the smaller church the pastor must often assume the role of landscaper, maintenance man, custodian, and a myriad of other responsibilities. As the congregation grows, he will be blessed with the services of other gifted persons who can do these things. Obviously, the pastor will be the vision caster, the motivator, the fund-raiser, and the administrator as well. But in the broadest sense of the term, he is first and foremost a pastor and a preacher: the shepherd and the feeder.

The ministry of the pastor is to shepherd the flock. This means taking time to know the people and being involved in their lives. At lunch, in the hallways, in their homes and in hospital rooms, the caring shepherd will know no greater joy than learning to appreciate each member of his congregation.

But he is the pulpiteer as well. His public ministry of teaching and preaching the Bible, explaining it to the people, and applying it to their lives is his supreme calling.

While both of these are distinct ministries, they are inseparably intertwined. A pastor will not endear himself to his people in such a way that they are prepared to hear his heart in the pulpit unless they feel they know him and he truly knows them. His personal ministry to the people will validate the authenticity of his public message. Both threads of ministry are intricately woven into the fabric of the pastorate. Precisely at this point, however, tension will arise not only within the heart of the pastor but between himself and his people.

Although it will not be easily developed in the mind of the minister, let alone that of his congregation, pastor and people must ultimately come to accept this observation: Great preachers are seldom great pastors, and great pastors are seldom great preachers.

Generally, these two individuals are two entirely different personalities. While human character can be changed, human personality rarely can. We are what we are. The personality and makeup of a great preacher might be described as a *racehorse*. This kind of man is not usually as comfortable in one-to-one counseling, spending time in the hospital, or visiting shut-ins as in the pulpit.

The personality of the person who is first of all a pastor, however, is normally quieter and more gentle. He is easy to be around and comfortable in circumstances that are moving a bit more slowly.

Predictably, when churches change pastors, they tend to seek out one who is the opposite of the pastor they just had. Some will say, "I want a man who is a good pastor. Brother Smith never came to see me when I was sick." After Brother Smith's replacement leaves, they will likely say, "I want a man who is a good preacher this time. Bro. Jones's sermons were boring, and I fell asleep when he preached."

That great racehorse in the pulpit will likely make you nervous in the hospital room. That great shepherd in your hour of bereavement may put you to sleep in the pulpit.

Ideally a pastor will have a large measure of both qualities and certainly be growing in both. But never forget that great preachers usually aren't great pastors, and great pastors are seldom great preachers. Let me make several observations:

1. *Scripture is clear that the body of Christ is filled with individuals of unique giftedness.* This is important. It makes for good, balanced, corporate, well-functioning ministry.

2. *The wise pastor will recognize and program to his weaknesses.* The weaker preacher might employ an associate who is a strong teacher. The weaker pastor will enlist staff members who are gifted at hospital visitation and counseling. By the way, before you terminate the services of a faithful staff member, reevaluate

whether they are in the right position. Reassigning our administrator to a pastoral care position years ago was one of the best decisions I ever made.

3. *Teach your people to understand and accept the difference between a pastor and a preacher.* God's people, given the facts, may be trusted to do the right thing. Help them understand what I am saying here. They will be supportive, and life will be better for you.

4. *Accept yourself.* Each of us possesses a different set of gifts and talents. Do your best to enhance and expand your abilities while accepting your own uniqueness. God made you a special person and placed you in the right church at the right time. Accept who you are, be yourself, and enjoy being you.

Part 6

WORSHIP SERVICES

Chapter 78

SEEKER FRIENDLY

The Seeker Friendly church has taken a bad wrap from mainline evangelicals. Is their criticism justified or is it jealousy?

Think about it. Did Jesus try to draw sinners or repulse them? Can we not reconcile "the common people heard him gladly" with being "seeker-unfriendly?"

The only motive I have observed in the hearts of pastors of Seeker-friendly churches, is a genuine desire to remove every barrier that would keep anyone from coming to hear the message of God's love and redeeming grace. And that's most commendable.

Some may exist, and if so, they are to be severely reprimanded. But I know of *no young pastors* who are compromising the purity of the Gospel, while removing barriers that would *keep people from hearing it.*

That is not to say they do not exist. It is to say, I have not observed them in mainline evangelical denominations.

Let this be the benchmark of how to "do church" at any level, and to all peoples and generations: THE MESSAGE MUST NEVER CHANGE, BUT THE MEANS MUST BE EVER CHANGING.

Paul's statement, "I have become all things to all men that I might by all means win some," *should forever settle the matter.*

Is knocking down barriers which keep people from hearing the Gospel something new? I think not. I sense that's what missionaries have been doing around the world for 2,000 years, by removing the language barrier and learning the language of those to whom *they speak*, not forcing them to learn their message *in order to hear*.

And isn't that what the men did who crawled up a ladder, cut a hole in the roof and lowered their friend into the healing presence of Jesus? I'd call that *pretty seeker friendly*.

Jeanie B. Cheaney in an editorial called *Gamble or Gimmick* May 8, 2010 edition of *World* Magazine, wrote about Bay Area Fellowship in Corpus Christi, Texas.

The church advertised "the ultimate give away" comprised of automobiles, bicycles, furniture and cash, each weekday of Holy Week. By Easter Sunday, thousands had received Christ as their personal Savior.

Ms. Cheaney wrote, "Bay Area Fellowship doesn't fit the stereotype of the glitzy megachurch with a shiny preacher who compromises the Gospel in order to swell the offering. The pastor isn't peddling seed-money promises to support his lavish lifestyle. He didn't twist arms to get donations; church members gave freely, not to receive tenfold back in material goods, but to bring in the unsaved."

"People originally came to Jesus because they wanted something from Him: healing, bread, political freedom or power. They weren't seeking forgiveness of their sins and life everlasting—but if they stayed, that's what they received. At Pentecost, everyone in that polyglot crowd heard the Gospel in his own language. Like it or not, materialism is the language of our culture, and the culture responded to Bay Area Fellowship on Easter Sunday. But once inside they heard a different message. They were told that the shiny cars would rust and break, but Jesus paid an inestimable price for something of phenomenal value, freely offered to all who would hear. No material gift can match the grace lavished upon us in Christ. Occasionally, giveaways may not be a bad way to make a point."

Oh yes, and I think I remember those good ole' revival days; something about pizza fellowships for the youth and hot dog parties for the kids, with a bicycle for the one who brought the most. Pretty seeker-friendly, I'd say.

> "For though I be free from all men, yet have I made myself servant unto all, that I might gain the more. And unto the Jews I became as a Jew, that I might gain the Jews; to them that are under the law, as under the law, that I might gain them that are under the law; To them that are without law, as without law, (being not without law to God, but under the law to Christ,) that I might gain them that are without law. To the weak became I as weak, that I might gain the weak: I am made all things to all men, that I might *by all means save some*. And this I do for the gospel's sake, that I might be partaker thereof with you."
> (1 Cor. 9:19–23, italics added)

Chapter 79

MULTIPLE SERVICES

I think it is best to use your existing buildings twice or even three times each Sunday morning before thinking about building new ones. Classrooms and worship centers used only an hour or two a week need to be considered for other purposes. Starting schools, scheduling additional services, and creating new Bible studies are certainly high priority in that consideration.

The question is, Do we start new services in order to grow, or do we start them because we are already growing? The answer to both questions is yes. Prevailing wisdom says that if your existing space is 80 percent full, it's time to build or start a second service. Frankly, I have a problem with that because another question must first be answered.

Is the facility 80 percent full because you are in a growth mode and have moved from 50 percent to 60 to 70, to 80, and it is obvious you'll soon be out of space? Or is it at 80 percent because you're *not* growing, and *once ran* 100 percent and then 90?

In the latter case factors other than space should first be addressed. Let me say that again. If you are at 80 percent because you're declining, starting more services is *not* the answer.

If, however, you have grown to 80 percent and are still growing, it is time to consider multiple services. Obviously you don't need more room until you reach 100 percent, but a church in a growth mode will likely be at or near capacity in a few months, and a great deal of advanced planning and preparation are required in starting new services.

One of the more appealing factors in starting a second service is that *people like choices.* All other things being equal, I will opt for the church that gives me a choice to come at 8:30 or 10:30 rather than the one that says I must come at 9:30.

If your worship service begins at 10:00 or 11:00, you should get immediate growth by adding an early option. I have found 8:30 or 9:00 to be a good option.

To your surprise, you may find some married young adults as well as senior adults will like the earlier time. Seniors are early risers. The majority of seniors arrive thirty to forty minutes before any morning Bible study or worship service, regardless of the scheduled time to begin. They just like to get there early. It is also a great attraction to seniors to be able to leave the facilities before the heavier flow of traffic comes in for the later services.

Additionally, many married young adults often find the early option to be attractive. Little children wake up early. Babies are sometimes wide awake and ready for that early feeding by 5:00 or 6:00 a.m. Remember, of course, that the nursery must be well staffed and functioning at least thirty minutes before the early service begins.

The same factors enter into the question of the advisability of multiple Sunday morning Bible studies. Here are several possible models to consider.

1. Sunday morning Bible study space is limited and cramped, but a lot of room to grow remains in the worship center. The answer? One central worship service at 9:45 a.m., with two Sunday morning Bible studies at 8:30 and 11:00.

2. Plenty of room to grow in Sunday morning Bible study with a worship service at near capacity. The answer? A central Sunday morning Bible study at 9:45, with worship services at 8:30 and 11:00.

3. Both Sunday morning Bible study and worship center have limited space; both are growing and approaching capacity attendance. There are two good possibilities:

Option 1: Flip-flop services: *Schedule A,* Sunday morning Bible study at 9:30; worship service at 10:45. *Schedule B,* worship service at 9:30; Sunday morning Bible study at 10:45.

Option 2: A staggered schedule: *Schedule A,* Sunday morning Bible study at 8:30; worship at 9:45. *Schedule B,* Sunday morning Bible study at 9:45; worship at 11:00.

I prefer option 2 for three reasons:

1. It is easy to understand.
2. It is naturally sequential.
3. Traffic flow is the best.

In option 2, be sure to factor in parking with both Sunday School and worship attendees on your campus at the same time at 9:45.

In multiple worship services consider the possibility of different kinds of music. One service might be traditional and the other contemporary. I think it would be fantastic for a church to offer four services on Sunday: traditional, contemporary, classic, and country.

In multiple Sunday morning Bible studies, every age should be given an opportunity to attend a class. Never allow a situation in which the young people or any other group can go to Sunday morning Bible study at only one hour if you have multiple Sunday School hours.

There is a danger that the quality of teaching might drop when you go to a second Sunday morning Bible study. Take your time and be certain you have staffed it with an adequate number of well-trained teachers.

Taking your time is always called for in preparing to go to multiple worship services and Sunday morning Bible study. For one thing people need time to decide which service or Sunday morning Bible study they wish to attend. Time will be required to take the survey, compile the results, enlist and train workers, and inform the people. If you jump up and start multiple worship services or Sunday morning Bible study units next week, you'll regret it.

Chapter 80

TRADITIONAL MUSIC

For many years the battle has raged over traditional music versus the increasingly popular new contemporary praise and worship music. Often it is called "The Worship Wars." Think of that. Aren't those two words mutually exclusive? Something like "dry water" or "cold heat."

If you haven't experienced the battle, you likely will in the future. I want to say three things that are critical. I ask for an open mind and heart as you consider them.

First, younger people should understand why the old music is so important to seniors.

1. *The old music has a dignity that older people feel is worthy of God.* It's never quite been said like: "When morning gilds the skies my heart awakening cries: May Jesus Christ be praised"[1] or: "A mighty fortress is our God, a bulwark never failing."[2]

This grand and glorious music is, to the heart and soul of senior adults, consistent with the majesty and dignity of the God whom they have revered since childhood.

2. *The old music emotionally ties senior adults to a better time.* What an unstable, frightening world we live in! In my city only one in ten dwelling places is inhabited by a traditional nuclear family. Nine out of ten are inhabited by homosexual couples, divorcees, live-ins, and other groupings. Everything that is nailed down is coming up. There is stability and security in the past, and the older we get, the more we need it. That great old music ties us to another

time when things were more stable. It is the music we grew up on. We sang the great Christmas carols at Christmastime, and "Power of the Blood," "Just as I Am," and "Saved, Saved, Saved" during revivals.

We want things like they've always been. Move the furniture, change the pictures, put the dresser on a different wall; that's hard for senior adults.

Changing cars is hard. Changing churches is awkward. Changing jobs is difficult. And certainly changing music.

Nothing stabilizes our heart like the Word of God and the music of our faith. It is the spiritual heartbeat, the soul of who we are as believers. Our music is everything to us. That's how we remember. It's how we express our heart. It's how we worship God. It's how we make it through the day. And to think of a world in which it is fast slipping away is extremely difficult for senior adults.

3. *It ministered to us in times of great need.* As I stood by mother's grave, we sang "In the Garden" and "Sweet By and By." The night my sister was converted, they were singing, "Pass Me Not Oh Gentle Savior." When I was tempted to go back into the world, I often remembered the words of "I'd Rather Have Jesus."

These songs are important to us. They represent spiritual markers in our lives. They are essential to the spiritual and emotional stability and security of many seniors. They ministered to us in the past, and we desperately long not to lose them. We need them today, and we will need them tomorrow.

Some time ago, a Navy veteran said, "Pastor, the new music is OK, and I'll never criticize it, but let me tell you why the old songs are so important to me.

"I was on a ship with three thousand other sailors in World War II. I truly believe I was the only Christian on board that ship. Living for the Lord was difficult. There was no help, no support whatsoever. Many evenings I would go to the back of the ship and sit for an hour to see the sun set and watch the waves separate behind the ship and sing those old songs. Had I not had 'The Old Rugged Cross,' 'Jesus Keep Me Near the Cross,' 'What a Friend We Have in Jesus' and 'Amazing Grace' to sing, I don't know if I could have made it. Those songs were my survival."

4. *Many of us learned our theology from those songs.* I grew up listening to topical sermons. My pastors always preached topical sermons. Seldom, if ever, did I hear a series through the Bible, verse by verse, from an Old or New Testament book as I do now. So we learned much of our theology from those great hymns. Songs of redemption and security. Songs of salvation and comfort. Songs of lordship and holiness. Sing aloud the five verses of "One Day." Those five verses contain virtually the entire New Testament story in a nutshell.

5. Older people love the older music because of the desire to leave a legacy. Every day I think about my children and grandchildren and the world we shall leave them, and it's not a pretty picture. Everything in my heart wants to leave a legacy of better times.

I want my children to know the joys I have known, the power of a great family, the blessing of friendship, the importance of integrity, and the peace of God. And much of that revolves around the music of my life. Frankly, I cannot conceive of a world in which my children never heard of "The Old Rugged Cross," "Love Lifted Me," "Down at the Cross," or "Since Jesus Came into My Heart." But I'm afraid that's the kind of world we're going to leave them.

And frankly, I think we owe something to our seniors. They paid the bills, they built the buildings, they perpetuated the faith, and *we* are here because *they* were here.

If you don't have a service where you blend the music and include the great hymns with contemporary music, consider starting a second service with only traditional music.

Endnotes

1. Katholisches Gesangbuch, "When Morning Gilds the Skies."
2. Martin Luther, "A Mighty Fortress Is Our God."

Chapter 81

CONTEMPORARY MUSIC, PART 1

Now I want to help those of you who are older understand why the new music is so important to the young. And I must tell you straight up that unless you can grasp this and find a way to include, even prioritize, this kind of newer music, your congregation will get more and more grey, and in fifteen or twenty years, you may have no congregation at all.

You resist the new music at your own peril. It's here to stay, and if you can't find a way to honor it and use it as well as the older music, you will not reach this young generation. During the first decade of the twenty-first century, with nearly fifty thousand churches, Southern Baptists baptized only one out of every thousand American teenagers.

We are losing the battle. We have a perishing generation, and unless something drastic happens, there's going to be no tomorrow. We must reach teenagers and young adults, and their music is their life and their language. If we do not understand that, we will fail as missionaries to a desperately needy generation.

Let me help those of you who are older understand why the new music is *so important* to the young.

The new music is to Jesus, not about Jesus. Get hold of that. It is *to* Jesus, not just *about* Jesus. Search the pages of your hymnal, and you will find that probably no more than 10 percent of the hymns and gospel songs are addressed *to* the Lord Jesus Christ. They are testimonies *about* Jesus. They do not address

239

Him and personally worship and connect with Him. Why is this connection absolutely critical?

To answer this you must understand what's happening in our world. There are three basic tenets in society: the home, the government, and the church.

In the *home* we have a 40 percent divorce rate. A large percentage of our residences are *not* inhabited by traditional families. Young people are quickly losing confidence in the home because most of them have never really seen a real home and family, let alone a Christian home and family.

The second tenet of society is the *government*. This young generation has lived through two decades and more of political scandal and corruption. In the *church* scandal after scandal arises. Virtually every month we hear of a new one.

The young people see the church as they see the government and the home and say, "There's nothing to it." Naturally, they are disillusioned—unstable, searching, seeking—their feet in the wet concrete of an undependable, unstable, and unrespectable society in which they have virtually no confidence.

They reject the establishment. They reject tradition. They largely reject denominationalism as they do virtually all structure and organization. They seem not to care about anything traditional at all.

But down deep in their heart is still a hunger for Jesus Christ. He is still the true Light that lights *everyone* that comes into the world. The problem is they don't know that Jesus is what they hunger for so they try to fill the empty spot with drugs, sexual immorality, and a thousand other things.

But every once in a while a young person gets hooked in to Jesus, and when they do, their level of commitment is through the roof. They're easily won to Christ. They're not anti-Jesus. *Many are simply antiestablishment.* And when they find Jesus, they are passionate about Him. They have found the only stable, secure, dependable thing they have ever known, and it's more important than anything—as it should be. And so for them to *praise* Jesus, to *love* Jesus, to *talk to* Jesus, to *sing to* Jesus, to *worship* Jesus in music is everything. They don't want to talk *about* Jesus; they don't want to sing *about* Jesus. They want to talk *to* Jesus; they want to sing *to* Jesus.

Examine the words of today's contemporary praise music. You may be surprised to find it is not *about* Jesus, it is primarily *to* Jesus. It addresses Him, it speaks to Him, and it is everything to the young. Because of the instability and unreality of the society in which they live, when young people today find a relationship with Jesus, they are passionate about it, and their love affair with Him scintillates in its expression through the music of their worship.

Have you noticed in many churches the pastor doesn't sit on the platform? There are few choirs and virtually no special music. This young generation doesn't care how we look on the platform. They don't care about hymnals. They don't care about being sung to by a choir. They don't care about bulletins and orders of service. They just care about Jesus. And how can we fault that? The new music is *to* Jesus and not *about* Jesus, and we should understand that, rejoice in that, and not discredit it.

Chapter 82

CONTEMPORARY MUSIC, PART 2

Contemporary music is the language young people speak. Their whole world is music. If you're going to communicate with young people today, *you have to speak their language,* and their language is music. CDs, iPods, iPhones, YouTube, My Space, cell phones, downloads; it's basically all about music. Music is their world, it sets their standards, it determines their priorities, it influences their lives, it sets their moral pattern and influences their convictions. It is everything.

If you're going to Germany as a missionary, you will have to learn to speak German. You don't make the people in Germany learn to speak English. If you're going to Nigeria as a missionary, you'll have to learn to speak Ebo, Swahili, Uraba, or Housa. Those are the languages Nigerians speak. You must speak to them in *their* language, not yours.

A few years ago *Time* magazine observed if a teenager today has money and is hungry, he will spend it on an iTunes card before he would buy a sandwich. Music is *their* language, and they're not speaking *our* language. We absolutely must put our message in their language if we're going to communicate the gospel to them.

Less than one-half of 1 percent of all music listened to today is classical music. It's fine to try to raise the level of *music appreciation,* but if we don't start raising the level of *Jesus appreciation* by communicating the gospel to this young generation in the language they speak, we're going to lose them.

When John and Charles Wesley were converted, they set out to get the gospel into the heart of the secular world to which they were called. They went to the bars and taverns and listened to the kind of music being sung. They took the melodies and wrote gospel lyrics to them. That is *exactly* what many young musical missionaries are doing today. Whether it is hard rock, soft rock, or in-between rock, music is still the medium through which we must preach the unchanging gospel of Jesus Christ to today's teens and young adults.

The new music is primarily Scripture set to music. And how can we fault that? Again, search your hymnal. Barely 5 percent of the hymns are nothing but Scripture set to music. In contemporary music barely 5 percent of the songs are not!

Things change. The apostle Paul speaks of at least three kinds of music: "psalms, hymns, and spiritual songs" (Eph. 5:19). Apparently there has always been a variety of music types throughout the history of the Judeo-Christian faith. Perhaps the apostle Paul had something like that in mind when he wrote, "I have become all things to all men; that I might by all *music* save some" (see 1 Cor. 9:22), or something like that.

The message must never change, but the methods and means must be ever changing to bring an ever-changing generation to the knowledge of the never-changing truth.

Have you ever wondered why God preserved the words of the oldest music of the Judeo-Christian faith in the Psalms? The hymnbook of the Old Testament is preserved for us in our Bible.

But why did He not see to the preservation of the music? We don't know how Psalm 23 went. We can't identify the melody of Psalm 51 or Psalm 91. Why did God preserve the words but not the music? I think it's because He knew every generation would write its own music.

Remember, there's nothing sacred about guitars or organs, bongo drums or violins, robes or blue jeans, fast or slow, loud or soft, E-flat or C-major. Music is amoral. Music is the vibration of air *from* a string or *through* a tube. Music is only a means by which we express what's in our mind and in our heart.

Please use the new music to express the old gospel to the hearts of a dying generation. If not, you will be part of the *problem*, not part of the *solution*.

Yes, things do change. If they didn't, you'd probably be singing Gregorian chants today. That's what we used to do, you know. Then came hymns; now comes contemporary music; tomorrow, probably something else.

When I began in full-time Christian ministry, I was a traveling evangelist. When we went to town to conduct an old-fashioned revival, we simply printed out a few dozen handbills, got a roll of scotch tape, and went to grocery stores, service stations, and drive-ins and put them in the window.

Today if you are going to advertise your campaign, you'd better get on your computer and your iPhone. One of my students said recently, "If I want to communicate with my teenagers, I have to text them. They won't answer a call or respond to a brochure or letter about anything."

Let's review. I have asked the younger people to understand why the old music is so important to those of us who are older. I have asked the older people to understand why the new music is so important to the young. Now let's look at what Jesus said to both.

Chapter 83

JESUS' ANSWER TO WORSHIP WARS

Surprise! Surprise! Neither kind of music is necessarily important to God. Think about that for a minute. Do you think God really cares whether music is fast or slow, loud or soft, old or new?

In John 4, Jesus said something that should forever *put an end* to the battle.

Jesus' conversation with the Samaritan woman was getting a bit too close for comfort. When Jesus was talking to her about her five husbands and the man with whom she was now living, she quickly changed the subject.

"Sir, you Jews say we should worship in Jerusalem. We Samaritans say one ought to worship here on Mount Gerizim." Let's talk about authentic worship.

Jesus' answer was wonderful. He said, "Woman, believe Me, the hour is coming and now is when neither on this mountain nor in Jerusalem will you worship the Father. You worship what you do not know. We know what we worship, for salvation is of the Jews. But the hour is coming, and now is, when the true worshippers will worship the Father in *spirit* and *truth*. For the Father seeks such to worship Him." "God is a Spirit, and those who worship Him must worship Him in *spirit* and *truth*."

Jesus refused to acknowledge the superiority of either Samaritan worship on Mount Gerizim or Jewish worship in Jerusalem. He cut straight to the chase and said, "Woman, worship style is not the issue. All that matters is one thing: that you worship God in *spirit* and in *truth*."

All the accoutrements of Jewish and Samaritan worship are irrelevant, nonessential, and unimportant. What matters is the way you worship in your heart.

Jesus tells us only two things are essential to *acceptable worship*. First, it must be *in spirit*. That simply means it must be sincere; from your heart. Second, it must be *in truth*, based on the Word of God.

If people are worshipping Jesus Christ with lyrics from the Word of God and doing it with all their heart, it doesn't matter whether they're dancing a jig or sitting in a cathedral—God is honored, and God approves their worship.

The devil has us running in circles over the issue of *how* to worship, when the answer is clearly stated in John 4. It doesn't matter about the physical accoutrements of worship; all that matters is that it be spiritually sincere and doctrinally authentic.

Let me ask you a question. Here is a group of young people singing choruses around a campfire at youth camp. Over here a southern gospel church sings Stamps Baxter music, barreling out "I'll Fly Away" from a shaped note-songbook. Over here a church in Africa worships: nationals dancing and chanting John 3:16. Here a great cathedral in London worships with a five-million-dollar organ, seven fold amen, and chancel choir. Do you really think God cares? And by the way, what are you going to do if you get to heaven and find out God likes rap?

The Samaritan religion was quite different from Judaism. The Samaritans were half Jew and half Gentile. They had nothing to do with the Jews, and the Jews had nothing to do with them. Their worship, their religion, everywhere there were differences. Here are but a few.

- The Jews worshipped in the temple in Jerusalem. The Samaritans' temple was on Mount Gerizim.
- The Jews believed they descended from Abraham. The Samaritans believed they were converts of a lion.
- The Jewish altar was small. The Samaritan altar was sixty-five by sixty-five feet with elaborate pillars and statues.
- In Jewish worship the Gentiles worshipped in the outer court. In Samaritan worship they sat together.
- The Jews were city people. The Samaritans were country people.
- The Jews believed Gerizim was cursed. The Samaritans believed Jerusalem was cursed.

Sound familiar?

Differences continue today throughout the body of Christ, but the worship of our Lord in spirit and in truth should be the greatest single unifier of our devotion to Jesus. We need to be wise as serpents and harmless as doves in this area—wise enough to include new styles of music and harmless in our gracious acceptance of those with different musical tastes.

Chapter 84

LEARNING FROM THE PAST

Samaritan worship differed from temple worship. Absolutely. But nowhere was the difference greater than in their music.

- Jewish worship was simple. Samaritan worship was elaborate, loud, and over the edge.
- The Jews sang straight ahead, side by side. In Samaritan worship two groups called rightists and leftists faced each other and sang antiphonally.
- The Jews ad-libbed. In Samaritan worship there was no ad-libbing; the melody was structured and unchanging.
- The Jews sang one text to only one melody. The Samaritans sang the same text to many different melodies.

L. A. Bernstein, noted authority on the Samaritan religion states, "The most obvious difference in the two forms of worship was the firm commitment to their musical traditions of the Samaritans."

They would not change; they would not bend; they would not adapt.

Dr. Bernstein points out that in Jesus' day, there were approximately 1,200,000 persons in the world practicing Samaritan worship. *Today, there are about 600.* One must wonder if there is any connection to those statistics and their refusal to change.

In my city new mosques are opening. Other religions are growing. Young people are being drawn into the occult, attempting suicide, hooked on drugs, dying of AIDS, and getting all their values from the Internet, their music, and their reality TV.

Let me ask you a straight-up question: Would you be willing to die in order to reach your grandkids for Jesus Christ? I know you would. Now another question: Would you be willing to *change your music* in order to see them come to Christ?

Imagine your church twenty years from now, at the rate you are going. Of this you can be certain: if you are not finding a way to embrace the new music, either in blended services or two alternative services offering a choice of both kinds of music, your church is likely getting older and grayer. And one day, your church may cease to exist.

We face two challenges.

The first is not to throw out the older music. It's great music; it's important; it meant much to us. And we need to honor it and embrace it.

Second, we need to find ways to incorporate the newer music. Either two services or blended services are the only answers I have found. But you must do both kinds of music. And remember, Jesus said the only worship acceptable to Him is that which comes from a heart of loving sincerity and doctrinal integrity.

I spent three years discussing, analyzing, and considering beginning an additional service in our church that was fully contemporary. Houston's First is beyond 170 years old. It is the second oldest Baptist church in Texas, second only to First Baptist Church of Independence. Things don't change easily in a church like ours. Finally I realized two things. (1) I *had* to begin a contemporary service. (2) I would have opposition.

With fear and trepidation, yet confidence in the leadership of the Holy Spirit, we began that service. We prepared for two hundred persons. The first service had nine hundred! By the time I left, there were eighteen hundred. Today there are thousands more than that as pastor Gregg Matte continues to provide both kinds of music with unparalleled quality.

Before beginning the new contemporary service, I called a Sunday school rally for our fifty-year-olds and above. More than two thousand were there. I spent an hour explaining why we were starting that new service.

I asked, "How many of you have kids or grandkids who don't go to church, don't love the Lord, aren't Christians, and it's breaking your heart?" Over half raised their hands.

I said, "When you walk down the hallway to your class next Sunday morning and you hear music coming out of the worship center you don't like, remember: it's not for you, *it's for your kids and grandkids.*"

Spirit and truth. From the heart and from the Word.

Chapter 85

USING THE ARTS

Houston's First is widely known for its annual Christmas pageant. For twenty-eight years Gerald B. Ray, the grand master of Christian pageantry and our worship pastor, led the church in presenting the annual Houston Christmas Pageant to approximately forty-seven thousand people.

It is, of course, not necessary for every church to attempt something on so grand a scale. The church for the deaf, one of our strongest missions, presents its own annual Christmas pageant in a small building to a few hundred persons at a cost of less than three thousand dollars. It is equally blessed of God. But few events will be better attended and provide more effective outreach than dramas and pageants in your church.

Hundreds of churches are discovering the benefit and impact of pageantry and drama. Many churches present an annual Easter pageant and Christmas pageant.

Who could overstate the impact of Jeannette Clift George, the Christian actress, playwright, and producer. She and her talented company of Christian artists have thrilled thousands across the world. This method of presenting the gospel through one of the world's oldest art forms is a powerful ministry, far too often overlooked by the church.

Somewhere in your congregation there is an artistic person who would love to lead this ministry. There are people in your church who are good at drama, videos, makeup, costuming, and a hundred other things, who have never found their niche in the kingdom. That long-sought place of service might be in just such a ministry.

Frances Schaeffer went beyond the importance of the arts as a reflection of the culture to emphasize the necessity of using the arts to impact the culture. Why has the church given so much attention to music and so little to art and drama, not to mention dance?

Our Catholic friends have outdone us in this area. Even the most casual tour of Italy cannot fail to impact the believer with the awesome power of the arts in the Christian faith.

But where to start? Perhaps a skit or a play, a small pageant, an art display, or seminar in your church. Sculpture and painting can have much the same impact as music in our churches and in our homes. But it is generally given little attention by evangelicals.

Contemporary services often feature skits and videos, and this is a good place to start. The younger people that will be drawn to your contemporary service are accustomed to a fast-paced, electronic environment. We often show a video clip from a movie with a scene and dialogue pertinent to the message. For a nominal fee you can get blanket coverage to do this. Today Pastor Matte does much, much more.

Your Christian bookstore has material available with many creative skits. Some of our best skits really get the point across with humor. Five minutes is the limit for a skit and one minute for a video clip from a movie. If they are powerful and pertinent, they can even be used as an introduction to your message.

Rick Warren of Saddleback Community Church goes beyond the video and the skit to the live presentation. In virtually every sermon, instead of telling the illustration, he prepares someone to come to the platform and tell his or her own story. If the person is unavailable, Rick will video the testimony in advance.

Sugar Creek Church of Houston has an awesome dance ministry. They use it about once a month. It is beautiful, effective, and presented in exceptionally good taste. It has a heavenly anointing and truly glorifies God.

Yes, you read it right, dear Baptist friend, Psalm 150 is still in the Bible. Try it, you'll be blessed.

> Praise Him with trumpet blast;
> praise Him with the harp and lyre.
> Praise Him with the tambourine *and dance*;
> praise Him with flute and strings.
> Praise Him with resounding cymbals;

praise Him with clashing cymbals.
Let everything that breathes praise the LORD.
Hallelujah! (Ps. 150:3–6)

The arts are powerful and God is their author. Don't let the devil's *abuse* of them stop you from *using* them for His glory.

Our Lord gave us all of these rich and powerful tools to arrest our attention and communicate His love. We have been embarrassingly negligent in doing so. Perhaps the time to start is now.

Chapter 86

CHURCH ATMOSPHERE

Each church has its own personality. Generally, five factors go into creating it: the architectural style of the building, the traditional liturgy of the church, the personality of the pastor, the socioeconomic makeup of the congregation, and the music.

For centuries churches were churchy. Robes and stained-glass windows, in the minds of most Americans, was synonymous with going to church. About 1960 that began to change.

As stated in our chapters on traditional and contemporary worship, the musical landscape of the American church has changed dramatically. Younger people like contemporary music. The church must, in some forum, offer this option.

While Houston's First offers both traditional and contemporary worship services, each has a bright and warm atmosphere. Structured formality and joyous freedom are *not* mutually exclusive.

Some Americans go to churches with guitars and videos while others worship with organs and robed choirs. Some people like church right down the middle.

At the risk of the mundane, let me tell you the philosophy that drives my approach to worship: *You can't hatch eggs in a refrigerator.* The purpose of the proclamation of the gospel of Jesus Christ is to change lives. It is that for which He came and that which only He can do.

There is a great distance from what I am to what I long to be. The transformation of human character brought about through repentance of sin and personal commitment to Jesus Christ is so radical that it can only be described in terms of people's becoming something they have never been before—born again! When He enters a life, everything is drastically changed.

The divine operation of the Holy Spirit which produces that change occurs more easily in an atmosphere conducive to freedom and fluidity. We are naturally resistant to God. We want our way. We want to do our own thing. But music, fellowship, and worship with other believers and fellow strugglers break down our inhibitions and resistance to the work of God's Spirit. To do something as radical and unstructured as allowing God to transform my life in an instant may certainly be done in a formal and structured environment. But it is *more easily* done in an unstructured, informal setting. Several factors go into creating such an environment.

1. Personal holiness. The Spirit of God has little freedom to circulate through a congregation of sinful, coldhearted people.
2. Warm music that stirs the heart.
3. A friendly and approachable pastor.
4. Prayer time. Nothing in the service warms the heart like the opportunity to kneel at the altar and pray and/or be prayed for by the pastor and congregation. Start a prayer time in your morning service. Dim the lights and invite your people to bring their burdens to the altar. Ask your deacons to come forward and kneel with them and pray for them. As pastor, pray audibly for the needs of the people. A special prayer time in each service can revitalize the worship experience.
5. Color and style of the worship center.

The atmosphere of your church is important. If people don't get past that, they may never get to what you have to say about the Lord and what He can do in their lives. In all things let love and warmth be your priority.

And that translates to dress, music, buildings, décor, love, laughter, and informality from everything from the architecture to the announcements. Go ahead, brighten it up. Warm it up. You'll hatch more eggs.

I have recently visited three or four churches with a Starbucks-like lobby.

Lots of coffee.

Lots of couches.

Lots of overstuffed chairs.

Lots of fellowship.

Lots of love.

I liked it.

Chapter 87

RECOGNIZING GUESTS

As Great Commission churches our magnificent obsession is to touch those outside our fellowship with the gospel. Worship of God and edification of one another are intended to build up the body that we might be his "sent ones."

Indeed, the message of the cross is an offense to them who perish, but that in no way implies the messenger is to be offensive. A consumer-friendly church and a noncompromising message are not mutually exclusive.

Truth with integrity and love is always in order. The wise pastor will remove every barrier to the unbeliever—from parking to greeting, from dress to decor. Everything must be done to say, "You are loved, you are wanted, you are welcome here—just as you are."

Every physical and spiritual effort must be made to make your guests feel welcome. I recommend referring publicly, and in print, to all who visit your church as "guests." The term *visitor* suggests a kind of intrusion into the status quo. It says, "You are an outsider; come in and watch us do our thing." The term *guest* says, "You are a welcome and special part of the family. Come on in!"

How do we best go about identifying guests in order to facilitate follow-up? The most important thing may well be what you do *not* do.

People do not like to be singled out. For years preachers asked guests to stand and be recognized. Believe me, that is *not the way to do it*. We began asking our members to stand in honor of the guests. That proved to be somewhat more effective. Although the members of our church sincerely greeted those guests seated around them, our guests still felt a sense of having been pointed out.

We found a better way to do this. Attached to our Sunday morning worship guide is a perforated guest registration form. At some point during the service when guests are welcomed, they are asked to fill out the form, detach it, and place it in the offering plates as they are passed. It is, of course, necessary to do this in the service before the offering. Another way is to place guest registration forms in the pew racks or seat backs, and invite your guests to fill them out in the same manner.

During the benediction the pastor should leave the worship center before the worshippers to *meet* and *greet*. Everyone may not be greeted individually, but the attempt should be made. Look into the eyes of the one to whom you are speaking, not over their shoulder. Those whom you did not have opportunity to greet will notice that you gave undivided attention to each person, and sense, "If I ever need the pastor, he will do the same for me."

Guest receptions are also profitable. When this is done, an invitation is given to the guests to join you for a cup of coffee at a designated area. A corner of the lobby will do well. A table with formal tablecloth, coffee urn, perhaps orange juice, and cups will have been prepared by a small group of hosts and hostesses who will serve the refreshments, form the greeting line, and assist the pastor. The pastor's spouse should accompany him.

The advantage is that you can spend more quality time with individuals. Those who choose to come to the guest reception are usually good prospects. The disadvantage is that you will seldom get to greet your own members personally, but you can do that before the service, in the lobby and aisles of the worship center. We have done it both ways at Houston's First, and you will find the best method for you.

Most preprinted registration forms contain boxes that say, "Interested in joining our church? Check yes or no." Customize your forms to include "undecided." Normally the registration form is filled out early in the service. Unfortunately, the individual is asked to indicate his interest in the church without the benefit of having experienced the full service.

The person who says no at 11:00 a.m. might say yes at 12:00 noon. Add a third box to the guest registration card. Give people a chance to say yes, no, or undecided. A *no* normally means no, but *an undecided is often a yes waiting to happen.*

Personal visits, phone calls, and other contacts by pastor and people to all guests should be made as soon as possible the following week. A Sunday afternoon telephone call to those who were in your service that morning is most impressive to a prospective member.

Don't let the prospect cool off. Don't let the ripe fruit lie on the ground. Woe to him who neglects the prospects.

"Share with the saints; pursue hospitality." (Rom. 12:13)

"An overseer, therefore, must be above reproach, the husband of one wife, self-controlled, sensible, respectable, hospitable, an able teacher." (1 Tim. 3:2)

"But hospitable, loving what is good, sensible, righteous, holy, self-controlled." (Titus 1:8)

"Be hospitable to one another without complaining." (1 Pet. 4:9)

Hospitality is important. Start brewing that coffee.

Chapter 88

PUBLIC TESTIMONIES

The first inclination of Andrew upon coming to believe in Jesus was to tell his brother Simon Peter: "We have found the Messiah!" (John 1:41).

New converts should be encouraged to "go home and tell." The value of personal and *public* testimony cannot be overstated. The new convert, however, should be both seasoned and instructed before public testimony is given from the pulpit.

When the conversion of popular and influential persons occurs, our first inclination is to put them up for a testimony. Far too often pastor and new convert have been embarrassed, not to mention the embarrassment brought on the name of Christ.

Anyone is subject to "going back," but the *high-profile* new convert is especially vulnerable. A time of personal discipleship must be spent and a solid sense of stability established before the new convert is encouraged to give a public testimony.

Announcing that on a given date an influential person will give his testimony can be of great value. Someone should assist the new believer in refining his or her testimony until it is just right. When the time comes, the wise pastor will encourage the person to write out his testimony, reading it aloud to himself or others several times. Those who give public testimony from the pulpit should be helped at three points:

1. *Timing matters.* Brevity is always in order. The individual must be led to understand the difference between a testimony and a life story. Most testimonies take longer than I want to listen and tell me more than I want to know. Few of us were born in log cabins. Seven or eight minutes is the outside limit for a testimony; five minutes is ideal.

2. *Every effort should be made to glorify Christ and not the individual.* Accounts of sin must not be overly descriptive. Good taste is always appropriate. Remember the children.

Frankly, few people inherently know how to give a good public testimony. The motivation might be pure and the concept beneficial, but the bottom line is that few people know how to do it. Help the new believer prepare.

3. *Every testimony should contain three elements:* (1) what I was and how unfulfilled I was, (2) who made the difference and how it came about, and (3) what I am today and how I feel about it.

The apostle Paul traveled the Roman Empire confronting both religious and political establishments. Although he was the great intellect of the New Testament, his message was not first theological but personal. His argument was himself: his personal testimony—his greatest defense. To the believer who knew Christ, he taught theology. To the unbeliever who didn't, he gave his testimony. Study the accounts. Three ingredients were always present—*who I was, what happened, and what I am today.*

Through the years I have confronted thousands of persons with the claims of Christ. These included atheists and unbelievers, the cultist and the curious, philosophers and intellects, rich and poor. Some were receptive; some were not. Often they debated the Scripture, the person of Jesus, even the existence of God. But one common thread ran through every response; *no one ever attempted to refute my personal testimony.*

"Let me tell you what happened to me" is the ultimate softener of the human heart. That you have sincere joy and care enough to share it is at once disarming and effective with the unbeliever.

Listen again to John 1:40–42: "Andrew, Simon Peter's brother was one of the two who heard John and followed Him. He first found his own brother Simon and told him, 'We have found the Messiah!' (which means 'Anointed One'), and he brought Simon to Jesus."

Notice the progression:

- He found his brother.
- He told him whom He had found.
- He brought his brother to Jesus.

In the traffic pattern of our lives, we regularly "find our brother." That which best prepares a person's heart and brings him to Jesus is following Andrew's example. The intermediate step between finding a person and bringing him to Christ is our personal testimony: "We have found the Messiah!"

In your personal witnessing as well as your public ministry, don't forget the power of the personal testimony, both yours and those whom you have led to Christ.

Use that personal testimony. It is the irrefutable argument for the gospel and the ultimate validator of its authenticity. It works!

Chapter 89

USHERS AND GREETERS

The first impression of your church is the one that will linger in the minds and hearts of your guests. An impression of a cold, uncaring congregation will not allow you that second and third chance with those you would reach.

I couldn't count the times I've walked into a men's clothing store, sized up the suits, and already said no in my mind before the salesman asked, "May I help you?" That first impression is important. Everything possible must be done to make those potential members who visit your church feel comfortable and welcome.

Your parking will make the first impression. Policemen or volunteer car parkers should direct the people as they approach your church and its parking lots. A sign that says, "Guests, Please Turn on Your Headlights," is the first order of business. Those cars are then directed to the priority parking you have reserved in the area of the parking lot nearest to the entrance.

Covered drop-offs for rainy days should be ample and obvious. Give consideration, as well, to special parking for expectant mothers, parents of infants, and small children near the nurseries. Ample parking for the physically disabled, as well as senior adults, should also be clearly marked and close to church entrances.

Shuttle buses from the extremities of your parking lot should be provided and captained by a friendly and faithful volunteer. Sunday morning worship guides can be distributed on the shuttle, and questions about locations and activities answered.

In addition to car parkers, shuttle drivers, and captains, the progressive church will have outside greeters and inside greeters, an information desk, and ushers.

Outside greeters are of two types: (1) those who open the door of the car, introduce themselves, offer to carry the baby, and escort the family to the front door; and (2) those who open exterior doors of the building and again welcome the guests. Those greeters will direct the guests to the information desk just inside the lobby.

Information desks should be located near each main entrance to your facilities. They should be staffed with knowledgeable, friendly volunteers, ready to go the second mile to answer the questions of your guests and make them feel warm and welcome. In cases of large facilities, information desk assistants may personally escort families or individuals to the nursery, classroom, or worship center.

The next personal touch will be by an inside greeter. Once inside the lobby, this person opens the door to the *sanctuary*, welcomes the people to the worship service, and hands them a bulletin, worship guide, or other pertinent material.

Once guests are seated, the service will begin. The atmosphere before the service is as important as the worship hour itself.

Church members should be encouraged to introduce themselves and welcome and assist new people who are being seated near them. If a parent brings a baby in arms, it would be nice to say, "If you would like to take her to our nursery, I would be happy to go with you." It is important to be sensitive to the parent's response. Should a parent not choose to do so, he must not be made to feel uncomfortable or uncooperative by not placing the child in the nursery or preschool facility.

Ushers may need training to be sensitive to the needs of the congregation during the service. If a child is crying, it may be appropriate to offer help. Again, this must be graciously done with no inference that the child is disrupting the service. If this impression is given, the young couple will probably never return.

Ushers should be sensitive to other disturbances in the service.

Occasionally, unintentional or even premeditated disturbances will occur. Two to four ushers in the area should go immediately to the person and deal with the situation without having to be directed to do so from the pulpit.

It is the responsibility of ushers to distribute the offering plates or other materials that might be called for during the course of a service. They should also be responsible for taking offering plates to an appointed place of security.

Greeters and ushers may or may not wear name tags. I strongly recommend that you have both male and female greeters and ushers.

Young adults add much to the perception that yours is an alive and invigorating congregation. Great sensitivity, however, must be exercised toward older ushers and greeters who have served faithfully for decades. It is possible to rotate or blend in new and younger ushers and greeters without giving the feeling that you are putting older ones out to pasture.

The Holy Spirit has blessed the church with members of varying giftedness. Two of those special gifts are hospitality and the gift of helps.

Within your fellowship are many wonderful persons who cannot sing a solo, give great sums of money, or teach a class. These are the helpers who make guests feel at home. Identify, enlist, train, and honor them. They are an indispensable part of a ministry that functions at maximum efficiency.

Chapter 90

SUNDAY NIGHTS

One of the more sensitive issues in the spotlight today is the value of the Sunday night service. Few churches in America, among all denominations, still have Sunday night church. Is this good, or is it not? Let's talk about it.

Dr. Herschel Hobbs, former pastor of First Baptist Church, Oklahoma City, and meticulous documenter of Southern Baptist history, writes that Sunday night church services were initially begun to appeal to people who were hung over from Saturday night and couldn't get out of bed Sunday morning.

Regardless of the reason for their existence, Sunday night services have been a part of the American landscape, particularly in Southern and rural areas, since the turn of the nineteenth century.

Many factors in American culture have caused the church to revisit the issue of the value and wisdom of Sunday night church. Probably the most significant is the emergence of the working mother.

In a large number of American families, both mother and father work five days a week outside the home. Evening family time is virtually nonexistent. Saturdays are spent going to Little League ball games, shopping, doing yard work, and running a variety of errands that have been pushed back to the weekend. Sunday morning is for church, leaving only Sunday evenings for a relaxed family time.

Sunday night has become stay-at-home night in America. Theaters are empty, bars are empty, shopping malls are empty. Americans are home watching videos and television. The only vestige of family night that remains in most American homes is Sunday night.

Let me ask you some questions.

- Are Sunday services simply a tradition you passionately preserve?
- Are they necessarily biblical?
- Does hurriedly running around to more and more church services truly enhance the spiritual quality of our lives, or does it simply relieve the guilt of discontinuing what we have been doing for decades?
- Do they help make the Lord's Day a *hallowed* day or a *hurried* day?
- Are Sunday night services counterproductive to the spiritual growth of quality families we are attempting to build through other means and ministries?

The purpose of this chapter is not to persuade you one way or the other, but to get you thinking. Above all, don't continue Sunday nights because "we've always done it that way." But don't drop them just because everyone else is doing it. Seek the heart of God. Talk with your people, and make the decision that is right for you. If that decision is to have Sunday night services, consider the following:

1. Don't make the Sunday night service a duplicate of the Sunday morning service. If I have pizza for lunch, I don't want it again for dinner. The evening service should be different from the morning service. With one exception. Due to parking restraints, three needed morning services are impossible at Houston's First. So the church conducts a duplicate Sunday morning service at 5:30 that night. Sunday morning worshippers are not expected to attend.

2. Start the evening service rather early—5:00, 5:30, or 6:00 p.m. at the latest. Early evening worship gives people time to get home and still enjoy an evening with their family.

3. Bring in guest speakers rather often, and let staff and laymen do some preaching. It is difficult to preach multiple services in the morning and then preach again in the evening, especially if you have to preach a different message.

4. Don't go too long. There is nothing wrong with a good crisp forty-five or fifty-minute service.

5. Don't put a guilt trip on your people. Let those who choose quality Sunday evening family time know they too are honoring God. The priesthood of the believer recognizes the privilege and responsibility of each person to find God's direction for his or her own life.

Again, as in all good decision making regarding major change, take your time and bring your people along with you.

Dropping Sunday night services will be unpopular among the majority of your senior adults. Consider a small evening chapel service just for them with 100 percent traditional music, an older preacher, and a dismissal time that allows them to get home well before dark.

Chapter 91

SUPPLY PREACHERS

We're not talking here about the seminar speaker who comes for a weekend conference or the evangelist who comes for a week's crusade. We're talking about the one-time supply preacher who is an occasional guest in your Sunday morning pulpit. Most of the time this person is invited only to preach in the pastor's absence. But I encourage you to think about bringing such persons in occasionally even when you are at home and presiding over the worship service.

It is important for your people occasionally to hear a fresh voice and different perspective, particularly in a pastorate of long duration. It doesn't have to be a holiday Sunday. Occasionally, it can be nice to invite a good speaker to your pulpit for no other reason than to bless your people.

Not only will it allow you to pace yourself in those times you need it, but it may be stimulating to your congregation as well. Special subjects will be in the area of such things as testimonies of celebrities, marriage and family, stewardship, prophecy, hot topics, or musical artists, to name a few.

Booking a quality speaker means extending the invitation well in advance. The person you want your people to hear is likely in great demand. He also has a schedule to control. Your best chance at getting him to come is probably to extend the invitation a year in advance. The lines of communication must be kept open and clear between you and your pulpit guest.

Discuss honorariums, travel arrangements, housing, subject matter, and other details. It is customary to pay all the expenses of your pulpit guest, including travel, airport parking, hotel, and meals.

Honorariums should be agreed upon in advance and presented in person at the conclusion of the service in which he speaks. Don't tell him, "Sorry, we couldn't get the check ready. We'll mail it to you." You've had a year to get ready, and everyone likes to be paid on time. "On time" for your pulpit guest is *at the conclusion of the service.*

Tickets for food are normally signed by the guest and charged to the hotel room, with the bill paid by the church. Most hotels will bill the church after the fact and want credit card information from the church in advance.

At the time of this writing, honorariums usually range anywhere from five hundred dollars to twenty-five hundred dollars. You rang? Smaller churches normally pay smaller honorariums while larger churches pay larger. Regardless of the size of the church, however, it is unthinkable to fly a guest speaker across the country, take two or three days of his time, and give him only a two- or three-hundred-dollar honorarium.

Remember, it takes a Saturday to get there, particularly if it is a Sunday engagement, and a Monday to get home. That thirty-minute message for your church probably cost that person three days of their week. Consider the time, as well as distance and value of the ministry, in determining the size of the honorarium.

Often you will be inviting a friend. But don't invite him just because you're comfortable with him or hope he'll invite you to preach in his church in return. If he's just another average, good preacher who will not really bring something new and special to your church, you might be better off just to go fishing with your friend rather than have him fly across three States to preach to your people. It's easier, and it's less expensive. A pulpit guest should be a special occasion, and his sermon should be a special message. If you're interested in someone you do not know personally, get references, check them out, and ask the hard questions.

One issue that always arises is the sale of books, tapes, and CDs by the visiting author or musical group. It is most appropriate to expand your guest's ministry, and the kingdom, by promoting such material for sale after the service. It is never appropriate for the guest to do that himself.

Enlist some of your members to set up a table and handle the sales. Let the pastor announce their availability just before the benediction, and let the guest sit at the table and sign his books if he desires. But for the visiting speaker to be seen as the money handler, the hawker, or the promoter is to *negate the good* that was accomplished through his message.

Expenses for travel should be mailed in advance or reimbursed at the time the honorarium is presented. The guest should be encouraged to stay and mingle with the people, greeting them, answering their questions, and praying for them when appropriate. If circumstances are such that he must choose between this and signing books, what to do is obvious.

It is always best to contact the individual personally in advance and follow up with a written, formal invitation. It is always appropriate as well to send a note of thanks.

Part 7

PROGRAMS AND MINISTRIES

Chapter 92

SUNDAY MORNING BIBLE STUDY—HOW?

The corporate worship of God's people is an indispensable part of the Christian experience. But other needs can be met only in a small-group setting. Here Bible study and interaction occur, and edifying personal relationships develop.

Many churches have changed the name of these groups from Sunday school to Sunday morning Bible study, Life groups or Bible fellowship. I think this can be wise. There is, particularly in the secular world, an image of Sunday school as something that children do. The name "Bible study" has a wider appeal to all ages and all kinds of people.

Questions abound as to the best way to do Sunday morning Bible study.

Shall we have small classes or large classes? Small classes are best. Admittedly, with fewer teachers and larger classes, the quality of teaching may go up, but a serious effort to train and develop good teachers can staff a large Sunday morning Bible study with many small classes.

Small classes are preferable not only for the purpose of building personal relationships but because of the opportunity to ask questions.

Large classes tend to become *mini-church* services taught by a *mini-pastor*. Virtually no opportunity is offered for the interchange of ideas, and many people will leave with unanswered questions. In a smaller setting, members are not only allowed but encouraged to raise their hands, ask questions, and join the discussion. *And we learn best by asking.* In the smaller class members have opportunity to learn the answer.

Further, good small classes become good big classes, and good big classes can be divided to create two good small classes, which can again become two good, big classes. New units grow faster than old units. There is no better way to expand the Bible-teaching ministry of your church than by the old Sunday school axiom "divide and multiply."

Should classes be age graded? Absolutely! Children should be in Bible study classes with other children their age, as should teenagers and adults. Singles should be given the opportunity to go to Bible study with other singles, young marrieds with young marrieds, seniors with seniors, etc. This grouping by age and marital status offers a natural mix that is essential in nurturing developing relationships.

Should the sexes be mixed in Sunday school? Should you have only boys' classes and girls' classes, or classes for only men and classes for only women?

The best answer is to offer an option. Certainly among children and teenagers, there is much to be said for classes for boys and classes for girls, but for adults offer a choice of classes. In Houston's First, we offer couples classes for married adults as well as men's classes and women's classes and often several of each within the same departmental age span.

Men often lag behind women in spiritual maturity and biblical literacy. And while we learn best by asking, many men in such classes will normally not ask questions in front of their wives. So there is a case to be made for both mixed and separated classes even among adults. I recommend offering a choice in each adult age division.

Most student divisions coincide with school grades from kindergarten through college. Beyond that, the age spread must be wider, normally every three to five years. When you get to the upper end, forget trying to get people to tell you their age. Just have a class for fifty and up, or sixty and up, such as the Golden Agers or the Prime Timers.

Growing churches often face the question of multiple services. I suggest four possible models, primarily determined by space limitations within your building.

1. A central Bible study hour with two worship services, one before and one after Bible study.
2. A central worship service with two Bible study hours, one before and one after the worship service.
3. Two worship services and two Bible studies that flip-flop.

4. A staggered schedule: Schedule A (Bible study, 8:30 a.m.; worship, 9:45 a.m.); Schedule B (Bible study, 9:45 a.m.; worship 11:00 a.m.).

There are three advantages to the staggered schedule.

First, it is easy to understand. You simply go to Bible study and church on one schedule or the other. You are either a "Schedule A" person or a "Schedule B" person.

Second, it is naturally sequential. Everyone goes to Bible study and then church. No one goes to church and then Bible study.

Third, it best facilitates traffic movement in your parking lots.

Sunday morning Bible study is a beautiful and wonderful thing. It can be most difficult to get your arms around hundreds of people. But in the Sunday Bible study, relationships flourish, needs are met, and the church is strengthened. It is a place to be known by name, missed when absent, and ministered to, when in need.

Sunday morning Bible study is not an organization *of* the church; it *is* the church, organized to do ministry.

Chapter 93

SUNDAY MORNING
BIBLE STUDY—WHY?

The purpose of organized Sunday morning Bible study is fivefold.

Religious Education

In the Sunday school we teach God's Word.

To teach the Word of God does not simply mean to explain it; it means to apply it to one's life. And in good Bible teaching, teachers will relate to their students, live among them, know their needs, and be conscious of meeting those needs as they prepare the lesson. Sunday school teachers should not simply appear and disappear after Sunday morning. They should be involved in the lives of their students.

Bible study teachers should be trained by the pastor or minister of education. They should meet the standards of holiness, calling, serious preparation, stewardship, and faithfulness. Any church will have gifted teachers who need little training. Many of your people will have been effectively teaching for years. But it is important to constantly develop and train a fresh group of new leaders if your Sunday Bible study is to divide, multiply, and grow.

Religious education is done in many ways. People learn through more ways than lecture and dialogue. Videos, for example, as well as object lessons can be most helpful.

Evangelism

The best way to do outreach evangelism is through the existing unit of the Sunday morning Bible study structure. There's no need to reinvent the wheel. The most likely person to visit a twenty-eight-year-old single woman is her teacher or another class member. Geographical proximity does not carry the weight of spiritual affinity. If I teach fifty-year-old men, I will likely drive across town to visit a fifty-year-old prospect for my class before I will go down the street to visit a teenager.

Assign prospects to the Sunday school. They may be visited through other outreach ministries of the church, but you can't show too much attention to a potential new member for your class.

Stewardship

Sunday morning Bible study is a great place to teach stewardship. Here the matter can be personalized and explained. Here testimonies can be given and questions asked.

Distribute offering envelopes each Sunday morning to everyone in Bible study above preschool age. You can't begin teaching stewardship too early.

Ministry

In a setting in which people are studying the Bible and praying together, personal ministry naturally occurs. Within each departmental age division of the Sunday school, you need outreach leaders and in-reach leaders.

The responsibility of the *outreach* leader is overseeing personal visitation of prospects. The purpose of the *in-reach* leader is meeting the needs of the class whether they are domestic problems, health needs, financial needs, discouragement, going through a divorce, absenteeism, etc.

Fellowship

The family that *prays* together stays together, and the class that *plays* together also stays together. Every month or two each Sunday school class should have a fellowship, a lunch, a social—perhaps a cookout, a beach party, or other event. Meet the social needs of your people within the Bible study unit, and build a solid church. Great classes build great churches.

Hyman Appleman told the story of an Indian chief who was a Bible teacher in a church in southeastern Oklahoma. Because of his knowledge of the oil business and his familiarity with the various languages spoken by the Indians in Oklahoma, a large oil company from another state repeatedly tried to hire him. He refused their offer, and they raised it again and again. Finally he told them, "I am not coming at any price. Your salary is not an issue."

Pressed further, he replied, "Your salary is big enough, but your job isn't." "Why?" they insisted. The answer of that humble Indian chief was simply, "My Sunday school class."

Out of that class came twenty-seven men who went into full-time Christian ministry through the years. Great was his reward where it really counts.

> And they devoted themselves to the apostles' teaching, to the fellowship, to the breaking of bread, and to the prayers.
>
> Then fear came over everyone, and many wonders and signs were being performed through the apostles. Now all the believers were together and held all things in common. They sold their possessions and property and distributed the proceeds to all, as anyone had a need. Every day they devoted themselves to meeting together in the temple complex, and broke bread from house to house. They ate their food with a joyful and humble attitude, praising God and having favour with all the people. And every day the Lord added to them those who were being saved. (Acts 2:42–47)

Chapter 94

MINISTRY TO ADULTS

The educational, spiritual, and social needs of various adults are as different as the needs of children and the needs of teenagers. As the church begins to grow, it is necessary that separate ministry and Bible study units be designed not only for married adults and single adults but also for the three broad age divisions within all adults: senior adults, median adults, and young adults.

Senior Adults

The ministry to senior adults is the largest untapped gold mine of opportunity and spiritual resource you have. Consider this: For the first time in American history, there are more senior adults than teenagers.

Senior adults are reachable. They are mature, serious, and they're thinking about eternity.

Teenagers feel they are immortal and will live forever. But the senior adult, as recently as his last medical checkup, came face-to-face with the reality of his own mortality. The older, more serious person is much closer to heaven or hell; and he knows it.

Senior adults have historically been considered hard to reach. Indeed, if a person does not respond to the gospel when he is young, he may become spiritually hardened. But people are living longer. Not only are there more senior adults, but they are more secular than their ancestors were.

Millions of them in our pagan culture have never been seriously confronted with the claims of Christ at all. Untold numbers of American seniors have never heard the gospel of Jesus and are most reachable.

Senior adults are best reached by other senior adults or their children or grandchildren. Cultivate friendships. Take a bus to a recreation park or a ball game or road trip. Have a picnic. Invite them to socials. Build relationships. Show them you care. They will respond to you and to the Lord. What a shame that most churches pay far more attention to teenagers than senior adults. They too are a field "ready for harvest" (John 4:34).

Senior adults have time. They make great volunteers for your church and are just waiting to be asked. They will count the offering, stuff envelopes, greet incomers, organize prayer meetings, build missions, wait tables, call prospects, and carry out special projects. They love to keep busy, and they have lots of time to fill.

Senior adults have financial resources. Realizing their own mortality, developing an increasing sense that "you can't take it with you," they will respond to charitable and Christian causes. They are often the first to give to advance the gospel, the most sacrificial in giving to the building fund, and the most consistent in mission contributions. Wow, what a group!

Median Adults

These marvelous saints of God between the ages of forty and sixty are usually the backbone of your church. They are different from married young adults, who are still uncertain who they are, up to their neck in debt, and looking for a good time. Their needs are also as different as those of senior adults and teenagers. The median adults in your church and their lifestyles may vary greatly from small church to large church, blue collar to white collar, large city church to small rural church. Analyze your median adults. Learn their uniqueness. Understand their needs, and program to meet them.

Married Young Adults

Married young adults *begin* at any age and are classified as high as thirty-nine or as young as thirty-four. Grade by the age of the wife.

Through the years we have experimented with many models. But to our surprise, we have determined that the best teachers for married young adults are often other married young adults. There will always be those among your young adults who were raised in the church and who, though still in their thirties, are spiritually mature beyond their years. These will be the best teachers for your married young adults.

Have a nearly married department for engaged couples and a newly married class. The nearly married department confronts the issues that couples will face in marriage and teaches appropriate Bible study material to meet them. This can be a specially designed fifty-two-week curriculum and is readily available. In this department friendships are already being forged that will tie them to your Sunday school and church for years to come.

The nearly married couple is encouraged to attend their department from engagement until marriage, whether their engagement lasts two months or two years. Newlywed classes are normally for young adults. Older newlyweds normally blend in with their age group regardless of length of marriage.

A sensitive pastor will design some unique approaches to these three widely varying age divisions within the adult division of the Sunday school.

Chapter 95

MINISTRY TO SINGLES

One of the most profound changes facing the church is the growth of singles. Fifty percent of the adult population in Houston is single.

Some have been married, others never have. Some are motivated career people; others are living day to day. Some are young; others are approaching retirement age. Some have discretionary income; others live paycheck to paycheck. Some are single parents; all are in life transition.

With such diversity, transition, and mobility, leading a singles ministry can be like preaching to a parade. The mobility of society, the transition of early adulthood, and the reluctance to commit have created a unique culture of adult singles deeply hungering for more.

Preeminently, singles desire an authentic relationship with God and others. Single adults want and need four things.

1. *The habit of studying God's Word.* Sunday morning Bible study and evening midweek studies are both effective.

2. *The practice of ministry application.* The maturing Christian single must engage in appropriate application ministry. Singles are prime candidates to put their training into practical ministry, but ministry needs to fit giftedness and personal interests, and they love doing ministry together.

3. *Christian community.* The key to Christian community is developing feelings of safety and enjoyment, and safety is paramount. Growth can come only when we feel secure enough to be ourselves without fear of judgment or attack and when we are safe enough to receive loving correction.

The Christian community must also be a place of enjoyment. Enjoyment breeds feelings of safety, and safety fosters the reality of enjoyment. What better place to have fun than a safe, loving, challenging, Christian singles group?

4. *Accountability.* This vulnerable time in life needs the one-on-one relationships found in a small group. The accountability component is the key to healthy Bible study, ministry application, and Christian community. In the personal accountability group, the single can say, "I'm not alone in my struggle with sin," and find confidentiality, acceptance, and support.

Singles want to enter into the group with a sense of anonymity and the ability to "check things out" safely before joining or feeling "checked out" themselves.

Another key to ministering to singles is to know that singles follow singles. Critical mass, or the feeling that there are "others like me," is key to creating an atmosphere where singles feel safe and are willing to stay around.

Singles, of course, want to be involved with other singles. Houston's First facilitates Metro Bible Study, an interdenominational Bible study ministry of fifteen hundred to two thousand singles every Monday night. Both large and small congregations use Metro as a connection point with other singles. One of my sons met his wife at Metro.

Perhaps more than any other group, singles have time and desire to serve the Lord. One of the great joys of my ministry in Houston was to watch our young singles grow in their passion for inner-city ministries. In the summer of 1995, 135 of our singles took a week of their vacation time to conduct Vacation Bible Schools, build churches, do street witnessing and other inner-city mission ministries. Today the number is several hundred! Many of these singles are now entering a lifelong career of serving others in the name of Christ.

Additional ideas for big-picture possibilities abound. Be creative. We did praise and worship nights called "Unplugged" (followed by Starbucks coffee), weekend retreats, and ski trips, all with the idea of creating places where singles feel at home.

Singles are special people.

> Now in response to the matters you wrote about: "It is good for a man not to have relations with a woman." But because sexual immorality is so common, each man should have his own wife, and each woman should have her own husband. A husband should fulfill his marital responsibility to his wife, and likewise a wife to her husband. A wife does not have the right over her own body, but her husband does. In the same way, a husband docs not have the right over his own body, but his wife does. Do not deprive one another sexually—except when you agree

for a time, to devote yourselves to prayer. Then come together again; otherwise, Satan may tempt you because of your lack of self-control. I say the following as a concession, not as a command. I wish that all people were just like me. But each has his own gift from God, one person in this way and another in that way." (1 Cor. 7:1–7)

Chapter 96

MINISTRY TO STUDENTS

Teenagers prefer the term *student* to *youth* or *teen,* and their staff leaders prefer student minister to youth director. The terms *youth director* and *youth ministry* are out. *Student minister* and *student ministry* are in.

More important are the paradigm shifts that have occurred in effective student-reaching ministries. The twenty-first-century student minister must be alert to these changes.

The heart of student ministry today is one-to-one relationships. Students are hungry for authenticity. They crave an up-close relationship with someone they can trust, who understands and cares about them.

Many students feel they are aliens in their own home. Their natural craving for deep family relationships often goes unsatisfied by insensitive or overly busy parents. Far too often an intimate relationship with her boyfriend is only a girl's substitute for a relationship with an absentee father.

There is potential danger here, of course. But the wise student minister will help develop deep, godly relationships within his students.

Formerly student ministries were characterized by a "compete with the entertainment world" approach. Bigger was better, and each weekly event had to be louder and greater than the one before. Auditoriums were often filled with big bands, bright lights, and burgeoning crowds. But the result was often little more than an emotional and spiritual roller coaster.

Articles in *Newsweek* which appeared the week after the shootings in Columbine High School in Colorado (April 21, 1999) stated that the students who make it in the real world have a significant adult besides their parents who invests time in them.

Students need a relationship with their student pastor and other Christian students. Life in middle school and high school can be difficult at best. Fellowship with other believers during student years makes it easier.

Student ministry should emphasize unity, friendship, fellowship, brotherhood, sisterhood, family, and the group. The affirmation and support of fellow *Christian* students is of great importance at a time when peer approval is *everything*. A young person's deepening relationship with God is greatly nourished by the approval and support of a peer, who also hungers and thirsts after righteousness.

A growing relationship with Jesus Christ transcends the student years and carries young people through college, marriage, and into parenthood. Your student ministry is a failure if your students do not know how to spend time with the Father, read His Word, and hear His voice.

Focused worship is another changing dynamic of student ministry. Students no longer just want to listen to music. They hunger to experience true worship of God through the music *they are singing*. Music that only excites is *out*. Music that is truly an avenue into the presence of God is *in*. Contemporary worship should not be divisive in our churches. It's time to come to the conclusion once and for all that we must meet students where they are.

Students in Houston's First often stand in worship and praise for an hour and still felt slighted when the worship time is over. There is a new hunger to worship among students. Never judge the authenticity of a student's worship because it's set to music they like and you don't.

Experiential, hands-on missions is another new and exciting paradigm shift in student ministry. There is a growing trend toward both local and global missions. In 1997 fifty-two students from our church went on mission trips. By 2010, the number was two hundred.

This new generation wants to be part of something significant and something God sized. Don't be surprised if more and more of your students feel a burning urgency to declare Christ to the nations.

And they have an increasing passion for personal evangelism. The dividing line between believers and nonbelievers is sharpening in public schools. Christian students are decidedly more bold in sharing Christ. Wearing Christian T-shirts, carrying Bibles to school, playing Christian music—all these are indicators of the heightened spiritual intensity of a new generation that is serious about their faith.

Who will ever forget the testimony of Cassie Bernall, who lost her life in the Littleton massacre simply because she answered yes to the question, Do you believe in God?

Christian students are bold. Christian students are winners. Show them how. Set the example. Believe in them and be patient. Exciting things are happening with students across the nation, and virtually every significant move of God in history began among students.

Encourage your student pastor, encourage your students, and encourage the parents of your students. You are doing more than building tomorrow's leaders today; you are tapping into the greatest potential resource in the kingdom of God.

> "Remember your Creator in the days of your youth: Before the days of adversity come, and the years approach when you will say, 'I have no delight in them.'" (Eccl. 12:1)

> "When all has been heard, the conclusion of the matter is: fear God and keep His commands, because this is for all humanity." (Eccl. 12:13)

Chapter 97

MINISTRY TO CHILDREN

The children's ministry is organized to reach boys and girls, first grade through fifth, with God's message through Bible study, fellowship, activities, and personal ministry. The foundation of this ministry is the Sunday school organization.

In age-graded Sunday school classes, children are led to discover Bible truths through activity-centered learning during small-group time, Bible teaching, music, dance, art projects, videos, drama, puppets, and many other creative forms. All Bible learning activities must relate to the specific biblical objectives of the Sunday school lesson. It's leadership needs a balance of men and women, young and old.

During large-group time children experience prayer, singing, Bible reading, teacher-led discussion, and application of the Bible study relevant to their age level. Children are also led to develop Bible usage skills and memorize at least one Bible verse weekly.

Children's workers should be carefully chosen leaders who enjoy and understand children. Children need teachers who understand that *there is more to learning than listening and more to teaching than telling*. Children need role models who accept them as they are and who use words and concepts they can understand—all in love.

Houston's First conducts a First-Grade Bible Presentation event each year in a Sunday worship service. As first-graders are becoming aware of words and learn to translate print into meaning, they are impressed by books. When we do special Bible presentation ceremonies, we communicate to the impressionable new reader that the Bible is an important book.

Christian fellowship is also important to children. Two enrichment activities that provide children with the opportunity to make new friends are Vacation Bible School and camp for third- through fifth-graders. Sixth graders are normally grouped with middle schoolers, not grade schoolers, in both Sunday school and activities.

The third- through fifth-grade camp provides an extended time of Christian discipleship training in a leisurely setting. Children grow through Bible study, worship, and fellowship as they swim and participate in other recreation, as well as arts and crafts activities together.

For many children, camp is the first extended break from the security of their home. Much sensitivity and personal attention is dictated here.

Vacation Bible School not only introduces many new families to our church, but fifty to a hundred children each year accept Christ as their personal Savior during the VBS decision service. See my chapter on Vacation Bible School.

Each Sunday morning an ongoing children's new members class is provided for boys and girls who have recently made a profession of faith in Christ. This class helps children understand more fully the decision they have made and helps them become established in the Christian life.

Children are also counseled individually about their salvation experience before their baptism.

Another vital part of our church's ministry to children is mission education. We invite children to learn to care about the needs of others around the world through mission study. Children are taught to become Great Commission Christians and are provided with opportunities to get involved personally in serving others. We also introduce children to missionary heroes and teach them our Christian heritage. More than half of our Southern Baptist International Mission Board missionaries are the product of children's mission organizations.

Additionally, children's church is formatted like a worship service. During this time children will experience all the elements of worship in "big church" except baptism, the Lord's Supper, and a formal invitation to make decisions and join the church. Children are taught to pray, sing, give offerings, and listen as the Bible is taught.

The ultimate goal of the children's ministry is to establish a solid foundation for each child's faith that will result in commitment to Jesus Christ as Savior and Lord, followed by a life of fellowship and service.

Everything children's workers do, from skating parties to Sunday morning Bible study, should help children come to know God's plan for their lives and experience it.

Give major priority to a sharp, "with it," children's ministry. Study churches that "get it," such as First Baptist Springdale, Arkansas; Grace Presbyterian, Houston, Texas; First United Methodist, Woodlands, Texas; and many others. Reach the kids and you *will* reach their parents.

> Said a precious little laddie to his father one bright day,
> "May I give my heart to Jesus? Let Him wash my sins away?"
> "Oh my son, but you're too little, wait until you older grow.
> For bigger folks 'tis true need Him, but little ones are safe, you know."
>
> Said the father to the laddie as a storm was coming on,
> "Are the sheep all safely sheltered, safe within the fold, my son?"
> "Ah, the big ones are, my father, but the lambs, I let them go.
> For I didn't think it mattered little ones are safe, you know."
>
> Oh my brother, oh, my sister; have you too made that mistake?
> Little hearts that now are yielding may be hardened then, too late.
> E're the evil days come near them, "Let the children come to Me.
> And forbid them not," said Jesus. "Of such shall My kingdom be."[1]

Endnotes

1. Source unknown. Author heard it and memorized it in Ireland fifty years ago.

Chapter 98

CHILDHOOD
CONVERSION

F ew issues in your ministry will need to be handled with greater sensitivity than the question of childhood conversion.

As with adults, the conversion of children must always be allowed to take place by the sovereign movement of the Holy Spirit, not through human manipulation.

The age of the conversion of children is not fixed in Scripture. Some children may be ready to make a profession of faith at six or seven; others will not be ready until eleven or twelve. Many factors enter into the timing. It should be noted, however, that children are becoming exposed to blatant sin much earlier today than in the past. It is important, therefore, to allow for the possibility of earlier conversion because children experience earlier exposure and subsequent earlier guilt.

Throughout the history of my own denomination, huge numbers of adults who made decisions as children have been "rebaptized." Often it is said, "The children didn't know what they were doing." I have observed however, that more often the adults who dealt with them didn't know what *they* were doing.

Parents should be cautioned to respond to the questions of their children without offering additional information that might create pressure on the child, resulting in premature professions of faith. Children want to please, and any authority figure must be cautious at this point.

It is important to separate conversion from baptism and joining the church in the mind of a child. For this reason we offered a six-week preparation for baptism and membership course for children as well as adults. The length of the time between profession of faith and baptism was generally much longer than that.

Children in churches that offer catechism should understand clearly that completing the catechism, answering the questions, and being baptized is *not* tantamount to being "born again."

If special "decision services" for children are offered during evangelistic crusades, camps, Bible schools, etc., they should always be only for older children. Preschoolers, first-graders, second-graders, and perhaps even third-graders should not be involved.

That is not to say some second-graders and third-graders may not be ready to make a decision for Christ. It is to say that we must not do anything that is conducive to hurrying the process. Conversions of children at earlier ages usually happen best at home. Several factors, however, support the validity of childhood conversion at virtually any age.

1. *The allure of sin.* Children are being exposed to sin at an earlier and earlier age. More than thirty years ago the *Dallas Morning News* ran an Associated Press story about New York City schools training kindergarten teachers to detect signs of drug addiction. Sin appeals and sin addicts. The older one becomes, the harder it is to turn from sin to Christ.

2. *The ability of the children to understand.* To become a Christian one must do two things—repent of sin and receive Jesus Christ as personal Savior.

Repentance and faith are at the core of the conversion experience. You don't need to worry about an adult's knowledge of sin. He has plenty of that by experience. You have to be concerned, however, about his faith. It is not easy for adults to believe.

With children, it is exactly the opposite. They have plenty of faith. It is easy for them to believe in Jesus. You do, however, have to worry about their knowledge of sin. Be certain they not only understand what sin is but also have a personal conviction of guilt about their *own* sin. Help them understand that sin is not simply disobedience to mommy and daddy; it is disobedience to God.

3. *Children are not ashamed.* Jesus said, "Confess me before men and I will confess you before my Father which is in heaven. Deny me before men and I will deny you before my Father which is in Heaven" (see Matt. 10:32–33).

When children "walk the aisle," looking around, chewing their gum, and smiling, it is not because they are not sincere. It is because they are not inhibited.

4. *Children don't have a lot of silly excuses.* How long since you heard a child say, "Don't push me; I don't have the feeling yet," or, "There are too many hypocrites in the church."

5. *Children have their entire life to give to Christ.* Charles Haddon Spurgeon stepped off the train upon his return from an evangelistic meeting in a small church. One of his men greeted him and said, "Pastor, how many were saved?" "Two and one-half," Dr. Spurgeon replied. "Two and one-half?" questioned the man. "Yes. Two children and one adult. The two children have their entire life to live for Jesus. The adult has only half."

Jesus said, "Let the little children come to me. Don't stop them, for the kingdom of God belongs to such as these" (Mark 10:14). He also said, "But whoever causes the downfall of one of these little ones who believe in Me—it would be better for him if a heavy millstone were hung around his neck and he were thrown into the sea" (see Mark 9:42).

Let God do the work. He knows the right time for each child. Don't do anything to manipulate the process, but don't stand in the way when it begins to happen.

Chapter 99

MINISTRY TO PRESCHOOLERS

The preschool ministry of the church has a major responsibility to two groups. The first and foremost ministry is to children. Each age and developmental milestone must be considered as children are taught in the church setting.

During these years of astounding growth, solid foundations must be laid in the life of the child. Research has shown that during the first six years the child learns half of all he will learn in his lifetime.

The second ministry of preschools is to their parents. Most couples come to the experience of parenting with little or no experience with children. Many know little about child development and realistic expectations for their children.

The range of parental behavior can swing widely from those who are unrealistic and unreasonable to those who will not challenge the child in any way. The wise counsel of Sunday school teachers and preschool workers can assist the parent in working with, playing with, and teaching their children.

As the child grows older, the challenge of the preschool staff is to take the Bible into the child's world of play. As a child colors, we thank God for his eyes. As a child sets a table in the family living area, we say thank you to God for our food. As a child hears the story of God creating the world, he plays with plastic animals like those God created. Blocks, books, the nature center, home living center, puzzles, music—all these present opportunities for the child to hear and internalize the truths of the Bible.

Since the language and vocabulary of preschoolers is limited, it is important that the child can relate the words he hears to reality. It is more important that a child *understand* what is being said than that he *memorize* it.

It is useless to talk about kindness to a child who has no idea what the word *kind* means. If we are to teach kindness, we must do it in the context of doing a kind act.

In addition, young children view the world literally. We must, therefore, be careful with the words we use with this age child. We need to use literal words like *Bible, church,* and *Jesus* rather than *God's Word, God's house,* and *Lamb of God.* Saying things in a manner the child can easily understand and make a part of his life is vitally important.

Sadly, the physical risk to the child's safety is greatly heightened in our violent and decadent society. Incidents have even occurred where a divorced or separated parent has attempted to "kidnap" a child from a preschool or nursery while the estranged spouse was attending a worship service. Even the most readily recognized member of your church may not pick up his child from preschool without following strictly enforced safety procedures. Systems must be developed to protect against this happening. See my chapter on *security.*

Adults working with children must be screened through a background check to ensure the safety of each child. And that includes *everyone.*

As life begins, the parents should receive an in-home visit from the preschool ministry. The birth of a child is a time of uncertainty, as well as joy. This is an important time for the preschool ministry to encourage and aid the family with concerns they might have about bringing their child into the world as well as bringing him to church. Such things as safety, personal attention, and hygiene should be ensured and strictly observed.

Enlisting committed preschool volunteers is among the most difficult tasks of the church, but nothing is more important. In addition to paid workers and volunteers, preschool parents should be challenged to serve one Sunday in six.

Preschool ministry is not religious babysitting. It is the heart and soul of God's promise, "Teach a youth about the way he should go, and when he is old he will not depart from it" (Prov. 22:6).

God just loves babies.

O little town of Bethlehem, how still we see thee lie!
Above thy deep and dreamless sleep the silent stars go by.
Yet in thy dark streets shineth the everlasting Light;
The hopes and fears of all the years are met in thee tonight.

For Christ is born of Mary, and gathered all above,
While mortals sleep, the angels keep their watch of wond'ring love.
O morning stars together proclaim the holy birth,
And praises sing to God the King, and peace to men on earth!

How silently, how silently, the wondrous Gift is given!
So God imparts to human hearts the blessings of His Heaven.
No ear may hear His coming, but in this world of sin,
Where meek souls will receive Him still, the dear Christ enters in.

O holy Child of Bethlehem, descend to us, we pray;
Cast out our sin, and enter in, be born to us today.
We hear the Christmas angels the great glad tidings tell;
O come to us, abide with us, our Lord Emmanuel.[1]

"This will be a sign for you: You will find a baby wrapped snugly in cloth and lying in a feeding trough. Suddenly there was a multitude of the heavenly host with the angel, praising God and saying: Glory to God in the highest heaven, and peace on earth to people He favors." (Luke 2:12–14)

Endnotes

1. Phillips Brooks, "O Little Town of Bethlehem."

Chapter 100

SPECIAL BIBLE STUDIES

S unday morning Bible study is the heartbeat of your church, but it should be
pumping its life-giving blood through many other opportunities for Bible
study beyond Sunday morning.

The healthy church will provide other types of study at other times of the
week. One of the most effective is the "support group" Bible study.

This is the type of gathering where six or eight people—perhaps even as
many as twenty-five or thirty—meet regularly around a common issue, with
a solid biblical base, and under the leadership of a fellow struggler who has
become an overcomer.

Please hear me clearly: Support groups in your church are not a *compromise*
but an *opportunity*. I would never suggest the Bible be left out or even watered
down to attract the secular person who is looking for a support group. There
is something special about knowing a church cares enough about a particular
need or addiction to offer help. But these groups should focus on Bible study.

Needs can be met through teaching, application, and discussion of
Scripture, prayer, and encouragement that "I can do all things through Christ
who strengthens me."

Houston's First offers support groups for alcoholics, drug addicts, recovering
homosexuals, families with homosexual members, grief after death, divorce recovery,
and post-abortion anxiety—to name a few. Find a need, meet it, and people will
come. Jesus always went to hurting people, and they always responded to Him.

Another category of special Bible studies are those led by your people in homes and marketplaces across your city. From 1971 until the present, Houston's First maintained a weekly Bible study in the downtown/business community of Houston. This lunch from 12:00 noon to 12:50 p.m. includes a twenty-five-minute Bible study and is a major entry point into the church.

I personally taught that study for twenty years. At the midpoint of that time, we relocated our church to the area of town where most of the attendees lived. Within the first six months more than a hundred families with members attending this study joined our fellowship. Across our city today, approximately twenty-five groups of our men meet at various restaurants for breakfast once a week for a time of sharing, Bible study, and prayer.

Weekday and evening Bible studies within the walls of the church also meet many needs. Houston's First women's ministry offers studies in "John," "Isaiah," "Prayer," "Missions," "Worship," "Breaking Addiction," "Revelation," "The Church," "The Character of Christ," and "the Financially Confident Woman" as well as "Becoming a Friend of God," and many others. What an opportunity for the women of the city!

The high point of the week is a Tuesday evening women's Bible study taught by Beth Moore. These Bible studies have a combined weekly attendance of several thousand.

Further, the church provides a weekly offering of seminars to both men and women. These meet Wednesday nights and Sunday nights. They offer such topics as: "A Biblical Portrait of Marriage," "Raising Kids Who Turn Out Right," "Experiencing God," "Grandparenting by Grace," "Finishing Strong," "When Life Caves In," and "Mastering Your Money," to name a few. They are taught in thirteen-week cycles by laymen and laywomen of the church who speak from their varied backgrounds and areas of interest.

Bible studies for men in the oil industry, quarterly men's barbecue with guest speakers, and men's ministry offerings are provided, including such topics as "Learning to Be a Man in Christ."

Home groups are popular today. Loyalty to the church and sound doctrine must be maintained, and that begins and ends with the facilitator.

Sunday morning worship and Bible study should be emphasized and doctrinal integrity protected. The key to both is the teacher/leader of the home fellowship group. Choose them carefully.

Houston's First offers many opportunities for Bible study beyond Sunday morning. Plan ahead. Use your people, stay well organized, meet needs, and be creative. The church should offer many opportunities for Bible study as entry points into the kingdom.

Chapter 101

SPECIAL MINISTRIES

While the doors of the church are open to everyone, there is wisdom in targeting special groups. People have a special openness to being a part of programs that have particular appeal to them.

Perhaps a hearing woman whose parents were deaf will come to you and say, "Pastor, I'd like to see us have a class for the deaf." Respond by saying, "Great idea. I want you to start it and lead it. We'll give you the room, the personnel, the publicity, and all the support you need to make it happen." If God birthed the idea in her heart, she is probably the one to do it.

That precise scenario birthed what became the largest deaf ministry in the Southern Baptist Convention at Houston's First over sixty years ago. Today it is a fully functioning deaf church. They have their own pastor, budget, and deaf deacons, their own campus, and many special ministries. Among them is the largest rehabilitation ministry to deaf prisoner parolees in America.

No more tender ministry exists than precious children with special needs. Their parents will thank you to their dying days, as you do it "for one of the least of these brothers of Mine" (Matt. 25:40).

Support groups are not only God's healing instruments in broken lives but special entry points into the kingdom of God and the life of your church. Cancer survivors, divorce recovery, single parenting, recovering addicts—the possibilities are endless. Unemployed job training and English as a second language are two of our most blessed ministries.

Our motives must begin and remain pure. Hurting people are not tools to get one more number in the baptismal total of your annual associational report. But people can and will be brought to faith in Christ because He alone is ultimately the only answer to all of life's needs.

Some of the best ministry in the kingdom is done through women's ministries and men's ministries.

Bible studies, retreats, trips, special speakers, everything from gourmet cooking classes to campouts and hunting trips are only part of the endless possibilities for changing lives and developing people into mature believers that exist in special ministries.

Share your dream with your people and ask them for ideas.

Chapter 102

THE ACTIVITIES MINISTRY

Christians ought to have fun. More importantly, they ought to *be* fun. The negative, sourpuss Pharisees drove everybody away. The happy Christian who is having a great time following Jesus draws people to himself and to his Lord. What better opportunity to meet the unbeliever halfway, as well as know and enjoy your church family, than playing softball together. An "activities ministry" or "recreation ministry" will greatly expand your outreach *to* the community as well as enhance fellowship *within* your church.

Everything from crafts and hobbies to roller skating and flag football can be enjoyed at relatively little cost. Houston's First has the luxury of a multimillion-dollar activities building with everything from saunas to racquetball and ceramics to bowling.

But your church is not limited if you do not have such a building. Basketball gymnasiums, public parks, backyards, bus trips, fellowship halls—many opportunities are available to enrich the lives of your people.

Again, many churches have large facilities and full-time staff in this ministry. But whether your activities ministry is large or small, its twofold purpose is to reach people for Christ and build that all-important fellowship within the congregation.

Before our building was built, committees spent two years studying the finest church activities centers, military bases, and Jewish community centers in America. They took the best ideas, put them together, and today the facility is a model for others. If you invest money in a building, take your time, look around, and build it wisely and well.

One afternoon, driving around the facilities of Bellevue Baptist Church, Memphis, Tennessee, with Adrian Rogers, I asked, "Do you reach many new members through your activities ministry, or is it primarily for your own people?"

"John," he replied, "it is the number one entry point into our church." Today I'm still staggered at that statement. Dr. Rogers, a powerful preacher, may have spoken modestly. One would think the persuasive pulpiteer would be the number one entry point into that church. But that's what he said, and that's the way it can be.

Adequate and accessible outdoor fields are important. Bellevue Memphis has more than I can count, and right on their property of over 300 acres. Houston's First is limited with only eighteen acres. Lease or buy property for fields as nearby as possible. Regardless of the quantity and quality of your buildings, you will be limited without playing fields.

Keep before your people, particularly those in charge of your activities ministry, the two goals of reaching the lost and building fellowship among the members.

Because acreage is limited on the church campus, our congregation conducts many outdoor activities at other sites, in addition to a massive offering of activities in our own facility.

Whether on your campus or off, keep activities focused on fellowship and evangelism. Houston's First requires that every team have at least two nonmembers who are required to attend our church twice a month. At halftime or before or after an event, the church offers prayer and a brief devotional or testimony. Christian sportsmanship is demonstrated and verbal witness given as unbelievers come to be interested in the things of God while recreating with our people.

Within the church's facility weight loss classes, Jazzercise, saunas, and many other opportunities are offered. The secular world is always responsive to something of interest in a Christian environment. Study the churches with great recreational ministries. Adapt them to your available space, expand your horizons, and get excited about developing a good activities program. You can reach people for Christ and have fun while you're doing it.

> How happy you are, Israel! Who is like you, a people saved by the LORD? He is the shield that protects you, the sword you boast in. Your enemies will cringe before you, and you will tread on their backs. (Deut. 33:29)

Happy are the people with such blessings. Happy are the people whose God is Yahweh. (Ps. 144:15)

Happy is the one whose help is the God of Jacob, whose hope is in the LORD his God. (Ps. 146:5)

The one who understands a matter finds success, and the one who trusts in the LORD will be happy. (Prov. 16:20)

Chapter 103

THE EVANGELISTIC CRUSADE

The first step in planning an evangelistic crusade is to seek the heart of God about who the evangelist will be. Evangelists are God's gifts to the church, and we should use them.

In addition to full-time or vocational evangelists, many gifted pastors have the gift of evangelism. The gifted evangelist is characterized by his passion for souls, his powerful delivery of the message, his unique giftedness in extending the invitation, and his special anointing.

The evangelist you want is not a manipulator. He is not consumed with himself, his personal convenience, his love offering, or a large numerical response to enhance his reputation. He is a humble, experienced man who loves people and loves lost souls, out of the pulpit as much as in, and tries consistently to win them to Christ in the normal traffic pattern of his life.

The delivery of the evangelist is nearly as important as his message. The ring of authenticity must be there. Credibility and genuineness must be obvious. The fire of his passion for the lost must come from his heart, not simply his mouth and hands.

Evangelistic sermons should be warmly illustrated and not exceed thirty minutes. The invitation should never be manipulated or overly extended. The evangelist should *give* God time to work but at no time attempt to *do* God's work for Him.

The first night or two of a crusade, the messages should be designed to stimulate the congregation to prayer, holiness, and bringing the lost. But the heart of the message for *most* nights must be to the lost. In any crusade such subjects as the new birth, the love of God, the second coming of Christ, the simple plan of salvation, the need for repentance, and heaven and hell should be included. And first and foremost, present the cross.

In giving the invitation, be authoritative, be specific, be urgent, and be honest. The battle is not won by the emotional manipulation of the people but by the passionate prayer of the pastor, evangelist, and congregation well before the crusade services ever begin.

The atmosphere of an evangelistic crusade must always be bright and upbeat. Sing the great old gospel songs. "The Old Rugged Cross," "Saved, Saved, Saved," "Are You Washed in the Blood?" and "Jesus Saves," are always appropriate. Sing choruses and sing the new songs as well. More young people will come if you do.

At some point in the services, everyone should stand and welcome one another with a warm handshake and greeting. Don't ask only the guests to stand. They already feel on the spot. Let them stand with everyone else.

The appeal for the offering should be clear and brief. Love offering envelopes and/or expense offering envelopes should be distributed. Be clear as to whether the offering is for expenses or a love offering for the evangelist. And under no circumstances should the evangelist ever take his own love offering. In the best-case scenario, crusade expenses are collected in advance or are in the church budget.

Use testimonies but rehearse them to ensure brevity. Have a crusade choir and/or praise team and use a good soloist. Special guests can make a great contribution to attracting the crowd and preparing the heart. But there is danger here because most special guests, having been flown in at somewhat great expense, will feel under pressure to "give the people their money's worth" and often take much too long. A personal testimony must be short, not exceeding ten to twelve minutes, no matter how famous the special guest may be.

Special nights are an important part of evangelistic crusades, such as children's night with a hot dog supper or youth night with a pizza party. In such cases it is best that the teenagers sit together. It is best that the children do not. "Pack a Pew Night," "Old-Fashioned Night," "Bring a Friend Night," "Prospect Supper Night"—all of these are wonderful ways to help promote attendance and enthusiasm for your revival crusade.

Open-air crusades in tents or stadiums as well as indoor crusades in off-site auditoriums and other venues are effective in cooperative crusades with several churches as well as crusades sponsored by just one church.

I encourage you to consider an interdenominational crusade. Methodists and Presbyterians, Nazarenes and Assemblies, Baptists and Lutherans can easily put aside their differences and cooperate in winning the lost to Christ. It is not difficult to find an experienced evangelist who understands the tact required to preach the gospel without causing division in such a setting, **yet** do so without compromise.

Follow-up should be done immediately. The best follow-up is done by the decision counselor who dealt with the person the night before. Contact either in person or by telephone should be made no later than the next day.

The old-time evangelistic crusade is a piece of Americana that is dying, but it ought not to be. I have never seen a Billy Graham crusade from the platform, from the audience, or on television that I did not weep throughout the invitation. Evangelist crusades inside and outside the church are wonderful. Let's not lose them.

Unfortunately, however, the fact is that the majority of Southern Baptist churches never have revivals anymore. You may say that crusades are old-fashioned and out-of-date. But I say, "To this younger generation, everything old is new again."

Chapter 104

WITNESS TRAINING

The Lausanne Covenant states, "Evangelism itself is the proclamation of the historical, biblical Christ as Savior and Lord, with a view to persuading people to come to Him personally and so be reconciled to God." Jesus called it going into all the world to preach the good news to every creature.

An unfortunate trend has developed, however, which calls evangelism everything from social ministry to fellowship to friendship. If we are to win the lost, our people must have not only a clear view of evangelism but equipping that is personal, precise, courteous, comprehensive, urgent, and bold.

As much as I love crusades, the personal one-to-one witness remains the single most important method of evangelism. Unfortunately, many church growth experts have been so galvanized around "friendship evangelism," they have rejected any sort of evangelistic visitation as confrontational as intrusive. I remember Jesus and the disciples were rather confrontational.

Every local church must provide training to equip its members in personal soul winning. To exclude training methodology means soul winning will be more discussed than done.

Structured, formal, witness-training opportunities should be regularly provided for your people. Sunday night classes are usually the best. The Roman Road, Christian Witness Training, Evangelism Explosion, and Faith are among the many successful programs available.

It is easy to teach your people how to lead someone to Christ. It's not easy to inspire them to *do it*. Classroom training should be followed by hands-on opportunity for in-home prospect visitation accompanied by a seasoned visitor. The best time is Sunday night, Monday night, or Wednesday night on the way home from church.

Teach your people to be "shrewd as serpents and as harmless as doves" (Matt. 10:16). Don't carry a big Bible to the door. Pray before you go. Ring the doorbell. Never ask, "Mrs. Smith?" Her attitude will be, "Maybe I am Mrs. Smith and maybe I'm not. That depends on who you are." Don't ask the person's name; state the person's name. If it happens to be wrong, they will tell you.

Ring the doorbell, step back as the door is opened, and all in one smiling sentence say, "Hello Mrs. Smith, we are Bill and Mary Jones from First Baptist Church. May we come in?"

Your opening sentence should clearly establish who you are, where you're from, who they are, and that you wish to come in.

Once you are seated, be sensitive to the mood in the home. Talk about them, learn their background, and determine their spiritual condition. Then present the gospel in the method in which you were trained and, if possible, lead them to Christ.

The best *lifestyle* evangelism is cultivating friendships in the marketplace and sharing Jesus in everyday conversation. But intentional, in-home visitation is *always* appropriate. This may best be done with prospects who have visited your church or through designated area canvassing or door-to-door visitation.

The missing ingredient in witnessing is the all-important personal testimony. Listen again to the record of Andrew, the master soul winner: "Andrew, Simon Peter's brother, was one of the two who heard John and followed Him. He first found his own brother Simon and told him, 'We have found the Messiah!' (which means 'Anointed One'), and he brought Simon to Jesus" (John 1:40–42).

Note the order of Andrew's masterful method:

1. He found his brother.
2. He told him whom he had found.
3. He brought him to Jesus.

Don't leave out that important second step. The force of the personal testimony, "Let me tell you about Jesus whom I have found," is at once impressive and disarming to the unbeliever.

And don't get stressed over looking for ways to bring Jesus into everyday conversation. Keep your heart and ears open, and virtually every conversation will contain some phrase which you can turn to talking about the things of God.

Remember the order:

> Contact
> Witness
> Win

Lifestyle evangelism is terrific. But keep on knocking on those doors as well. It's not an either/or situation.

> Hark! 'tis the Shepherd's voice I hear,
> Out in the desert dark and drear,
> Calling the sheep who've gone astray
> Far from the Shepherd's fold away.
>
> Bring them in, bring them in,
> Bring them in from the fields of sin;
> Bring them in, bring them in,
> Bring the wand'ring ones to Jesus.[1]

Endnotes

1. Alexcenah Thomas, "Bring Them In."

Chapter 105

PLANTING
NEW CHURCHES

O n a warm, sunny afternoon in 1988, God tugged at my heart. His
instrument was the chairman of the "declining churches" committee
of our local Baptist association. For over an hour we viewed pictures of sixty-
seven churches in Houston that were near extinction. With windows boarded
up, grass grown high, and other obvious signs of decline, it was apparent that
someone had to do something to help those precious little congregations.

God spoke to my heart, "I want you to be that someone." I called a meeting
of the pastors and asked, "What can we do?" Their answer was predictable:
"We need prayer, people, and money."

The overwhelming majority of these at-risk churches were in transitional
communities. As sometimes happens, Anglos were moving to the suburbs, and
the remaining faithful few had no idea how to go about reaching the tens of
thousands of ethnics who lived around them.

Since that time, Houston's First has helped virtually all of those churches.
The overwhelming majority have become strong enough to spin off and
become self-sustaining congregations. Today the Sunday morning attendance
in those spin-off mission churches, and the missions *they* started, when added
to the number of current mission churches, equals the size of the home church
and more. Through the years more than five hundred of our members have

gone back into those churches, many of them, the very congregations from which they came.

A special offering is received fifty-two weeks of the year to support this ministry. Sunday school departments additionally give time, money, and service to assist in everything from repairing roofs and building baby beds to distributing food and visiting prospects.

Our people love the missionary spirit of their church. From these missions alone have come hundreds of converts, at least twenty-five full-time Christian workers, and a benevolence ministry distributing more than $300,000 a year in food, furniture, clothes, and direct financial support to the needy.

But reclaiming small churches is only a part of the "kingdom mind-set" of Houston's First. Special ministries to jails and prisons, transients, alcoholics, and countless others are a part of the mission ministry. The church leads as many people to Christ outside the building as inside.

Would these persons ever have come to us? Probably not.

Would someone else have reached them? Perhaps.

But this I know: they were born into the kingdom, at least in part, because the Holy Spirit birthed a passion for the larger kingdom of God in the heart of one pastor and his people.

Dear pastor, hear my heart. Our church is a megachurch, but churches will never win the world by *addition*. The need is *multiplication*. The size and influence of your church is not paramount; the expansion of God's kingdom is. New works grow fastest.

There's no greater joy than giving yourself away for the work of the Lord. Every Sunday I gave two invitations; join the church and leave the church. As we sent people out to minister in these dying congregations, God blessed us exponentially.

1. Get a kingdom mind-set.
2. Give yourself away.
3. Send your people out.
4. The world is at your doorstep.

Upon my retirement Sunday, our church presented me with three scrapbooks containing more than eight hundred names of our members who were ordained, went to seminary, and entered full-time Christian ministry during our thirty years together.

We created an atmosphere of "give yourself away," and the more we did, the more the Lord brought to us.

At Pentecost, God brought people to the church from every nation under heaven. He has done the same thing again. The people are right there at your doorstep.

Of course, Houston's First has established traditional church plants as well. The above has been our primary approach.

> And there were dwelling at Jerusalem Jews, devout men, out of every nation under heaven. Now when this was noised abroad, the multitude came together, and were confounded, because that every man heard them speak in his own language. And they were all amazed and marvelled, saying one to another, Behold, are not all these which speak Galilaeans? And how hear we every man in our own tongue, wherein we were born? Parthians, and Medes, and Elamites, and the dwellers in Mesopotamia, and in Judaea, and Cappadocia, in Pontus, and Asia, Phrygia, and Pamphylia, in Egypt, and in the parts of Libya about Cyrene, and strangers of Rome, Jews and proselytes, Cretes and Arabians, we do hear them speak in our tongues the wonderful works of God. (Acts 2:5–11)

Chapter 106

SUMMER CAMPS

How can I adequately state the vital importance of the ministry of retreating in the life of the church? Weekend retreats, overnight trips, lock-ins—all are of tremendous value in the spiritual development of God's people. There is, however, something special about a week at camp. I admit to being a bit prejudiced. I was born again at just such a camp. Falls Creek Baptist Assembly in Oklahoma is the largest youth assembly in the world.

I was the first person to walk down the aisle on that hot Oklahoma summer evening. Beneath an old oak tree, I fell to my knees as someone prayed with me and led me to faith in Christ in a life-transforming experience. In that moment Jesus not only came into my heart but called me into full-time Christian ministry. Six weeks later I would stand before the Immanuel Baptist Church of Pryor, Oklahoma, give my testimony, play the trumpet, and lead worship in my first service in the ministry.

Happily I report to you that I never looked back. I wouldn't trade it. The trail has been long and joyful, and the blessings far outweigh the heartaches.

And it all happened because thousands of wonderful Oklahoma Baptists provided a youth camp for teenagers to get away from the crowd and give serious consideration to the claims of Christ on their lives. Let's talk about that.

We live in a fast-paced world. Thousands of impressions fill our minds every single day. There is so much to distract us, so much to deter and confuse us. The heavenly transmitter is speaking clearly, but our earthly receivers are so

313

crowded and clouded they rarely hear the voice of God. Camp is a great place to get away, slow down and listen.

Another great thing about a large camp is the inspiration of the sheer numbers who are there. Countless numbers of young people come from small churches and feel they are virtually the only young Christians in the world. What a powerful impact is made when they realize Christianity is no offbeat cult but the most powerful force on earth, as they join with hundreds or even thousands of other Christian kids at youth camp.

Another beauty of summer camps is their built-in attraction, which appeals to all young people. Many of the teenagers who go to Falls Creek or any other summer camp probably don't go primarily for spiritual reasons. They go because it is fun. The gals go because of the guys, and the guys go because of the gals. There is swimming, softball, music, and just hanging out.

What teenager, Christian or not, will not get excited about an invitation to spend a week having fun with hundreds or thousands of other teenagers? It always takes two or three days for them to deprogram from the clamor of the world. Young people should not be allowed to take electronics to camp. It's a time to get away from secular distractions. After a few days minds clear, and the Word starts to get through.

Non-Christian, as well as Christian, students should be not only allowed but encouraged to attend.

Every effort should be made to keep the tuition well within reach of everyone. There are always wonderful people in your congregation who will happily provide half or full scholarships for those unable to pay.

Mornings should be reserved for Bible study and worship, allowing ample breaks for refreshment and relaxation between each. Afternoons are for recreation and leisure. Evenings are for worship. Young preachers are the best camp pastors, and it's not difficult to find qualified, mature young men who can relate to students. Let the kids have fun. Let them be themselves. Rules must be enforced, but the secret is: *don't have too many rules.*

I recommend not giving an invitation for salvation, rededication, or full-time Christian ministry until the last two or three nights of the camp. Give God time to work. Let the conviction build.

Have ample sponsors. Have various kinds of competition between the different grades and cabins or dorms. A joint sponsor-parent-camper meeting should be held in advance of the camp so both parents and young people clearly understand the rules. Every sponsor must be able to give spiritual counsel to their kids as well as be able personally to lead them to faith in Christ.

Following the evening decision services, each sponsor should take those making decisions from his group to a quiet place for reflection, personal counsel, and prayer.

Camp sponsors should meet each evening for forty-five minutes to an hour before dinner to coordinate activities and events, discuss problems, and pray for the kids.

It may well be that more young lives have been changed in Christian youth camps than in all other programs combined. The International Mission Board of the Southern Baptist Convention reports that more of their missionaries made their decision for special service at Falls Creek Assembly than any other entity in Southern Baptist life.

What a great ministry it is. By all means, *take those kids to camp!*

Chapter 107

VACATION BIBLE SCHOOL

E very church should have a summer Vacation Bible School. In the old days these lasted for two weeks. Today most last only one.

In Houston's First, we had Bible school immediately after school was out. The theory was that in doing so, we could get the kids before their parents left on vacation. I have often wondered, however, if the end of summer might be better. Perhaps in the dog days of summer, when kids are getting bored and are not quite ready to go back to school, they might have a heightened interest in something to do. The best advertising for VBS will not be done through traditional media but through the Internet and through the invitation of excited children to their friends.

Times are normally 9:00 a.m. to noon, Monday through Friday, with attendance peaking on Thursday and dropping off on Friday. I have wondered, therefore, if Monday through Thursday would be better. But it could well be that attendance would then simply peak on Wednesday. Be aware that if you plan a decision service on the day when attendance is the highest, it will likely be the next to last day.

The Bible school must be directed by a trained, committed leader. If the church does not have appropriate staff leadership, enlist a talented church member who has it on his or her heart. Good Vacation Bible School materials abound. Check with your local Christian bookstore or denominational headquarters.

During Bible school the children meet in various classrooms for unique activities: hand painting, model making; the opportunities are endless. One year in our Bible school, my wife taught a class of fifth graders. One of their projects was to write a script for a television newscast, in which each was a reporter or news anchor or witness, reporting the resurrection of Christ, His ascension, and the day of Pentecost. Their video was a classic.

Time-outs for playground activities, snow cones, etc., are always appropriate. One central rally should be held at the beginning or the end of each morning where all the children assemble together.

I recommend only one decision service. The message should be delivered by the pastor. It should be brief, simple, well illustrated, and totally without pressure. And no deathbed stories or tear jerkers. After a week in the Bible school environment, most children simply need to have the gospel clearly presented with an opportunity to respond.

In our church the annual decision service was only for third-, fourth- and fifth-graders. Our sixth-graders were part of our middle school division; and they, along with high school students, joined adults as Bible school workers.

A Friday night graduation service in which a program is presented, projects displayed, and diplomas awarded, is a good attraction for parents of the children as well as a good entry point into your church. Even with kindergartners, everyone likes to see their kids graduate.

Expedite the process of follow-up for those who make decisions, but don't rush them into baptism and church membership. The following Monday, begin visiting the homes of boys and girls who have made decisions. If the parents are receptive, schedule a series of classes for the children to learn more about Christ, baptism, and church membership. These visits are most conducive to reaching the parents of children for Christ.

Houston's First is thorough in following up children who make decisions, doing their best to determine that they have truly come to know Christ in a personal way. Each child gets a personal interview, and the quality of their decisions and church membership has been rather high through the years as a result.

I encourage you as pastor to give high priority of your own personal time to being seen at Bible school. Go to the classes, learn the names of the children, romp with them, and eat snow cones with them. It is a wonderful time of bonding for pastor and children. Our pastor, Gregg Matte, is a master in this area.

Bible school is an important ingredient in building great families and great churches. Plan your vacation time around Bible school. Postpone that golf game until the afternoon. Enjoy the Vacation Bible School experience with the children. You'll be glad you did.

And never forget the importance of reaching adults by reaching their children. McDonald's has built one of the largest businesses in America by selling fun to kids. Ed Young at Second Baptist Houston is a great proponent of reaching the parents by reaching the kids. They have thirty thousand each year in Vacation Bible School. Check it out.

Chapter 108

SPECIAL DAYS

I love holidays, especially the holy days. What can compare with Easter, Thanksgiving, and Christmas? Secular holidays are also important, particularly Memorial Day, Independence Day, Labor Day, Mother's Day and Father's Day. Let's talk about these special times.

Encourage your families to enjoy the holidays, and enjoy them yourself. Don't put a guilt trip on your people because they are out of town on a holiday. The annual Thanksgiving trip to grandma's house strengthens the family, which in turn strengthens the church. Encourage your people to go. Tell them to have a great time and assure them you will be praying for their safety as they travel.

Capitalize on difficult holidays. Labor Day can be a great time for a concert or church picnic. Fourth of July weekend can be a special time. Place flags around your church. Ask the choir to sing "Battle Hymn of the Republic." Have a color guard. Salute the flag. Sing the national anthem. And by all means, recognize and applaud your veterans as well as those now serving in the military.

Have a testimony from a war hero or bring in a great preacher known for stirring patriotic sermons and advertise it well. Your attendance will go up, not down, if you make lemonade out of the lemon of low attendance on holidays.

Memorial Day weekends are wonderful times to recognize families who have lost loved ones that year, as well as those who have lost loved ones at any time in the military. List their names, recognize them, and pray for them.

Preach on heaven. Preach on being grateful for the sacrifice of others. Be creative and turn holidays into special days.

Be flexible. Be willing to adjust schedules and times. The Sunday after Christmas, we have no Sunday morning Bible study groups and only one morning service. The consolidation of two low attendances into one strong attendance is "making lemonade."

Christmas morning is a special time. Children squeal with glee as they open their presents. Families gather around the table for a special breakfast.

Encourage your people to observe their family traditions and be willing to adjust your schedule occasionally to fit in. There should be nothing sacred about a schedule. Make good plans and advertise them well in advance.

Easter Sunday brings the largest church attendance of the year. On this day consider having an additional morning service. Sunrise services appear to have lost their popularity, but they can be exciting and new to a younger generation. Everything old is indeed new again, and many of your folks have never *even heard of the old*. Others will nostalgically appreciate your "bringing back the old days."

Place lilies or other flowers around the church platform. Use banners. Enlarge the orchestra. Make it special. There is no Sunday morning in the year like Easter. And don't make an issue out of whether it was initially a pagan holiday and how too much emphasis is placed on new clothes and bunny rabbits. Point to new life through faith in the resurrected Christ of which these things are only a reminder. Don't attack the negative, especially not on Easter. Magnify the positive. Jesus Christ is alive and well.

Now hear this! Preach a *short* sermon on Easter Sunday morning. The crowd will be large and filled with guests. This might be the only chance you will have at them until next Easter. Seize the moment. Be positive, and above all, *get out on time*. Better still, get out early and then do good follow-up visitation. You'll get more back that way. Bore them with a two-hour service, and they won't be back at all.

Easter week services may precede the great day. Noonday services are particularly attractive. In Houston's First we commemorate the death of Christ through a beautiful Lord's Supper service on Thursday night. The holiday week begins on Friday. Although your people will be there in great numbers on Sunday, they are usually nowhere to be found on Friday. Move your Good Friday service to Good Friday Eve. Your attendance will be low on Friday but high on Thursday.

Thanksgiving is family time. What a beautiful season of the year it is. Leaves turn, sweaters come out, football games abound, and people take trips to grandma's with turkey dinners and all the trimmings. Who doesn't love Thanksgiving? Years ago I was preaching a crusade in Canada, where Thanksgiving comes a week before Thanksgiving in America. What a deal! Two Thanksgivings in one year!

Thanksgiving services at the church on Thursday will be poorly attended. Thanksgiving eve will be the same. Tuesday night is the night to have your Thanksgiving service. Again, the Lord's Supper, special decorations, great music, and personal testimonies of gratitude, with a brief message by the pastor are in order.

Thanksgiving services should conclude with a special benevolent offering for the poor. Church offices should be closed on Thursday and Friday. Give your staff the time off, allowing them to enjoy this great holiday with their families.

Christmas Eve services are special. Many churches offer more than one, some as many as four or five, even beginning in early afternoon. Multiple services may well be conducted by different pastors and staff. There is, however, something special about 11:00 p.m. Christmas Eve services. Dim lights, processions with candles, the singing of hymns by children and adult choirs—these are a treasure. Again, the message should be brief. One year I simply read the Christmas story without comment.

Chapter 109

SPECIAL EVENTS

U nder this broad umbrella, the creative pastor will find the latitude to meet the special needs of his people and his community. Of course, there are church picnics and fellowships, after-church socials, Bible schools, choir concerts, etc. But I refer particularly to those one- and two-day opportunities that present themselves from time to time, primarily because of the availability of special speakers or musicians. Often a seminar speaker, author, or outstanding personality will be in your area. You might learn either directly from them or by the grapevine that they are going to be available.

Make a list of all the speakers you would like to have and contact them for available dates and/or find out when they are coming to your area. Many singing groups and seminars, for example, have a fairly large travel expense budget which can be cut in half if they are coming from one thousand miles away to be in your church one day and a church in a neighboring city the next.

I am often asked, "Did you allow such secular meetings as a chamber of commerce banquet or Rotary Club Convention to use your facilities?" The answer is yes.

Is it not much wiser to welcome a hundred unbelievers who need a place to have their annual meeting about gardening or the environment than to have the annual meeting of the mission society in your facility? If we indeed exist for those beyond our membership, anything we do which brings the unbeliever into the brick and mortar of our facilities is worthwhile.

They have probably requested the use of your church because you have ample room and are well located. Having a good experience, learning your location, and enjoying your gracious hospitality might establish the best relationship with an unbeliever your church could ever have. These kinds of people are likely to return on Easter or Christmas. Then you can meet them, cultivate a friendship, and perhaps lead them to faith in Christ. I urge you to dispense with any policy that does not allow secular groups to meet in your facilities. These are the kind of people you *want* in your facilities. And you may be certain they will respect your no-smoking policy. If someone doesn't, get over it.

Too often people feel we view them only as prospects to be targeted for our own ultimate gain—their money. Illustrating that we exist not for what we can *get* but for what we can *give* is a wise approach to the secular society we are trying to reach.

Throughout the course of a year, many "crossover" events will present themselves to you. These are the types of activities that will minister to your people and be of interest to the general public as well.

You will want to clear your calendar for speakers such as these and have them in your church any time you can get them.

Programs and seminars that offer help to the family, the hurting, the depressed, or the addict are always helpful to your people and attractive to the secular person. Who doesn't want help with a child addicted to drugs or assistance with a troubled marriage?

Concerts are of particular interest to both believer and unbeliever. Often costs appear to be prohibitive, but this can usually be overcome by selling tickets. Local Christian radio stations will often provide free advertising and even joint sponsorship of the concert in return for a ten-minute spot at intermission to talk about their station's ministry. Honorariums, expenses, and other arrangements should be clearly spelled out in advance. These are often negotiable and best done by contract.

When you have committed to pay the expenses and honorarium of an artist or group, you will need an offering to help cover your own expenses such as advertising, security, etc. Of course, you cannot sell tickets *and* receive an offering. If tickets are sold, they should be sold at a price that will cover anticipated expenses, including honorarium for the artist with enough left over to cover your own expenses. But be prepared to underwrite it all from your budget if ticket sales come up short.

And, of course, the artist, group, or their representative should not be allowed to make a financial appeal for their ministry. If an offering is received, it must be taken *only* by the pastor.

Outside speakers and musicians usually have books, CDs, or other merchandise for sale. Selling socks, T-shirts, and ties is strictly profit motivated and should not be allowed. Carrying home a book or CD is spiritually uplifting. Wearing "Sammy the Singer's" T-shirt is not.

Special events play a great part in reaching the unbeliever and ministering to your own flock. They also give a sense to your people and your city that yours is the church "where it's at." By the way, put some of those big events on holiday weekends, which normally have low attendance. You can make lemonade out of that lemon.

Chapter 110

MULTIPLE CAMPUSES

Many new models exist in the landscape of church planting. You must find what is right for you, but whatever you do, one thing is primary: your church should be growing. I would caution against starting somewhere else because we're "doing so poorly where we are." Transferring failure from one piece of dirt to another doesn't change much.

Houston's First relocated in 1977, not because we were doing so poorly but because we were doing so well and had no room to grow. Looking back we may have considered starting a second campus.

I'm thinking of three major churches where the satellite church became so strong the pastor moved and became its pastor. Today they are megachurches.

Some models, like Second Baptist Houston, have as many as six or more locations. Some have virtually started their own denomination with as many as two hundred to three hundred churches across America. Some start a second campus and a third with the intention of all three permanently remaining under the umbrella of the mother church. Some are begun with the intention of turning them loose.

Again, many models abound. As you seek the Lord for His will, consider these things:

1. *Don't do anything just because someone else is doing it.* Find God's plan for you and your church.

2. *If you abandon a declining location, give serious consideration to converting your facility into a mission center or church or some kind of ministry in the community around that location.* This is a major issue. Going into all the world includes, not stepping over that part of the world the Lord has placed at your doorstep. Houston's First has now helped establish nearly one hundred inner-city churches in this manner.

3. *Don't speculatively invest in real estate.* Don't buy a new piece of property on which you "might build" someday with an ulterior motive, "If it doesn't work out, we can always sell the new property for more and pay off our debt." Shamefully, some have done precisely that. We're in the soul-saving business, not the real estate business.

4. *Don't build more than you realistically need.* We all can suffer from delusions of grandeur. Ask the tough questions. Do the math and get real. What age am I? What is the age of my church? What is my track record? What is the economic potential of my congregation? What is the area in which we are located and in which we are considering purchasing? Realistically in my ministry, what can we reasonably expect our church to have in attendance?

In doing the calculation, don't forget the wisdom of multiple usage of your buildings. If that realistic number is a thousand on Sunday morning, you may not need over fifteen to twenty acres. As you calculate that attendance number, factor in multiple services.

5. *Nothing is more important in the decision of multiple campuses than an honest soul searching of the question, Why am I doing this?* Your pride and reputation were left at the cross the day you walked the aisle. Remember? Whether it's best for me is a nonissue. The only criteria is what is best for the kingdom? I can't answer every question you may be asking about multiple locations. But I can tell you that you must honestly answer the question, Why? And make sure in the deepest part of your soul, the answer is, "Only Jesus and those for whom He died." And if that means that all three hundred of the people I now have leave and go to the mission field and I end up with none, so be it.

Part 8

THE CHURCH STAFF

Chapter 111

THE PASTOR
AND HIS STAFF

The new way of designating church staff is titling each as "pastor."

Senior Pastor
Worship Pastor
Student Pastor

I like that. We are first of all pastors/shepherds to those within our area of ministry.

As the church grows in size, it will become less and less possible for the senior pastor to minister personally to the entire congregation. No more difficult issue will confront the senior pastor who truly has a shepherd's heart than the challenge of priorities.

What do you do when you can't return every call, grant every request for an appointment, contact every guest, or visit each member in the hospital? Inside Information! You must pastor your leadership. You pastor those who pastor others. Staff, elders, deacons, group leaders, committee members, and teachers are those people.

There is no greater blessing and no greater need than a smoothly functioning, well-trained, hardworking staff of loyal, godly men and women assisting their pastor in the work of the ministry. Aaron held high the hands of Moses, and deacons freed the apostles to give priority to the ministry of the Word and to prayer.

In the same way, today's church staff allows the pastor freedom to do what senior pastors/shepherds are called to do. The things we have discussed, not to mention countless others, consume the time of any pastor. Thankfully, God has given us many wonderful people to help.

Often I see a worship guide or newsletter with the following listing of pastors:

The Church Staff

John Doe	Senior Pastor
Jim Doe	Worship Pastor
Jerry Doe	Student Pastor
Judy Doe	Children's Pastor

With all due respect, let me point out, the senior pastor is not *on* the church staff. The senior pastor *has* a staff with whom to do the work of the church.

I loved my staff. Many of them are still the recognized gold standard in their fields. But they recognized, and the church recognized, the calling and position of the pastor as chief elder of the local congregation is a unique role in a New Testament church.

Let me point out the obvious.

- Loyalty to the pastor is supreme.
- Freedom to be productive and creative is allowed and encouraged.
- Accountability is not negotiable. As senior pastor, you are ultimately responsible for what happens in your church and on your staff.
- Friendship is essential.

The wise pastor will make *developing personal relationships* the number one priority within his staff.

Unity within the staff is paramount. And your people will be sensitive to the presence or lack thereof. And that lack will be devastating to the effective leadership of any pastor and staff.

As pastor to your staff, you are not only their manager but their spiritual leader and friend as well. And the balance can be as difficult as it is delicate.

Division must never be allowed to grow. Free expression of opinion and disagreement should be allowed and encouraged. But division, dispute, and hurt feelings must be resolved *before the sun goes down.* As pastor you must immediately initiate restitution of broken relationships within your staff.

My pastor, Gregg Matte, is a master in relationships. He recently made a staffing decision in our church which at first glance was a surprise but which was, upon further consideration, a stroke of genius.

Three associate music staffers were placed under the leadership of our worship pastor. One strong in contemporary worship; one strong in traditional worship; one strong in technology, sound, lights, media, production, etc.

The worship pastor, Stephen Smith, who Pastor Gregg placed over the music team, was one of his best friends. In Christ their hearts beat as one, and the church senses it deeply.

Longtime friends and brothers, they are "joined at the hip," and the result is beautiful. No relationship is more important than senior pastor and worship pastor.

One closing thought. I am increasingly appalled at the number of pastors and staffers I see who are unwilling to leave their geographical comfort zone. "Wherever He Leads I'll Go" doesn't mean as long as it's not out of the Bible Belt or not too far away from friends and family. The best position you will ever have may be awaiting you just around the corner or just across the state line.

Sing that song again. And this time *actually mean it*.

Chapter 112

ADMINISTERING THE STAFF

The priority of personal friendship may well be the missing ingredient and is certainly what lifts a staff from a *professional* staff to a *powerful* staff. Jesus elevated His staff to a new level of intimacy when He said, "I do not call you slaves anymore. . . . I have called you friends" (John 15:15).

When you expand your staff, give consideration to the importance of personal friendship. Look first for someone you already know and trust.

Few things are more important in a good staff than building good personal relationships. Strangers can indeed bond into spiritual unity of mind and purpose, but often longtime friends in other settings make some of the best staff members in the new setting of your current ministry.

But whether lifelong or new, developing friendships between pastor and staff is high priority.

The best pastor and staff relationship is not "employer and employee," but "friend and friend." This, of course, begins by calling staff with which you are personally compatible. "Can two walk together without agreeing to meet?" (Amos 3:3).

Friendship develops out of time and trust. To keep confidences, be honest with one another, admit an error, confess a fault, forgive and overlook, and really like one another are essential ingredients in building high level quality within a church staff.

Make the effort to build personal relationships with your staff and their families. They will be the most loyal supporters and productive helpers in your ministry.

In spite of the best relationships, there will be times when correction must be given and decisions overruled. When you do, never talk about a staff member behind his back to another person. And always be the initiator of reconciliation in damaged relationships.

The busy pastor will always attempt to be accessible to his people. They are never an interruption to our ministry; they *are* our ministry. However, there will be those times when a response to a member's request for your time must be delayed or delegated to another staff member. But the staff should know your door is *always open* to them.

It is not possible to pastor individually every person in a large church. The wise pastor, therefore, will pastor the staff, who in turn, pastor their individual segment of the congregation. Be available to the staff and always be supportive.

And please note again, the pastor is not *on* the church staff; the pastor *has* a staff with whom to work.

I am often amazed to learn of some churches who never have a regular staff meeting. That's like a contractor trying to build a house without a blueprint. If the carpenter doesn't know what the plumber is doing and the electrician doesn't know what the tile man is doing, the result will be disastrous. For many years we used the following schedule for Tuesday staff meetings:

1. 8:30 a.m.—individual staff division leaders or program staff met with their personnel, assistants, secretaries, etc.
2. 10:00 a.m.—program staff (division heads) met for one hour and a half. This included fifteen minutes of prayer and one hour and fifteen minutes of discussion. The pastor was in attendance, but the associate pastor presided. A printed agenda was distributed, reports were given, and decisions made.
3. 11:30 a.m.—all employees—including cooks, custodians, and secretaries—joined the entire staff in prayer until 12:00.

All of this was preceded by a weekly Monday lunch in the pastor's office or at various restaurants as the senior staff met with the pastor and prepared the Tuesday agenda. At this meeting many of the major decisions were made before the Tuesday 10:30 meeting, enabling us to facilitate the decisions made on Monday.

Chapter 113

THE EXECUTIVE PASTOR

This is a luxury you may have to await until your church gets larger. But as soon as it's feasibly possible, find this person.

Titles, like most things, change through the years. The oldest for this position was "assistant to the pastor." Then came "assistant pastor." Both were viewed more as a helper doing details, errands, and hospital visitation for the pastor. Neither had the sense of importance inherent in the name "executive pastor."

Next came the title "associate pastor." It was more a combination of the above plus administrative authority and oversight. The executive pastor is the right name for the position. While he will also do pastoral ministry, as will all in ministry, it is viewed by the staff and congregation as an extremely important position of leadership. And it is.

The executive pastor speaks for the pastor. When church members or staff members have talked with him, they are confident they have heard the word and will of the senior pastor.

Dr. David Self serves in that position at Houston's First. He writes, "'Executive' is not a title of privilege but rather a description of service." An executive pastor should implement the vision of the pastor and the church. *Executive* describes the administrative side, while *pastor* refers to the ministry side. An executive pastor should be a minister first and an executive second. It's not an easy balance but one that is critical. Never the tough, demanding

Donald Trump executive; always the tender shepherd who gets the tough things done with the shepherd's touch of "people first."

As the executive pastor, 100 percent understanding of the pastor's heart is essential. That's where the importance of personal friendship comes in. After fifty-seven years of marriage, I don't have to ask my wife what she thinks about this or feels about that. I already know. I know her that well. That is precisely the relationship that must develop between the heart and mind of the senior pastor and his executive pastor.

Generally speaking, the executive pastor should have oversight of personnel, finance, and operations. Nothing could be more biblical than for a pastor to have help in *all the other things,* that in prayer and study he might prioritize *the main things.*

One of the special experiences of my ministry was having Jake Self as my executive pastor at First Southern, Del City, Oklahoma, and his son, David Self as my executive pastor at Houston's First. Jake never finished grade school and David earned a Ph.D. Both were special men. Both had the same special ingredients. They were:

- Smart as a whip
- Sharp as a tack
- Undyingly loyal to me
- Deeply mature, godly men
- Great people skills
- Unparalleled work ethic
- Genuine love for people
- Wisdom that came only from God

Chapter 114

CALLING
A STAFF MEMBER

The easiest thing in the world to do is to add a staff member. The hardest thing is to release one. This is not to say that every staff member is not a wonderful Christian and a dedicated worker. It is to say that sometimes the right person is serving at the wrong church. Therefore, it is essential that you take your time and be sure you have the right person *to begin with.*

Employees such as secretaries, assistants, cooks, and custodians should be employed by the staff member with whom they work and are not the responsibility of the personnel committee. *Employees are hired;* staff members are *called.*

The calling of a staff member to lead a major division or ministry in your church is best done in concert with the personnel committee. In certain cases a related committee might be involved, such as a student pastor, with personnel committee and youth committee, or a minister of activities with the personnel committee, and the Christian Life Center committee. In some cases where committee responsibilities overlap, it might be best to bring both committees together. In other cases representatives from each committee will suffice.

A church will recognize that the ultimate weight of the decision to call a high-level staff member must rest on the pastor. There is a sense, therefore, in which the committee is really assisting the pastor by counseling him with well-thought-out wisdom and input. But he must make the final decision.

Don't let this concept frighten you. If God has brought mature believers to the committee, they will want it no other way.

Call four or five good friends in other churches and ask them to suggest names. Solicit names from the congregation. Soon a list of fifteen to twenty names will emerge. Think and pray over these and eliminate several.

Next, call the committee together with resumes and pictures of the three or four persons you consider to be the best candidates. Pastor, personnel committee, and any related committee will determine the priority order of these three or four.

Start with number one, and interview three or four people and decide. Try to determine the best candidate, the one to whom you feel the Lord is leading you, and deal with that person exclusively to a final yes or no. Don't deal seriously with two or three at the same time.

Contact the prospective staff person and determine their level of interest. The phone call should be to that person's home, not their church. Most of the time they will say yes or no regarding their level of interest on the first call. If they have some interest, ask them to pray about it a week or ten days; then call back.

Visit the person in their city, away from their church, field for a face-to-face meeting. As pastor, you will want to take the appropriate committee chairperson with you and perhaps an associate. If all parties are still interested, invite them to come to your city for an afternoon and evening and look over your church and church field and meet with the committee.

Don't make a decision on the spot. Ask the prospective staff person to return home and pray. Assure him that you and the personnel committee will pray and meet again. Meet a week later. Hear the heart of the committee, get their counsel, ask everyone to be frank and honest. If all concerned feel this is the right person, ask him officially to come to your church.

Depending on the level of the position, some prospects will be invited to the position by the pastor and personnel committee. Some will be called by the church.

Maintain confidentiality throughout the process. Don't let the name of the potential staff member leak to the congregation. The first information the other church should have that the staff member is coming to your church is *after* the decision has been made and announced simultaneously at both churches and not leaked to either.

And don't even think about asking someone to come in view of a call if you don't intend to call them. Coming in view of a call should only be done at the level of pastor and senior staff.

When the pastor, committee, and potential staff member have agreed on a date to come before the church, the staff member should go immediately to his current pastor and share his decision in confidence. The pastor should then release the information to his congregation in concert with the release of information to your church.

If the whole church votes to call the staff member, do so on the spot as he steps out of the sanctuary at the conclusion of the service in which he has been presented to the congregation. The staff member should be prepared to announce his acceptance on the spot. Waiting a week or two to vote, or voting and waiting a week or two for an answer is not a good idea. It will set the ministry of the staff member ahead by six months if you allow for an immediate bonding with the people as they rejoice and embrace the new staff member at the moment of their acceptance.

Responsibilities, salary and benefits, moving expenses, dates, and other details should be clearly spelled out between the church and the new staff member. Discuss health insurance, retirement benefits, the furnishing of an automobile, gasoline expenses, vacation time, etc. Leave nothing to chance. The church should pay all travel, motel, and food expenses for the staff member during visits to your church for interviews and in view of a call.

Chapter 115

REASSIGNING
AND RELEASING

When a staff member is deemed unproductive or uncooperative, every effort should be made at redemption. Have you clearly communicated? Does he know you are dissatisfied? Have you shown him how to improve?

Have you pointed out why you are displeased? It is incumbent upon you as his pastor, friend, and employer that you go the second and third mile to help save this person. Remember to put yourself in his shoes. Kindness and charity are always in order.

One of my most effective ministries was reassigning staff members who were good and faithful persons but in the wrong position. Each of us has our own giftedness. If a person has a loyal heart and a great spirit and you cannot make him into what you feel you need, the first step is to examine the possibility of reassigning him to a different position on the staff. A different ministry might be a better match for his spiritual gifts.

We shuffled some of our staff about more than once in my thirty years in Houston, and every move proved to be a good move. Talented staff members can serve in many positions. Always ask, "Is this person serving in the right position on our staff?"

There will, however, be times when problems are unsolvable and differences irreconcilable. When a staff member must be dismissed, it should be done with the consultation and support of the personnel committee. Every staff member will have a following. Their constituency might comprise 5, 10, or 20 percent of your church. Among them will be personal friends, and therein is the potential for problems.

Just as a good personnel committee can be insulation between you and making bad decisions in the first place, so can they be a buffer between you and the reaction that may result when tough decisions must be made. That the personnel committee made the determination to release a staff member is more palatable to the congregation, and certainly easier on you, than that *you* made the decision to release them.

At such times the importance of grace cannot be overstated. Facilitate their exit from your church with dignity and respect. And consider the potential for future ministry elsewhere for that staff member and his family.

They have a reputation to maintain, feelings to be considered, and bills to be paid. We have continued to pay staff members for many months on occasion to help them land on their feet in another church. Above all, put yourself in their shoes, be considerate, and be gracious.

Occasionally a situation will arise where a staff member may have no future and you cannot in good conscience recommend him to another church. From time to time, people in this situation will be considered by another church whose pastor will call you for a recommendation.

There are many ways to handle this delicate situation. For me, the best, was not to return the phone call. Soon the pastor gets the point, and I am free from having put out the bad word on a fellow servant of the Lord who might have an effective ministry elsewhere.

If a person is unworthy of future employment, that responsibility will be the Lord's. If moral failure is involved, make every effort to assist the fallen brother or sister in getting counsel and spiritual therapy aimed at restitution. While he can't continue to serve on your staff, he may be restored to ministry elsewhere.

Put yourself in this person's shoes, and go the second mile in this difficult situation.

Chapter 116

DELEGATING RESPONSIBILITY

I magine trying to lead two million persons across a desert with no map, no food, and no water. Moses had an administrative nightmare not only in leading the Israelites and providing for their needs but also in judging them in matters of personal and national decisions. His was an impossible task.

You know the story. Moses' father-in-law, Jethro, helped him get organized. The people were divided into groups, assistants were named, and the work efficiently done. Our Lord, of course, referred to Himself when He said, "On this rock I will build My church" (Matt. 16:18). Yet he poured his life into developing twelve leaders who would be the human instruments through which he would do the building.

The pastor of a growing and vibrant church must learn that he cannot be a jack of all trades, make all the decisions, and do everything himself. He must have help. Staff, secretaries, deacons, teachers, and the church members comprise a large reservoir of talent and abilities. Right now there is probably someone in your congregation just waiting to help you do the job.

Your senior adults will visit shut-ins for you. A retired minister in your congregation can help visit the hospitals. Women can beautifully plan the churchwide Thanksgiving banquet and men who can build that new mission. People in your congregation know how to design ads, take surveys, handle legal work, and do a hundred other things that need to be done in a church.

But don't delegate responsibility at random. The new member's packet should contain, among other things, a talent survey card. Keep a master file of your people's talents, hobbies, and occupations. When you need something done, go to that file.

A mechanic who cannot teach a lesson can repair the church bus. A carpenter who cannot give great sums of money can build bookshelves for the children's department. A talented lady can help improve the quality of the church meals. A grocer can assist in ordering foods in quantity for weekly church meals.

When you have a job to be done—whether painting a room, following up new members, or recruiting and training ushers—get laypeople to do it. Invite them to your office and have a heart-to-heart talk. Tell them you need them. Tell them how much you are counting on them and how important they are to the work of the kingdom.

Ask them to enlist others, oversee the job, carry it through, and give you a report when it is completed. And thank them publicly when the job is finished. Think! You'll find an easier way and someone who can do the job. You can't do it all, and a hundred good people are wanting and waiting to be used.

Larger churches, of course, have the luxury of being multistaffed. While some are called and paid to assist you in the work of the ministry, don't forget the wealth of services available within the laity of the congregation.

One Sunday morning I preached on the importance of being available to God for His service. I will never forget a man who approached me.

"Pastor, I would never come forward on an invitation to be one of the crowd to say I am willing to serve," he said, "but if you ever pick up the phone, and tell me there is something special you need me to do for the church, I will never turn you down."

Even though you have a paid staff, give equal importance to the volunteer spirit of your people. Within the staff structure at Houston's First were many levels of administration—directors of education, music, counseling, cleaning, school—each with a level of leaders under them who administered others within their area. One thing in common made each of these leaders effective: they were all good delegators.

Being a delegator, getting people to help and trusting them to do it, begins with a sense of personal security that rests in our security in Christ.

Insecure leaders feel the need to do everything themselves, check up on everybody, look over every shoulder, and trust no one else to get the job done.

The apostle Paul tells us our Lord is the head in heaven and we, various members of His body on earth (see 1 Cor. 12:12–20).

The beauty of the body is its diversity. As a functioning body has various organs and limbs, so the members of the body of Christ bring varying gifts and talents to the service of our Lord. So turn it loose. Let the church be the church. Let someone else do it, and trust them to get the job done. A few will disappoint you. Most will bless you.

This is particularly true within the church staff. Early in my ministry I greatly belabored the matter of checking up on my staff. Finally, I decided if I were to do my job and theirs, I might as well get paid my salary and theirs!

Make every effort to hire competent, committed, hardworking, talented people and turn them loose. Even the member of the smallest staff, whose commitment to our Lord is high, is probably capable of doing more than you imagine.

Chapter 117

INTERNS

The best thing about interns is probably not so much about what they'll do for you as what you'll do for them.

Interns are usually college or seminary students, part-time, paid by the hour or full-time for the summer.

Children's ministries and student ministries are particularly highly programmed in the summer months. VBS, camps, mission trips, and retreats are great times to get your staff some help.

Most of what they do will be physical labor and running errands. But they're there because they love the Lord, want to help, and are eager to learn about His work. Your staff and congregation will be aware of several potential interns. After school and weekends as well as summer are good times for them.

As pastor, spend some personal training time with your interns. Explain what you are doing and why. Be patient. Love them. Show them what they did and didn't do right. Pray with them and help them fulfill their potential.

Let your interns observe some staff meetings and divisional planning meetings. Learning their way around the inside of a good church with actual hands-on, up-close, and personal experience may be the best education they'll ever receive. I couldn't number the young men I know who are pastoring great growing churches who learned their way around on the staff of a megachurch and simply began doing what they observed.

Teach them the importance of punctuality, persistency, hard work, integrity, kindness, patience, and respect. And don't just talk about it, demonstrate it. Go the second mile with your young interns. Even the smallest church can afford one, once in a while. And remember what you do for them may be more important than what they ever do for your church.

It's a win-win situation. Even consider putting them in your missions budget. It's a great investment in the lives of young men and women who will one day impact the world.

Part 9

THE CHURCH FINANCES

Chapter 118

NEW TESTAMENT TITHING

How often someone says, "I don't believe in tithing, that's under the law." Indeed it is. But let me show you that in everything Jesus ever said, taught, or did, He exceeded Old Testament law. He went far beyond the law. Love always does.

Jesus said, "Don't assume that I came to destroy the Law or the Prophets. I did not come to destroy but to *fulfill*" (Matt. 5:17). He came to *fully* fill a *partially* full law.

The Moral Law—The Ten Commandments show us *our need of God.*

The First: "Do not have other gods besides Me" (Exod. 20:3). *Jesus said,* "The Father and I are one" (John 10:30).

The Second: "Do not make an idol" (Exod. 20:4). *Jesus taught* loving family and possessions more than Him is idolatry.

The Third: "Do not misuse the name of Yahweh your God" (Exod. 20:7). *Jesus said,* don't even take God's creation in vain by swearing an oath by it.

The Fourth: "Remember the Sabbath day, to keep it holy" (Exod. 20:8). *Jesus said* the Son of Man is *Lord* of the Sabbath (see Luke 6:5).

The Fifth: "Honor your father and your mother" (Exod. 20:12). *Jesus taught,* Honor them by caring for them financially, even until death.

The Sixth: "Do not murder" (Exod. 20:13). *Jesus said* to hate your brother is to murder him in your heart (see Matt. 5:21–22).

The Seventh: "Do not commit adultery" (Exod. 20:14). *Jesus said*, adultery is lust in the heart (see Matt. 5:28).

The Eighth: "Do not steal" (Exod. 20:15). In John 10:10, Jesus taught that while the thief comes to *steal* treasure, He comes to *give* the greatest treasure of all—life—and is Himself the treasure in abundance.

The Ninth: "Tell the truth" (see Exod. 20:16). Jesus said, "I *am* the truth" (see John 14:6).

The Tenth: "Do not covet" (Exod. 20:17). Paul taught *Jesus did not* commit the ultimate act of covetousness by clinging to equality with God, but came to earth as a man and died on a cross.

The Ceremonial Law shows us *how we come to God*. Within the ceremonial law were many ceremonies, feasts, ordinances, special days, sacrifices, festivals, celebrations, buildings, and temples. They all pointed to Christ, previews of the main event (see Phil. 2:5–8).

The Jews revered Solomon's temple. Jesus said, "something greater than Solomon is here!" (Matt. 12:42).

Thousands of young, unblemished, male lambs were sacrificed for sin. John the Baptist introduced Jesus, "Here is the Lamb of God, who takes away the sin of the world!" (John 1:29).

Jesus is greater than the altar. Hebrews says He was the Lamb *and* the altar.

Earthly priests annually went behind the veil of the temple to make atonement for the sins of the people. Jesus was *forever* our high priest, after the order of Melchizedek, eternal, without beginning or end of days (see Heb. 5:10).

Jesus is greater than the mercy seat. The high priest repeatedly placed blood on the mercy seat. Jesus ascended into the holy of holies not made with hands, placed His blood on the mercy seat and *forever sat down* at the right hand of the Father. Once for all it was done.

Inside the ark of the covenant were the Ten Commandments. Jesus exceeded the Ten Commandments.

In the ark was an opher of manna from the wilderness. Jesus said, "I am the bread of life" (John 6:35).

In the ark was Aaron's rod. When Moses lifted his hands, the waters split. When Jesus raised His hands on the cross, He parted the waters of sin, death, hell, and the grave.

The Civil Law shows how, rightly related to God, *we now relate to one another*.

Roman law required a citizen to carry the pack of a Roman soldier one full mile. Jesus said carry it two. If a man requires your coat, give him your cloak also. If he smites you on one cheek, turn the other cheek. Bless them that curse you. Pray for them that hate you and spitefully use you.

The law said to forgive your brother if he asks.

Jesus said if your brother has something against you, don't wait for him to initiate reconciliation. You initiate the reconciliation and forgiveness whether you are at fault or not. The law said forgive three times. Jesus said, seventy times seven. And He didn't mean, don't forgive offense number seventy-one. It was simply a metaphor which meant "never stop forgiving."

Tithing—under the Law? It certainly is. And this is why we are to give more not less than 10 percent. Grace *exceeds* the law, and love *outgives* it. Read it again and again. "Don't assume that I came to destroy the Law or the Prophets. I did not come to destroy but to fulfill" (Matt. 5:17).

Chapter 119

STEWARDSHIP PREACHING

For a Jew to give more under the law in a simple tithe than a Christian gives under grace is a disgrace to grace. If Jesus exceeded the law in everything he said, taught, or did, how can it be that this includes everything except the most important thing in the Christian life—the stewardship of our possessions?

On what basis do I say our relationship to money may well be *the most important thing* in the Christian life? For starters, Jesus said, "Where your treasure is, there your heart will be also" (Matt. 6:21). The two are inseparable. You cannot love God with all your heart and not love Him with all your treasure. Two entire books of the New Testament, 1 John and James, were written to say that our actions validate the reality of our profession of faith.

We can *talk* a good game, but unless we *do* there is no salvation. Our good works do not contribute to our salvation, but they are the major authenticator which validates its reality.

Jesus paid it all, and by grace we are saved through faith, *not* by our works. But where there are no works, faith without works is *dead*. Faith that produces no works is *empty* faith. Faith that produces good works demonstrates it is *saving* faith.

And what is the most difficult of all human works for most believers if not giving their money? We work hard for our money. It is our retirement, our savings, our family, our food, our clothes, our home, our children's education, our car, our vacations, our fun, and our holidays. It is *central* to our lives; it is truly who we are.

Is not, therefore, where our affections lie the most significant indicator of our relationship to Christ? Are not our possessions the tangible, measurable expression of who we really are?

- There are 2,250 verses in the Bible about money.
- More is said in the New Testament about our relationship to our possessions than is said about prayer, hell, and faith combined.
- The number one theme of the parables is our relationship to our possessions.
- Stewardship is the number two theme of the New Testament, second only to salvation.

Giving 10 percent was indeed under the law. And does the principle of exceeding the law apply to everything except the main thing? I think not!

Ten percent? That's just for starters. Our Christian faith exceeds the Old Testament and fulfills the law. And that not only includes but exceeds the number two theme of the New Testament, *our relationship to our money.*

For a Jew to give more under the law than a Christian under grace is indeed a disgrace to grace.

Stewardship preaching. Not seeker friendly? More importantly, it's not kingdom friendly to ignore it. In so doing, you do your people a great disservice.

You sacrifice much blessing on the lives of your people when you fail to teach the second most prominent theme in the New Testament. They can never be fully blessed until they "get it" here. Nor can your church.

You will only raise a church filled with immature, undeveloped believers if you fail here. If Jesus gave our relationship to our possessions second billing on the marquee of the New Testament, so must you.

One's relationship to his possessions is inextricably bound up in his relationship to his Heavenly Father. "Don't collect for yourselves treasures on earth, where moth and rust destroy and where thieves break in and steal. But collect for yourselves treasures in heaven, where neither moth nor rust destroys, and where thieves don't break in and steal. For where your treasure is, there your heart will be also" (Matt. 6:19–21).

Chapter 120

OVERSEEING THE BUDGET

Our Lord warned against the folly of failing to plan. The cost of everything from the next big event to next year's operating budget must be thought out well in advance. When you fail to plan, you plan to fail.

The order is:

- Enlist the budget committee.
- Prepare the budget.
- Adopt the budget.
- Administer the budget.

The finance committee, appointed by the committee on committees, is to be comprised of persons who are tithers to the church, mature, supportive, knowledgeable, and who have great faith. They should represent a broad section of the congregation and be instantly recognizable as men and women of respect and integrity. No church member should ever be able to say, "He's on the finance committee? You're kidding!" Budget and personnel are the two most important committees in your church.

Budget preparation should begin three months before each new fiscal year. And the best fiscal year is January 1 to December 31, not the associational year, October 1 to September 30.

Hearings should be held with the staff and representatives of various entities within the church allowed to present their program budget and explain and support it. The finance committee will, with the pastor, make the final determination on which line items are increased, decreased, or eliminated in the new budget to be recommended to the church for adoption. And the finance committee, not a separate budget preparation committee, should prepare the budget.

Annual budget increases should reflect a measure of optimism and anticipated growth. Nonproductive ministries should be reduced or eliminated. New ministries and programs should be funded adequately to ensure they are birthed with a good chance for survival and success.

When the budget has been recommended by the committee and approved by the deacons, it should be voted on by the entire congregation.

Few things should be voted on by the congregation. The annual budget is one of those things.

On a given Sunday morning, the budget should be adopted by the entire congregation with a commitment to its support. Discussion of individual items within the budget should, however, be done on Wednesday night preceding the Sunday morning worship service in which it is adopted.

Wednesday, discussion without vote.

Sunday, vote without discussion.

Simultaneous with this process, a special budget promotion committee appointed by the pastor or committee on committees should conduct a thirty-day annual stewardship campaign to prepare the church for adopting the budget. The stewardship campaign should be simple—comprised of a publicity committee, two sermons, two testimonies, and at least one Sunday school lesson on stewardship. Stewardship testimonies to fellow class members during Sunday morning Bible study are most effective.

Administering the budget should be done on a weekly basis by the executive pastor or administrator. Monthly finance committee meetings should be conducted to oversee the budget.

Let there be no secrets. Full disclosure is important to the financial health of the congregation. The budget committee will take under consideration any necessary seasonal spending in dealing with overages in particular line items.

Midyear adjustments to the budget may be made by the finance committee, requiring no other authorization or action. Salaries should be lumped together by division. Individual salaries should not be printed or disclosed to the congregation. That's where you learn to trust the personnel committee.

Care must be taken to seek the Lord for a good balance between faith and reason in planning and administering the church budget. Here we will do well to observe our Lord's admonition to be as "shrewd as serpents and as harmless as doves" (Matt. 10:16).

> Encamped along the hills of light,
> Ye Christian soldiers, rise.
> And press the battle ere the night
> Shall veil the glowing skies.
> Against the foe in vales below
> Let all our strength be hurled.
> Faith is the victory, we know,
> That overcomes the world.
>
> Faith is the victory! Faith is the victory!
> O glorious victory, that overcomes the world.[1]

Endnotes

1. John H. Yates, "Faith Is the Victory."

Chapter 121

FISCAL RESPONSIBILITY

L et me put it bluntly: I have personal knowledge of at least two cases in which handling the church collections on a regular basis was too great a temptation for a church member. Not only shalt thou not tempt the Lord thy God; thou shalt not tempt thy brother, the offering counter. Cash should never be handled except in the presence of three or more persons.

Ninety-nine out of one hundred Christian people are honest. But even the best among us are capable of yielding to temptation, particularly when there is overwhelming financial need in one's own life.

Even the smallest church can afford a safe. At the conclusion of the offering, the ushers should take the offering plates to a designated secure place. At least two persons then secure the money in the safe to be counted on Monday.

Ideally, a safe should be purchased that requires two persons to open. Each person should have different parts of the combination in his or her mind. Deposits should be removed from the safe and counted in the presence of three or more persons with money counts and deposit slips completed appropriately. You may save yourself and someone else a lot of heartache if this procedure is diligently followed.

Money should never be left overnight in the possession of only one person—pastor, staff, or church member. Money should not be kept locked in a staff member's drawer to be placed in the vault the following day. It should never be kept in the possession of any individual at all.

As I write these words, I am vividly reminded of a heartbreaking situation. An employee was terminated from Houston's First because he was videotaped removing $1,600 from a staff member's desk that had been left there overnight in violation of church policy. The employee was arrested and the staff member reprimanded.

God's people trust us with their money. It should be well secured as well as well spent. The wise minister will keep himself above possible reproach and never handle the church's money.

"Stay away from every kind of evil" (1 Thess. 5:22).

The finance committee, with pastor and administrator is responsible to oversee the church budget. Depending on the season and the need, the church finance committee of Houston's First met at least monthly and sometimes weekly, with full accounting given to the congregation in regularly scheduled business meetings.

The other side of the coin is that the finance committee is to be entrusted with the responsibility of expending funds previously approved in the adoption of the church budget. Once the budget has been adopted, the church should not *reapprove* individual expenditures *within* that budget. That is the responsibility of the pastor, staff, and finance committee.

What good is a system in which authority is given to a finance committee, only to have other committees and boards look over their shoulder and second-guess them? The finance committee is to be entrusted with the business of the church.

Each year a professional audit of the church's finances should be conducted by an outside accounting firm. Seldom, if ever, will improprieties be found, and finding them is not the primary purpose of the audit.

The purpose is to ensure the congregation that professionalism prevails at every level of the church's finances. A good firm will occasionally recommend procedural changes to enhance the effective functioning of the church's finances.

Annual audits can cost as little as a few hundred dollars or, as in the case of large churches, tens of thousands of dollars.

Given the occasion to do so, the first thing the secular world will jump on your church about is your finances. Here you want to be squeaky clean. Seize the initiative and see that from collection to deposit, to expenditure, to accounting, your church finances are above reproach.

More than one pastor has brought embarrassment to himself and his church in failing to do so.

- Don't handle church money.
- Don't have secret accounts.
- Don't set your own salary.
- Have an entertainment budget set by the finance committee and use it with integrity.

Stay squeaky clean. You'll be glad you did.

Chapter 122

BORROWING MONEY

There is no way to overstate the problem and burden of debt in our time. Individually and corporately we should aspire to be debt-free.

Some churches, however, are confused over the issue of borrowing money. The church should have a balanced perspective of the biblical view of borrowing and lending. It is erroneous to extrapolate from Scripture a teaching that borrowing is unbiblical and, as taught in some quarters, downright sinful.

At the root of this issue is an erroneous interpretation of Romans 13:8: "Do not owe anyone anything, except to love one another, for the one who loves another has fulfilled the law."

Even the simplest exegesis of the context verse makes clear that the subject is not "money" but "love."

Because of Christ's love for us, we owe a debt of love others. Paul is simply saying, "Pay the debt. Don't fail to meet the obligation you owe." The issue is not owing; it is not paying what you do owe. It is an amazing stretch to extrapolate this clear teaching into a prohibition against borrowing money.

The eminent Old Testament scholar, Dr. Phillip Williams, stated, "The earliest record of borrowing and lending was done as an honor to the poor, to allow them to save face by not having to take charity." It added to a person's dignity and sense of self-worth to say to them, "I believe in you; I believe in your future; I believe you can pay this money back."

In Old Testament days lending money was an honored profession among the Jews. There are important issues, however, regarding the matter of usury—

charging exorbitant interest. Taking advantage of one's brother in this manner is an obvious breach of ethics.

Deuteronomy 28:44 is often cited as a proof-text against borrowing money: "He will lend to you, but you won't lend to him. He will be the head, and you will be the tail."

Verse 12 of the same chapter, however, casts a different light on the subject. "The LORD will open for you His abundant storehouse, the sky, to give your land rain in its season and to bless all the work of your hands. *You will lend to many nations*, but you will not borrow."

Read the entire chapter. In context, God is clearly saying if Israel honors and obeys Him, He will prosper and bless them so greatly they will not need to borrow money. They will, in fact, be in a position to lend money to others. Conversely, God says in the last half of the chapter, if they do not obey Him, they will not prosper and will have to borrow money.

Is it possible our Lord is promising Israel if they will obey Him, they will be in a position of doing something sinful—i.e., lending money? Clearly, if it is a sin to be a borrower, it is a sin to be a lender.

And what of our Lord's statement in Matthew 5:42, "Don't turn away from the one who wants to borrow from you"?

Jesus taught four parables about lending and borrowing. In no case did He infer there was a moral issue connected to either. The issue was the attitude of the borrower and the manner of repayment.

Borrowing for you and your church might or might not, at any given time, be the right financial decision. Many factors will go into determining that. But solid biblical scholarship dictates that we clearly understand that borrowing is not a moral issue *in and of itself*.

There may be *related* moral issues such as usury or failure to repay, but the issue of the morality of incurring debt through borrowing is, biblically, no issue at all.

I have great respect for those who teach "save up the money, and don't build until you have the cash in hand."

Consider:

1. As you wait, the price of construction goes up. The interest you save may be less than the increased cost.
2. Lost momentum can slow the growth of your church.
3. While we do not reach people to get their money, the fact is, new people you reach with that new building will help you pay for it.

Think about it!

Chapter 123

THE BUILDING PROGRAM

The first issue to be resolved is this: Are we absolutely certain that now is the time to construct the new building? Has every other possibility been explored?

Has dual or triple usage of existing buildings been considered? Has serious consideration been given to beginning new missions? Have the people been given adequate information about projected cost, options, and the pros and cons of building and not building?

Take your time and bring along your people with you. Start on your knees, and when the Lord has given you peace, first present the dream to your leadership. Don't stampede your people. Most of them are "not there yet."

Measure the pulse of your congregation about the proposed building program.

- Do they truly love the Lord and hunger to see the church grow? There is often some apprehension among longtime members about all those "new ones" coming in.
- Is the church financially able to build?
- Has it been long enough since the last building campaign and accompanying capital campaign?
- What were the problems then, and have they been resolved?
- Is the church in unity?

- Do the people truly believe in the program?
- Do they love and follow their pastor?

Things must be *just right* to enter a building program. Building programs can be a tremendous blessing, or they can cause great stress within the fellowship.

Once these matters have been satisfactorily resolved, the first step is to appoint a qualified building committee. This can be done by either the pastor or the committee on committees. The building committee for the new facility is different from the existing property and space committee that is charged with the responsibility of the maintenance of existing facilities.

The committee's first act should be to interview potential architects. This process should be open to members as well as nonmembers of your congregation. Be advised that church members under consideration for architect may end up with hurt feelings if they are not selected.

Nonetheless, select the best architect for the job. The person should be a Christian with knowledge of how churches operate and one who has done other church projects.

Discuss fees, concepts, dates, and other details. The architectural fee is normally in the 7 percent range and includes both designing and overseeing the building throughout its construction, in concert with the building contractor. The selection of the architect, determined by the building committee, should be approved by both deacons and church members before documents are signed by the trustees.

The people should be invited to submit ideas regarding areas of interest to them, including everything from hallways to classrooms to color of bricks, etc. Let the people take ownership. Encourage their input. Jesus said, "Where your treasure is"—and this includes the treasure of time and ideas—"there your heart will be also" (Matt. 6:21). The architect will need approximately three to six months to put the ideas of your people into blueprints, in a finished form to be approved by the building committee and church.

Next, a general sketch will be made of the floor plan with an exterior sketch and a model of the building. Once the plans have been approved, display the model in the lobby of the church. Ask for people's opinions and input. After blueprints are drawn by the architect, ask him to estimate approximate costs. The church will then approve the project and the cost and vote to proceed.

Once final plans are approved, they are put out to bid to a select list of five or six potential bidders. A list of qualified contractors, who will be allowed to bid, should be prepared in consultation with the architect.

You will need to determine whether you will simply accept the lowest bid. Surprisingly, other factors come into play. Inform potential contractors whether you are committed to accepting the lowest bid, and stay with it.

The architect will help you determine a closing date for bids to be received as well as a time line for completion of construction. The building schedule will be built into the contract with appropriate penalties included for time overruns. Weather delays will, of course, be part of the equation. Expect the time from the first meeting of the building committee to the groundbreaking for the new building to be fifteen to eighteen months. The drawing of plans will take about six months. Construction time will average nine to twelve months.

In your cost projections include building construction costs, architect fees, any special site work, paving, ample contingency, landscaping, furniture, and equipment. And be prepared for this: The entire project *will* cost more than you anticipate and take longer than you expected.

Two months before the building is completed, plan a dedication ceremony and move-in date. But know that you may have to change it. And try to get the plans right the first time. Those change orders will be expensive.

Chapter 124

THE CAPITAL CAMPAIGN

Once you have determined to buy land, build new buildings, or remodel existing facilities, the next step is to determine the method of financing your project. Normally called "the capital campaign" or the "fund-raising campaign," raising the money to build can be as exciting as the building project itself.

Fund-raising programs are normally conducted to finance five types of projects. The excitement level of the people in descending order of projects is as follows:

1. Complete relocation.
2. Worship center.
3. Other buildings.
4. Remodel existing buildings or parking lots.
5. Reduce/retire existing debt.

People give to vision, more than need. If they gave to vision, the neediest organizations would not be the neediest. Sell the vision.

"We're reducing the debt in order to _____." Fill in the blank and emphasize it.

In rare circumstances, if the giving potential of the church is extremely high and the financial need is not overwhelming, it may be possible to excite the people and stimulate them with the challenge of giving all the money in a cash offering on one Sunday. Seldom, however, is this possible.

The better way is to think in terms of three-year pledges. People are accustomed to signing three-year notes for appliances, automobiles, etc. Over a three-year period they *can* and *will* give much more than on any single day.

Some church members will say, "I don't believe in pledging." Help them to see that, in fact, they do.

We pledge virtually every day to those things that are of value to us. Every time you write a check, you are making a pledge. Each time you use a credit card, you are making a pledge. If you have served in the military, stood at the marriage altar, or signed a mortgage, you have pledged. The issue is not, "Do I believe in pledging?" It is, "Will I pledge to that which is far more important than any of these lesser things—the expansion of the kingdom of God?"

Share with your congregation that a pledge is not a legally binding document; it is a good-faith commitment that helps the church plan its work. When adequate pledges are in hand, borrow the money for interim, short-term financing and begin construction. Some banks might wish to hold the pledges, but they are never to be used as collateral for the loan. If all the money does not come in during the three-year pledge period, extend the loan or get a new loan for a short duration.

Waiting three years until all the money is in hand to begin building is counterproductive. Escalating building costs mean the project will cost much more three years in the future than it does today. People will also grow discouraged as they see nothing happening. Construction stimulates giving. Conduct the campaign, get the pledges, secure interim financing, and start building!

The typical pastor will want help in conducting a major capital campaign. Let me urge you never to borrow materials from another church that have been purchased from a professional fund-raising organization. It is unethical and might be downright illegal as well. Several opportunities of assistance are afforded to you.

Many large professional firms such as the Gage Group, Eklund Stewardship, In Joy, and Generis handle capital campaigns. Denominational programs are also available that are conducted by full-time denominational employees. Additionally, several small firms and individuals do a good job. I don't know of any bad capital campaign consultants.

You may choose to conduct the campaign yourself. The only book on the subject I know is my B&H book, *Successful Church Fundraising.*[1] Some pastors are comfortable with doing their own programs. Most pastors and churches, however, feel the need to have a consultant actually visiting the field and giving personal direction.

Public announcements of a person's pledge are never in order. Campaign goals can be reached without that or any other embarrassment or high pressure.

Beware of setting unrealistic goals. One fund-raiser asked a church that could not reasonably pledge over $300,000 how much they would like to raise. "One million dollars," the pastor replied. Anxious to get the contract, the fund-raiser responded, "Good. The goal is a million dollars." How sad! A reputable campaign consultant will help you determine how much you can realistically expect to pledge.

Above all don't let anything deter you from going forward. Budget, building programs, and capital campaigns are always to be done in faith.

"Now without faith it is impossible to please God." (Heb. 11:6)

I have never found economic downturns to impact negatively the capital campaigns I conduct. At the height of the 2007–2008 economic downturn, I had the joy of leading Champion Forest Baptist Church of Houston in a successful $39 million campaign. The money came in over budget, and three beautiful buildings were built.

Press on!

Endnotes

1. John Bisagno, *Successful Church Fundraising* (Nashville: B&H, 2002).

Chapter 125

THE BENEVOLENCE
MINISTRY

Jesus made clear He has little patience with those who think only of themselves. So much of His ministry was directed to the hurting and the poor. It has been no surprise through the years to find the secular world often measures our sincerity as believers by our compassion for the poor.

Admittedly, there are always phonies among us. The Pharisees asked of the woman who broke the alabaster box, "Why wasn't this perfume sold and the money given to the poor?" (see Mark 14:3–9).

They didn't care about the poor. They only cared about trapping Jesus. I once asked an antagonistic reporter, "How much does your newspaper give to the poor?" But compassion on those who have nothing might be the most consistent badge of our sincerity as well as the most natural response of our hearts.

Determining the reality of a need can be difficult. For years a woman stood at an intersection near our church, begging every car for money as hundreds of exiting worshippers passed by. One day we asked the motel just across the street to give her a room in conjunction with our adopting her other needs as a church. The hotel manager laughed. "Why, we offered that woman's husband $36,000 a year as a maintenance man, plus free room and board for her family." Her response? "Why would we want to do that? We're making $600 a day on the streets."

I seldom drive by a beggar on the street without rolling down my window and giving him something. But I never do so without thinking of that woman. Perhaps if we err, it should be on the side of doing too much rather than too little.

But through the mission ministries of our church and a hundred other avenues, we are well aware of an endless stream of hurting people who genuinely need our help. Generally, at Houston's First we attempted to meet benevolent needs in three ways.

Within the scores of Sunday school classes in the church, we encouraged an atmosphere conducive to helping one another. Thousands of dollars every year flowed around the church budget directly from one person to another within the Sunday school classes. I knew of cases where people had lost their jobs, had their house burn down, or had great illness where classes gave them $1,500 to as much as $10,000, and that's all right. These compassionate givers are generally those who have learned the joy of giving by being consistent tithers to the church budget.

A second source of benevolence was special offerings in the services of the church. Six times a year, at Christmas Eve services, Thanksgiving eve services, and four Lord's Supper services, we received an offering for the poor. These were second offerings received at the door after the regular offering for the church's budget had been received. These gifts totaled several thousands of dollars a year.

The third avenue of meeting needs was through our missions center. One of the many mission ministries of our church was called the Mission Training Center. This was the drop-off and distribution point for food, clothes, furniture, appliances, etc. Financial assistance ministry was coordinated through the center. Well over a quarter of a million dollars in food, cash, clothing, and other items are distributed there annually in the name of Jesus.

In some ministries a nominal fee—perhaps ten cents for a pair of shoes or a dollar for a suit—is charged. There is something to be said for this. If a person pays at least something, it may enhance his sense of dignity and self-worth. God will lead you to the best way for you and your church.

But develop a well-planned and coordinated benevolence ministry. Jesus said, "You always have the poor with you." And you will. It is a ministry without end but one that is vitally important.

Some of the most gifted servants of God in your congregation are just waiting to be asked to direct the work of this ministry. They may not be able to give great sums of money themselves, but they can give themselves if this is where their heart is.

Nothing will bless you more than helping people as Jesus did. He reminded us that even a cup of cold water given in His name would receive a disciple's reward. Never have we more the opportunity to be His hands and feet than here. A smile, a touch, a tract, a kind act—these "cups of cold water" given in His name and with His love are of high priority to our Lord and should be to us as well.

In being a generous church, you create an atmosphere in which people become givers. They give more time, more money, more love, more forgiveness, more prayer. They've experienced the love of Christ in giving to the poor, and that cross principle impacts every area of their lives.

> "As He stepped ashore, He saw a huge crowd, felt compassion for them, and healed their sick." (Matt. 14:14)

> "This is how we have come to know love: He laid down His life for us. We should also lay down our lives for our brothers. If anyone has this world's goods and sees his brother in need but closes his eyes to his need—how can God's love dwell in him?" (1 John 3:16–17)

Chapter 126

LEGAL LIABILITY

I n the not-too-distant past it was virtually unheard of for a church to be the
object of litigation. Unfortunately, such is no longer the case. In recent years
there has been a proliferation of lawsuits against churches and other community
organizations. Not only are churches being sued with regularity, but they are
losing virtually every case—either through out-of-court settlements or judicial
verdicts.

In 1993, Houston's First hosted a seminar helping churches learn how to
protect themselves against lawsuits. To my amazement one of the attorneys
stated in his lecture, "In the past five years, more than a thousand churches
have been sued; in every case the church lost."

The good news is, your church can greatly reduce the risk of financial loss
and a tarnished reputation in the community due to an unsavory lawsuit. *This
is an extremely serious matter.* It is vitally important that you protect your people
not only from individual harm but collective liability as well.

Understand clearly that the church is generally responsible for everything
that takes place in its buildings, on its premises, on rented equipment or
property, and virtually everything under the influence or sponsorship of staff
and other persons, whom the court would identify as, "an agent of the church."

This means the church is legally responsible not only for activities that
occur on its property but would, for example, include incidents that occur away
from the church in a vehicle that had been rented to transport students to a
youth retreat, as well as at the retreat itself.

In the same manner you make certain your church is adequately insured against fire and other catastrophic events, make certain your church carries adequate liability insurance. Such insurance should cover everything from broken legs incurred during church-sponsored softball games to food poisoning at a restaurant recommended by a staff member, to leading an out-of-state mission trip, to sexual misconduct by a staff member—*and everything in between!*

The church's greatest exposure to being found negligent lies in the area of *child abuse.* Every pastor should lead his church in establishing policies and procedures that reduce the risk of child abuse occurring in the church. And the law *requires* you to report *known* and even *alleged* incidences of child abuse. Abuse can happen anywhere, including *at church.*

Every New Testament church must make a commitment to minister to children in ways that are scriptural, loving, safe, *and legal.* Children are precious, and anything that threatens them—including physical, emotional, or sexual abuse—is unacceptable and absolutely not to be tolerated.

Developing a *children's protective policy* must be done with a broad base of understanding and support from your church's leadership, staff, and laity. As you develop and implement child-abuse prevention policies and procedures, give heed to this statement made by an attorney who specializes in defending churches against allegations of child abuse: *"The only thing worse than not having formal policies against child abuse is having such policies and not enforcing them."*

Your children's protective policies and procedures obviously relate to preschool, children, and youth ministries. However, make certain that your policies also include ministries related to music, recreation, missions, and any other programs which involve "children" (legally defined as anyone under eighteen years of age).

Any large church will gladly share a copy of their child protection policy. It is absolutely essential that you have one, that it is public knowledge and diligently enforced.

Terminating staff is an area fraught with liability potential. Minimize it by doing the following:

1. Document all meetings with staff members in which you discuss performance dissatisfaction.
2. Document the time and nature of the meeting, and have the staff member sign it.
3. Make repeated attempts to teach them to minister to expected levels of performance.

4. Only one reason given for termination can guarantee iron-clad safety against legal recourse. Simply say, "We're letting you go." Or, "We're going a different direction."

"Look, I'm sending you out like sheep among wolves. Therefore be as shrewd as serpents and as harmless as doves. Because people will hand you over to sanhedrins and flog you in their synagogues, beware of them. You will even be brought before governors and kings because of Me, to bear witness to them and to the nations. But when they hand you over, don't worry about how or what you should speak. For you will be given what to say at that hour, because you are not speaking, but the Spirit of your Father is speaking through you.

"Brother will betray brother to death, and a father his child. Children will even rise up against their parents and have them put to death. You will be hated by everyone because of My name. But the one who endures to the end will be delivered." (Matt. 10:16–22)

Chapter 127

A FINANCIAL POTPOURRI

Here are several small flowers to brighten the garden of your church's financial health:

1. *People give more money in colored envelopes than in plain white envelopes.* Perhaps subconsciously they feel you have cared enough to make the offering special by preparing special envelopes. Perhaps it is that lovely pastel colors such as yellow, pink, green, or blue are more pleasing to the eye. But for whatever reason the fact is that, on average, people give more through softly colored envelopes. Pink seems to be the most commonly used color.

2. *Distribute the envelopes before the offering appeal.* They may be mailed to the home, placed in chair backs, distributed as inserts in the bulletin, at the door, or in the plates, or some or all of the above. However you distribute them, give your people the opportunity to receive their envelopes in advance, see them, touch them, and hold them before the appeal for the offering is made.

3. *When offering envelopes are mailed to church members in advance, don't assume that everyone will bring them back.* Some will. Many will not. Distribute envelopes again and again. If they have brought their envelopes from home, they will simply bypass the opportunity to receive another. Just as church members will give more through pink envelopes than white envelopes, they will also give more with envelopes than without them.

4. *Allow your people to give as they wish.* Frankly, I preferred that every member of Houston's First give one offering check per week to the unified church budget. I recognized, however, that some of them preferred to give only

to debt retirement or a favorite mission project. Giving in any manner is to be encouraged, not discouraged.

5. *Encourage noncash gifts in the form of stocks, bonds, automobiles, notes for property, real estate, beach homes, jewelry, etc.* All of these may be given to the church for tax-donation credit if one prefers them to cash. This, too, should be encouraged, not discouraged. While we prefer cash, it is possible to encourage noncash contributions without discouraging cash.

When this type of contribution is made, the church should translate it into cash as soon as possible. We are not in the real estate business, nor are we in the business of speculating in the stock market. Sell stock gifts the next business day. Convert every noncash contribution into cash at the earliest possible moment after the gift is received.

The person making a noncash contribution has the responsibility of placing a value on the contribution and reporting it to the Internal Revenue Service. The church is not allowed to estimate the value of such gifts and give the individual a receipt for that estimate. It is only allowed to give a receipt that states the nature of the noncash gift. The amount claimed is between the donor and the Internal Revenue Service. In such cases the member is wise to obtain a professional appraisal of the value of the gift for his records.

6. *Make it possible for your people to give online, by credit card, or automatic debit.* This is the twenty-first century.

7. *When a special offering is to be received on a certain day for an important need, write a personal letter to ten or twenty of your largest contributors.* Encourage them to give generously and remind them that the offering will not be successful unless a few of the church's special contributors come through in a special way.

8. *Be an opportunist.* Keep your eyes open. Be alert to things that happen spontaneously in the course of a stewardship campaign. Sharing the news about a $15,000 pledge by a nonmember that actually occurred in the course of a stewardship campaign made an impact on the church.

9. *Report the results.* If the occasion is just right and you are relatively sure a goal is going to be reached—or at least an encouraging amount will be received—ask the finance committee to count the offering during the service. Then make a victory announcement at the close of the service. The people's response will be inspiring.

10. *Consider consolidating various special offerings of the same type into one major offering.* In my denomination churches normally receive three special mission offerings per year in addition to Sunday-by-Sunday offerings for the unified church budget and the Cooperative Program.

In our church, however, rather than three separate weekly mission offerings, we had one big missions month offering. The corporate effect was that by strongly promoting missions annually, rather than laboriously returning to it three times a year, we gave much more to each of the three causes than before.

11. *Mail offering envelopes from the church on a monthly or quarterly basis.* By the time summer and fall arrive, most members have misplaced the offering envelopes they received back in January. A monthly or quarterly mailing of packets of envelopes to church members is a regular but gentle reminder of the church's need and of their obligation.

12. *Give the congregation the opportunity for special, selective giving through the offering envelopes.* Two boxes of envelopes marked "budget" and "building fund" are not enough. A third box is needed labeled "other/specify." This is another way to encourage giving. Why make it hard for people to give? Do everything possible to make it easy!

13. *Install offering boxes on the wall at the rear of the worship center and in the main lobby.*

Part 10

FACILITIES AND OPERATIONS

Chapter 128

RELOCATING
AND LOCATION

P eople cannot attend a church they cannot find, nor will they likely attend one that is hard to find. Three things are important about the public's ability to find you: location, location, location.

Houston's First is blessed, located at the intersection of the two major arteries of the city. The geographical heart of the county crosses on the church property. Each day more than 125,000 cars pass our site. Visibility and accessability to those who pass by your property are important.

If relocation is impossible and you are not satisfied with your present location, do the best you can where you are. Make the buildings look nice. Pave and restripe the parking areas. Advertise the church. Maximize entering and exiting. And be alert to the possibility of purchasing additional land.

Adjoining land is best, particularly if it has frontage on a major road. But it is not out of the question to consider the purchase of land within a short distance of your church and use a shuttle system.

Often businesses with ample parking will either adjoin the church or be located nearby. Virtually all of them will consider entering into a relationship with you that allows you to park on their facility Sunday morning while allowing them weekday access to your parking.

But if your church continues to grow and you are simply out of space, five possibilities are discussed at length elsewhere in this book: (1) multiple services,

(2) buying additional property, (3) relocating, (4) sending your members out to start new missions, or (5) multiple campuses.

The fourth option is what Houston's First chose when no more property was available and multiple services were full and running over.

Nearly one hundred local missions have been established by the church since 1986.

Relocation should not be done because things are not going well in your church and you feel they will get better by moving. Indeed, you might have a short burst of interest from people in the new area, but the probability is that if you're not doing the job where you are, you'll not do much better in the place to which you move.

How many restaurants have you been to that had the reputation of being the best in the city, always packed, and were difficult to find? If the product is exceptional, they'll find you.

If, after serious prayer and discussion with your leaders, you determine more services and the purchase of adjoining property are not feasible, you must at least *consider* the possibility of relocation.

In making the decision to relocate, the church must give serious consideration to the following essentials:

1. Has every other possibility been explored and exhausted?
2. Have we prayed about the matter and determined it to be the will of God?
3. Do the people favor it? It is doubtful that 100 percent of your congregation will affirm any move, but the strong majority of the people must be behind it. I don't like minority rule, and neither do you. But a church that votes 55 percent to 45 percent to relocate needs to question seriously whether it is the thing to do *at that time*. It might be the right decision but the wrong time. Timing is important to God. *When* He does something is as important as *what* He does, and now might not be the *right* time to relocate.
4. Are we prepared to buy an adequate amount of property? Houston's First relocated because the church was landlocked downtown. Unfortunately, the congregation bought only eighteen acres and is landlocked again. God has used this, however, to thrust the church into the mission-planting business. Consider buying twenty to one hundred acres when you relocate.
5. Are you moving to an area with high growth potential? Is the area growing now, and/or will it grow in the future? Don't move to an area the population has already grown past.

6. Does the new location offer high visibility to the public? Proximity to freeways and major arteries is important.
7. What kind of businesses and neighborhoods surround the new location?
8. Is it possible to purchase the corner? If so, do it.
9. Can we afford to pay for the new property?
10. What is the salability of our present property?

Giving thorough and objective consideration to these issues, and taking plenty of time in doing so, assures the church of making the right decision regarding its all-important location.

Chapter 129

THE IMPORTANCE OF PARKING

Your people will never grasp the importance of parking until they get hold of this statement: "The church is the only organization in the world that does not exist for the sake of its members." We are more than willing to endure inconvenience in parking as well as other areas in the life of the church for His sake. The unbeliever who attends your church is not.

For me a ride on a shuttle bus or walk two blocks across a rainy parking lot matters little. But the unbeliever is looking for a reason *not* to go to church. Inconvenience in parking might be just the excuse he needs.

Studies of young adults indicate five things are important to them in choosing a church: relevant sermons, warm spirit, the opportunity to develop personal relationships, great children's ministry, and good parking.

That which may be most difficult to change is the inclination of your people's willingness to sacrifice their comfort in parking for the sake of reaching others. This includes giving money to construct covered drop-off entrances, parking in the extremities of the parking lot, and even riding a shuttle bus.

Close-in parking should always be reserved for guests, seniors, parents with small children, and those with special needs. Parking lots should be well marked and well lighted with greeters on location to escort guests to the nursery, classrooms, or sanctuary.

If you want your church to remain small, buy three or four acres. If you want it to grow, buy thirty or forty acres and cover most of it with good, well-drained, well-lighted, nicely landscaped parking. "It's nothing to us," you say, but it is everything to those you are trying to reach. All other things being equal, prospects will opt for the church with better parking.

Some churches attempt to enhance existing parking by getting more cars in fewer spaces through striping particular areas for compact cars. Usually this doesn't do much good. If it is raining, if it is hot or cold, or if they are running late, people are going to park where they want to park. Big cars will simply take two spaces. They will park in the handicapped zones; they will park in the flower beds and drive over the bushes to park close to the building. My opinion on striping for compact cars? Don't go to the trouble.

As you make projections for future growth, consider this. Allowing for entrances, exits, and parking, you can put 110 to 120 cars per acre. Survey your people to determine how many come per automobile each Sunday, averaging it out over four Sundays. With the large singles population of our city, our average is about 2.2 to 2.3. If your anticipated percentage of singles is less, these numbers can go up to 2.5 or 2.6.

Suppose the number is three. If you realistically believe within the next ten years you can grow to nine hundred people in attendance, you will need three hundred parking spaces or about three acres. Add the number of acres needed for other buildings, allow for future growth, add an additional few, and you have the amount of land you need.

I strongly urge you to consider the purchase of every piece of adjoining real estate that comes up for sale. First Baptist Church in Orlando, Florida, has one hundred fifty acres. Bellevue Baptist Church in Memphis, Tennessee, has over three hundred. Often costs will be prohibitive. We quit purchasing available adjoining land when it went to one million dollars an acre.

When this happens, only two possibilities exist: run shuttle buses to other lots or build parking garages.

The wisdom of building parking garages is, in part, determined by entrance and exit points from your church property. If they are limited, they may only compound the problem. In such cases rent or buy shuttle buses to run to other available parking areas as nearby as possible.

Shuttle buses should ideally be driven by one person and "captained" by another. Think how nice it would be on your shuttle bus next Sunday morning if a person with a warm, vibrant personality greeted all riders as they boarded, called each person by name, gave everyone a "worship guide," and told them about the events of the day.

Just for fun, go to Disney World in Florida. Study the shuttle system and learn from the best. And why not have shuttles with upbeat music, free candy, and Mickey Mouse (oops, make that Moses) painted on the side.

Have cool shuttles. Make some lemonade out of the lemon of parking problems.

Real estate, parking garages, and shuttle buses cost money. But most costly of all is the decision not to invest in good parking.

Chapter 130

BUILDING AND GROUNDS

The word *church* in the Bible has two meanings, the church universal and the local congregation. Neither refers to physical buildings in which you gather, but the local church needs a place to meet. That place should be well located, functional, comfortable, attractive, and well kept. You may have the most wonderful services within the walls of your sanctuary, but large numbers of people will never come in and experience them if they can't get past those rundown, outdated buildings on the outside.

Whether your building is metal or wood, brick or marble, large or small, you should do everything possible to maximize its appearance. In many of the towns and villages I drive through, church signs on the edge of town have faded and crumbling paint. On vacation I always look for a church to visit. I often seek out denominations other than my own to expand and enrich my own worship experience. But I never stop at a church with a crummy sign or rundown buildings.

The steps may be wooden, but they can be in good repair. The lawn may be small, but it can be well manicured. The sidewalk may be old, but the holes can be filled.

Put the book down for a few minutes. Walk around your church. Look in the closets. Check out the bathrooms. Go into the nurseries and Sunday school classes. Is the paint peeling? Are the floors unpolished? Are the windows broken and the trash uncollected? Are the Formica countertops from the 1940s? Do the carpets need replacing?

If you think people are going to live in a beautiful, well-kept home six days a week and go to a crummy-looking church building on the seventh, think again. It doesn't take a lot of money to buy fifty gallons of paint or a pickup load of new boards. It isn't difficult to plant flowers. It's not costly to wax the floors. Your church facility might not be valued on the real estate market at more than $50,000, but it can and should "look like a million."

Drive around your town and look at some other churches. What is your first impression of each? Do you like it? Does its condition say, "We care. We think the house of the Lord is important. You'll like it here. Come on in"?

Years ago I heard a woman singing on the radio. Her voice was off-key and her guitar out of tune. As she began, she said, "You know, folks, this here ain't gonna be too good, but just anything's good enough for my Lord."

Somehow, I don't believe that. Nothing is good enough for our Lord unless it's the best. It should be done right if it is done at all. To fail to do our best is to dishonor Jesus Christ.

Build a line item for "upkeep and building repair" into your church budget, and keep things fixed up and "in the pink." In Houston's First, we had a properties committee that worked with our systems manager, maintenance people, and grounds keepers to oversee the maintenance and repair of the facilities. It was a serious matter with us and one to which we gave much attention. I considered our "building and grounds" or "properties" committee to be among the most important committees of the church.

As your church grows, you will need more and more specialty help. Our church had a full-time painter; electrician; systems manager for telephones, computers, etc.; a kitchen crew; a maintenance crew; and a grounds crew. Your church might not yet be at the place where you need such a large staff, but employ people who really care about the beauty and efficiency of your facilities. To bring honor to God's house is to bring honor to Him.

Special consideration should be given to the lobby. Hopefully, it's large. If not, find a place nearby that is and create a homey, casual Starbucks type atmosphere. Lots of couches, free coffee, great fellowship, conversation, and laughter. People love it. Don't hurry your people through the morning schedule. Don't herd them like cattle, let them relax and enjoy the fellowship. The expression, "my church home," should express exactly that.

Chapter 131

YOUR PHYSICAL ENVIRONMENT

The comfort, sound, lights, colors, and room arrangement of the building in which you worship are important. Most things are obvious. Adequate offices, well-located classrooms, and ample restroom facilities are important parts of good facilities. But to the preacher, what surrounds him in the worship service is most important. Let's consider four areas.

Size and Shape

Too many sanctuaries are overbuilt. A one-thousand-seat worship center with three morning services is better than a four-thousand-seat sanctuary with three thousand in one service. And remember, people want options.

Construction costs, utility costs, maintenance, and, most importantly, options for the worshipers—all these play an important part in determining the size of the worship center. Great worship centers that seat eight to ten thousand people dot the American landscape. But I think the wave of the future is smaller buildings with multiple uses.

The traditional church building is rectangular. Modern church architecture, however, follows the rule of thumb, "more people, closer in."

Sloping the worship center forward, bringing the balcony closer, expanding the sides, and other creative options abound. But having the maximum number of people as close to the front as possible is important.

The attraction of the new professional football and baseball stadiums across America is the proximity of the people to the action. I never understood the inadequacy of our own Houston Astrodome until I attended a baseball game at The Ball Park in Arlington. What excitement! You will have to experience it to understand it. The stadium is so designed that you feel you are part of the game. I can't wait to get back there for another.

In 1972, we set out to relocate our church and build a new worship center in a new location. Ideas were solicited from the people. Suggestions regarding everything from restrooms to colors poured in from the congregation, and many were used. I made only one: Build an auditorium conducive to giving an invitation. We now have a worship center about which everything physically and psychologically says, "Come on down."

Our architect went back through history and came up with a Roman amphitheater style that is marvelous. The lower floor is sloped downward toward the front, with side balconies as wide as the rear balcony. Everything flows together to a common front. The feeling is created that whether upstairs or down, you are part of the same congregation.

Pulpit

Preaching from a manuscript, preaching without notes; standing still, moving around; stationery microphone, portable microphone—all these factors help determine the size and style of the pulpit. Everything should be done to keep the pulpit from becoming a barrier to good communication from pulpit to pew. The popularity of conversational communication over oratory has increased the popularity of preaching with no pulpit at all. If a pulpit is to be used, it should not be one the preacher "gets into" but "stands behind," and it should be "just what our pastor wants." And consider the significance of a centered pulpit in contrast with Roman Catholicism which makes the "Mass" the visual centerpiece.

Sound

The church is in the business of communication. The apostle Paul asked, "How can they hear without a preacher?" (Rom. 10:14).

I ask, "How shall they hear without a good sound system?"

Through the years I have probably preached in a thousand different church buildings in America. I have heard only a handful of really fine sound systems. The pastor might be a great speaker, but of what value is that if he cannot be heard? *Invest in a good sound system. Borrow the money. Pay it out. Do what you must,* **but get the best**.

The right place for the speakers is immediately above the pulpit. One speaker is never enough. A cluster of several is required. Sound technicians will determine the right amount and quality of mixers, tweeters, woofers, etc., but get help and do it right.

To get the best sound company in the city, find who does the sound for the rock concerts in your area. Hire the company that does the sound when the bands come through, and you will have the best.

The goal of a sound system is "presence." The Reliant Football Stadium in Houston seats seventy-two thousand. The speaker system sounds like someone seated next to you is speaking conversationally.

Lights

Well-placed, modern, uniform lighting is equally important. Dimming capability in various places in the worship center is important. Brighten up your auditorium with good colors and bright lights. It is a great honor to Him who is the Light of the world.

Chapter 132

SECURITY

God's loving arms protect His people, often through human instrumentalities. In the church we are that instrumentality. As leaders of the congregation, we are responsible to ensure the safety of the people and their possessions to the fullest extent of our ability.

The initial implementation of safety procedures for your church begins as the people enter your parking lot. Policemen and volunteer car parkers add to safety, both perceived and real, as people approach your church.

Tragically, recent events have again emphasized the vulnerability of even the smallest churches in our land. Protection and assistance must be visible and efficient. One additional officer or more inside the church gives an additional *sense* of security as well as *real* security.

Someone in the worship center should be designated to keep an eye on the service. In a larger church more are needed—some in uniform, some in plain clothes. Hopefully, you will spend your entire ministry without incident. But precautionary measures, which prevent just one, are well worth it.

This person or persons should have the ability to communicate electronically with an officer in an instant. In the event of a problem, ushers should be trained to go instantly to the assistance of the "inside watcher" who will be the first to respond. Occasionally a person may be so disruptive to a service he or she must be removed from your facilities. Your policemen will be trained to handle and enforce such situations. At this writing Houston's First has fifteen such officers, including traffic officers.

In larger cities and congregations, an added sense of security may be achieved by the presence of one or two designated persons who continually drive their cars through the parking lots at peak attendance hours. A simple, battery-operated, yellow flashing light on the roof of that car will suffice. Vandalism and theft will stop immediately, as will a sense of insecurity by your people.

Safety for worshippers as they leave the property is also a high priority. After the services there is a high concentration of automobiles exiting the property in a small amount of time. Again, one or more officers should be employed to expedite the flow of traffic, as every church parking lot exits to a public street. In some cases the city traffic department can be petitioned for traffic lights at your main exits. Officers may then hold those lights on green, waving through large numbers of automobiles as they leave the church parking lots.

Officers may also be of great assistance in the event of threats to the pastor. High-profile ministers and preaching on controversial subjects are connected to such threats. This problem may increase because of increasing hostility toward Christianity in our world. There are two subjects, which shall remain unnamed, that have generated at least six such threats in my ministry. Inform the officers in such cases. They are well qualified to take it from there.

The medical security of your congregation is equally important. Again, someone in your worship center should be prepared to identify any medical problem and contact security instantly. Our people are prepared with stretchers, oxygen, and other first-aid assistance. Seizures, strokes, heart attacks, and accidents are not uncommon in public gatherings.

Through the years I was proud of the professional manner in which our volunteer leaders and staff handled these situations. A doctor, paramedic, or nurse should be on call at every service. Consider a church committee to coordinate securing the medical welfare of your congregation. An incident that saves only one life is more than worth the investment of time and preparation.

The securing of possessions is also important. Purses left in choir rooms, desks left unlocked, offerings left unsecured—these things are trouble waiting to happen.

Protect the valuables of your people, but also protect them against temptation as well. One incident, improperly handled, can cause your church great damage through the negative publicity it receives. A word to the wise is sufficient.

Growing up in church in the 1950s was a lot different from today. Churches across the nation left their front doors open so a wanderer could come in to seek refuge from his troubles in the house of the Lord. Today only a few churches in America leave their doors open. Crime is a cruel reality even for the church, and you must address this growing issue.

Always practice the "two adult" rule that stipulates youth and children are never left alone with just one adult. In case of an emergency, one adult can secure help while the other assists in the emergency.

Tell your people that the worship service will never have a drama that includes violence. Explain that guns, knives, and other tools of violence will never be part of a worship experience, and a church drama will never surprise the congregation with *shock and awe.*

Chapter 133

FOOD SERVICES

E arly Christian history makes clear the importance of Christian fellowship to the people of God. Within the New Testament community, the practice of breaking of bread from house to house, so often mentioned in the Gospels, likely refers to the Lord's Supper. But fellowship around good food is certainly biblical.

Today's version of church fellowship has its roots in the New Testament community. An unbroken thread runs from Jesus feeding the disciples a breakfast of bread and fish at the Sea of Galilee to today's "all-day singing and dinner on the ground" at the country church.

Christian fellowship around eating together is here to stay, and well it should be. From Sunday school fellowships to church wide ice cream socials, God's people like to "meet and eat." The growing church will, however, have needs far beyond those which can be met by the traditional "potluck supper."

Even the smallest congregation needs a volunteer church hostess who has likely been in charge of cooking and coordinating church dinners since the days of Noah's ark. In those rare cases in which no such person exists, seek out the volunteer services of a good church hostess. This person will have a warm personality, good cooking skills, and be a gifted administrator. Hospitality is one of God's gifts to the church, and someone in your church has it.

Enlisting and coordinating volunteer workers for those weekly church suppers will be as important as getting the seasoning "just right" in the meat loaf. One of the wisest investments a church can make is to include some level of monthly financial reimbursement for this type of person.

As the church grows, consideration should be given to the addition of a food services director to the staff. Appropriate hourly kitchen staff can be added part-time and/or full-time under the direction of the food services director as church membership grows.

Coordinating the calendar of activities is always done with the involvement of the food services director. Many factors go into church programming. Such matters as time, place, date, public-address system, lights, chairs, tables, advertising, ordering, cooking, serving, and cleaning require the attention of one person with responsibility for coordinating all of them. An uncoordinated church calendar that gives too little attention to even the slightest of these details can leave your church programs in shambles.

As with other important positions, the food services director will be interviewed, employed by, and made accountable to the personnel committee, or the food services committee, and the appropriate staff member. That person will generally be the church administrator and/or minister of education.

Some churches choose to outsource food services. The reason may be such things as additional food service needs for a school or day care housed within your church facilities or insufficient food preparation areas. Regardless of the sophistication of your food preparation and distribution system, volunteers are always appropriate.

Our Wednesday night church supper was high priority. Hundreds of our people came straight from work and then went directly from the evening meal to various kinds of education, music, and mission meetings. At each of these Wednesday night dinners—the centerpiece of our food-service ministry—a different adult Sunday school class volunteered to serve. Not only was money saved, but the opportunity to be of service was afforded and fellowship enhanced.

In the integration of the food-services ministry into the life of the church, accurate records must be maintained. Requests for food service for a Sunday school class dinner, for example, must include all pertinent information about type of food, numbers, paper plates or china, etc. These should be forms written in triplicate—one copy for the administrator's office, one for the food services director, and one for the properties director, who will be responsible for setup and cleanup. Forms should be completed in writing a month in advance when possible. All things should be done decently and in order. Our Lord is not the author of confusion.

The food and fellowship aspect of your church is important. Your people will be coming from various walks of life, representing many races, geographical locations, socioeconomic statuses, and ages. In Christ's church they find common meeting ground. Here everyone is equal.

Relaxed times to get acquainted and come to know and care about one another are essential. In planning to build this dimension into the life of your congregation, never forget the importance of breaking bread together.

And make it first class.

Part 11

OTHER IMPORTANT MATTERS

Chapter 134

ORDAINING
AND LICENSING

Each denomination acknowledges God's call and legitimacy of its ministers in its own way. In many churches the first step is licensing the minister, to be followed subsequently by ordination. In Southern Baptist life both of these steps are done by the local church. In other traditions they are often performed at the denominational level.

In a Southern Baptist church, a license means, "You tell us God has called you into full-time Christian ministry, and we believe you." An ordination means, "We have had time to observe you, and we also believe God has called you." The first says we believe *you* believe it; the latter says *we* believe it.

After a person has made public his certainty of a call to the ministry, he will petition the church for a license. In Baptist life a license is primarily a pat on the back, a "God bless you; we're behind you; now go prove yourself."

Ordaining a minister, however, is different from licensing him. In many denominations seminary graduation and proven service are necessary for ordination. In Southern Baptist churches proven service is normally required; seminary completion is not. Ordination at the hands of a Southern Baptist church means the ordained person may perform marriage ceremonies as well as the ordinances of the church—the Lord's Supper and baptism. Ordination and license certificates should be registered with the appropriate government agency for the marriage ceremonies performed to be legal in most states.

While models vary from denomination to denomination, both license and ordination certificates may be revoked by the ordaining church for reasons it deems appropriate. These would normally include such things as immoral behavior, uncooperative spirit, or aberrant theology.

The Southern Baptist Convention has no official position on the issue of either licensing or ordination. Even if it did, it would not be binding on the autonomous, self-governing, local church. Many Southern Baptist churches do not ordain divorced men as deacons or preachers. Some do so. (See my chapter on deacons and divorce.)

Generally, women in ministry are licensed but not ordained in Southern Baptist life. The position of most Southern Baptist churches is that a woman may serve in any position except senior pastor. I concur. "But I do not allow a woman to teach or to have authority over a man" (1 Tim. 2:12).

The gifts and calling of God are without repentance. God doesn't change His mind about planning to use us. He intended to do so before we were born. God told the prophet Jeremiah, "I chose you before I formed you in the womb; I set you apart before you were born. I appointed you a prophet to the nations" (Jer. 1:5).

The ordination process of the church is an *earthly* expression of its affirmation of the *eternal* ordination of God upon the life of the minister. Let the ordained minister respect the high level of confidence placed in him by the ordaining church that affirms his call from God. If the time should ever come that the minister no longer holds to the doctrines and standards of the ordaining church, he should voluntarily relinquish his license or ordination.

Ordination services are normally held on Sunday afternoon to facilitate the participation of other Southern Baptist pastors on the ordaining council. It includes:

- Recommendation of the ordaining council (preceded by examination of the candidate)
- Scripture
- Music
- Prayer
- Candidate's testimony
- Ordination Sermon
- Laying on of hands

The ordination certificate is signed by the pastor, clerk of the ordaining council, and other ministers. Both ordination and license certificates are available at LifeWay Christian Stores.

Chapter 135

THE CHURCH LIBRARY

B e advised: the above name is not in vogue today. The new name is "media center" or "resource center," and it's about a whole lot more than books. A well-stocked, well-run resource center is a valuable tool for the personal enrichment of the congregation. The persons who impact tomorrow are those who write or record their ideas today. I have a high regard for the value of church libraries. Thankfully, men and women of noble character and keen insight are still writing today.

We are the benefactors of the legacy of great books left by those who have gone before. Imagine life without the writings of Charles Sheldon, Andrew Murray, C. S. Lewis, Oswald Chambers, Charles Spurgeon, and others, not to mention today's many outstanding writers. I could not have pastored my church without the benefit of commentaries and word studies of those who have gone before.

In our church we have the benefit of a highly dedicated and competent full-time resource center staff. But virtually every small church has, among its members, a gifted person who will gladly volunteer or who can be paid a part-time salary.

Don't see the church librarian as a stuffy old lady. This stereotype is a gross injustice. He or she is a bright and productive person whose value to the kingdom of God is incalculable.

Our church is blessed with a large, two-story resource center of approximately five thousand square feet. It contains fifteen thousand books, not to mention tapes, films, videos, and CDs. Our resource center staff advises pastor, teacher, and laity where to look for resources, what to look for, and then help them do it. They are organized, trained, disciplined, knowledgeable, thorough, and most helpful.

During the course of writing this book, I called Nancy Squires, our resource center director, at least a hundred times to look up something for me. Within ten minutes she was back on the phone with the answer.

Our resource center has several reading areas with couches, upholstered chairs, and good lighting. Among my greatest joys are the two children's reading areas. Here the children sit on stuffed sheep and big floor pillows and read children's books or watch children's videos in different areas appropriate to their age group.

There are also weekly children's reading times when parents can bring their children to hear a story. Our resource center is widely used and greatly contributes to the spiritual life of our church.

The resource center also administers the ministry of films, DVDs, videos, and CDs. A wide selection of each is available. It is also the responsibility of this ministry to record the weekly sermons of the pastor on audiotape, video, and CD, and offer them for sale at a nominal price to church members and the public.

Our resource center director/librarian was also an unspeakable value to me personally. She regularly did research for me. Two or three hours on a difficult part of the sermon with her help meant two or three hours freed up for ministry for me. And she was good at it, both in books and on the Internet. What would have taken me an hour or more, she could do in five to ten minutes.

Whether through print, audio, video, television, the Internet, or any other means, it is important to disseminate God's Word. Give attention to developing an excellent media center in your church. Somewhere in your congregation a gifted person is waiting to administer it, and a room is available to house it. There's no better time to find it than right now.

"But as for you, continue in what you have learned and firmly believed. You know those who taught you, and you know that from childhood you have known the sacred Scriptures, which are able to give you wisdom for salvation through faith in Christ Jesus. All Scripture is inspired by God and is profitable for teaching, for rebuking, for correcting, for training in righteousness" (2 Tim. 3:14–16).

Chapter 136

THE CHURCH SCHOOL

Houston's First was instrumental in starting three schools in our city. Houston Christian High School was begun in cooperation with First Methodist, First Presbyterian, Grace Presbyterian, Spring Branch Community, and First Nazarene. Each church was pastored by a warmhearted, conservative, Bible-believing pastor; and it was an experience of great joy. We agreed on an extremely tight, conservative doctrinal statement of faith at our first meeting. Today beautiful facilities stand on forty-five acres, housing Houston's largest Christian high school.

First Baptist Academy is a beautiful six-million-dollar kindergarten through eighth grade school located on our home campus. Enrollment is approximately four hundred students.

First Kids, our child development center, has approximately two hundred children and is located within our current facility, while First Baptist Academy was a new addition to it. The child development center is for children six weeks through four years of age.

Few experiences have been more rewarding in my ministry than being a part of starting these schools. From six weeks through the senior year of high school, a child can be taught the Word of God five days a week in a classroom setting through the ministry of our church. Let's talk about that.

American education is built on three primary foundations: public education, private and parochial education, and homeschooling. As a church we fully support all three.

No one inspired me more than the young people, teachers, and administrators who were being salt and light in the public education system. We recognized them, honored them, encouraged them, and prayed for them daily. Many Christians who work in public schools do so at a great price.

Private Christian education will continue, however, to be more important with each passing year. Our country is losing its soul, partly because God has been removed from the public classroom. Someone asked, "Where was God in the massacre at Littleton High School?" Unfortunately, God wasn't allowed in and hasn't been since the Supreme Court so decreed in 1962.

Homeschooling is growing at an awesome rate.

But the subject at hand is the beginning of private Christian schools by your church. If God leads you in this direction, be aware that start-up costs are high. City and state ordinances governing fire codes and other safety issues for children are many and strict.

Schools that exist within your facilities and share Sunday school classroom space can create problems of coordinating desks, cabinets, posters, scheduling, etc. Occasional tension between Sunday school teachers and schoolteachers using the same space is to be expected.

Requirements for weekday care exceed those for Sunday-only occupancy. There are state requirements for licensing as well, such as the training and quality of your teachers and director. He or she must be licensed by the state. This means paying a salary for a person who has paid the price to become qualified to do this kind of job. Good consultants are available, who will advise you regarding the ramifications of starting this or any other kind of educational ministry.

Schools should never be started only to teach children. They should also be started to offer an opportunity of ministry to both child and parent which may, in turn, present an avenue of entry into the kingdom and the church.

Don't start a school and forget it. Walk through the halls. Meet the parents. Be involved with the children. Eat lunch with them. Go to their plays. Pick up the little ones and become pastor to the school. Not only will you enrich their lives and offer ministry to their families, but many will also one day choose you as their pastor.

The church may be faced with hiring teachers at a rate higher than public school teachers with less financial ability to do so, because Southern Baptist churches and schools do not accept financial support from the government. Many excellent teachers are willing to teach in a private setting because they feel called of God to do so. But know that there will be these kinds of difficult issues. Confront them before you open the doors of your new school

Teachers in Christian schools must be Christian. They should also love to teach, love the Lord, and truly love children. A child should be encouraged not ridiculed, commended not humiliated. The Bible should be taught regularly in the classroom with at least weekly chapel services conducted. In Houston Christian High School, every teacher is additionally committed to personally discipling a specified number of students.

Consider making the investment of time and money required to begin a good Christian school. And be warned, all Christian schools tend to drift to the left. Christian schools don't remain Christian by accident. Diligence must be constant to keep the school true to "the faith that was delivered to the saints once for all (Jude 3)."

Here the trustees are the key.

Chapter 137

HOMESCHOOLING

The American educational system was largely built on four institutions of higher learning: Harvard, Yale, Princeton, and William and Mary. Their founding charters declare unapologetic commitment to the Word of God and the lordship of Jesus Christ.

Things have changed.

Colossians 1:17 says, "By Him all things hold together"—hold together. Schools, like nations and families, fall apart without Jesus Christ. Music, media, classrooms, and peer pressure virtually overwhelm even the most devout Christian families and their children, and this stressor is generally centered in seven intense hours called "school."

The Christian family is confronted with the decision: public school, private school, or homeschool. The good news is, most private schools are Christian schools. The bad news is they are beyond the financial reach of most families. Two options remain: public school or homeschool.

Public education today is presented in an academic environment of secular humanism, a secular worldview, evolution, and a total disregard for sexual abstinence while allowing full tolerance of the gay and lesbian lifestyle.

Regardless of their commitment to homeschooling, believers should highly value the ministry of Christian faculty and administrators attempting to be salt and light in the spiritually hostile environment of today's public education system. Prayer, encouragement, and support for them should be at the top of the list for every church.

Serious issues must be faced in the decision whether to homeschool children:

- What does God want for my children?
- Am I truly qualified to teach them?
- Can my home provide the required structure and discipline?
- Is the family in agreement?
- What are the financial costs?
- Are support groups, combines, athletic leagues, arts, and other systems readily accessible with other homeschoolers in my community?

Perhaps the biggest question in the list above which a parent must answer is, Is this really for me? An easily distracted, undisciplined, unstructured parent needs to think twice about homeschooling children. It is much more difficult than you imagine.

Some children have been spiritually shipwrecked in the forum of public education. Some have stood tall and strong, impacting their peers for Christ. They are the result of homes where parents paid the price and had the discipline to build strong children at home before they entered the public school system. Either way, there is a price to pay and major parental responsibility to assume. Again, it is a decision only the parent can make under the leadership of the Holy Spirit.

The position of the church in all of this is obvious. The pastor must encourage his people to seek the Lord and teach them how to do so in this and every important decision. The responsible pastor will give full respect and support not only to these three means of education but also to the parents who choose one over the other two, regardless of their decision.

Chapter 138

THE USE OF RADIO

We live in a day of the greatest opportunity to communicate the gospel the world has ever known. Opportunities abound. Facebook, texting, e-mail, Internet, radio, and television are only the tip of the iceberg in emerging electronic technology.

In the day of state-of-the-art, super-tech communication, don't overlook radio. That men such as Chuck Swindoll and James Dobson choose radio is significant.

There are many reasons for this, not the least of which is the high cost of television. You can probably have a daily radio program for less money than the cost of a weekly television program. By all means, use television to advertise your church and televise your services if you are financially able to do so. But don't ignore radio.

Radio is inexpensive. Radio is everywhere. Radio is readily accessible. Television sets are rarely in automobiles and never in the front seat. Radios, conversely, are in virtually every automobile.

How can we say enough for the rich ministry of Christian radio? Knowing I can turn the dial to any of several Christian radio stations in Houston is a great blessing. How often have I been listening to the news—murders, fires, burglaries, rapes, pressure of world events—and said, "Who needs it?" Then with a touch of the dial, I changed my environment to a beautiful song of praise to our Lord Jesus.

Three uses of radio may be within the reach of your church budget.

The first is spot announcements. Being on the radio, like being on television, spreads the gospel and advertises your church and its events.

It also gives a good sense to your congregation that what you are about is important. Your people take pride in the fact their church spreads the gospel through radio and television and does it well.

Spot announcements can be purchased inexpensively when contracted in large quantities. Fifteen seconds is enough—thirty seconds at the most.

Keep it happy, bright, and short. Don't preach. Just give listeners the facts about your church and/or the event you are publicizing. Purchase spots in drive time. More people are in their cars between 6:30 and 8:30 a.m. and 4:30 and 6:30 p.m. than any other time of day. The increased cost for an ad time during these hours will be well worth it.

Another possibility is a daily radio program. Many local churches now have three- to five-minute programs every day of the week. To tell the truth, most say it just about as well as they would in fifteen or twenty minutes.

If you commit yourself to a daily radio program, be prepared to pay the price in time and preparation. If you want me to talk on any subject for an hour, I'm ready to ramble. If I have to say it in three or four minutes, it will take me a while to get ready. And don't take the time to edit your sermons down to five minutes. Get an editor. Once again, someone in your congregation is just waiting to help.

The third use of radio is the live or delayed broadcast of the weekly services of your church. For more than thirty years, we broadcast our Sunday morning services live on the largest Christian radio station in the city as well as an early tape-delayed broadcast on the NBC radio affiliate. If possible, broadcast your service live. There's something exciting and special about that.

Above all, move the service along and don't let the music portion of the broadcast drag, or you will lose your audience. Make announcements to your congregation *before* or *after* the broadcast. And be certain to get the entire message on the air. It is extremely frustrating to your radio audience for you to go off the air the last two or three minutes of the message.

I love radio. Worldwide ministries have been built through radio. Undoubtedly, that was at least part of what Jesus had in mind when He said, "This good news of the kingdom will be proclaimed in all the world. And then the end will come" (Matt. 24:14).

Chapter 139

THE USE OF TELEVISION

Let me put it simply: If you can get on television, do it. The advantages are obvious. A few words to the wise, however, are in order. The television ministry of your church will be costly and time-consuming. Often it can be done only at the sacrifice of other valid ministries. It should not become the tail that wags the dog. I know a few churches that have a television ministry. I know a lot of television ministries that have a church.

You might need to employ a part- or full-time, paid technician or director. But the best service is performed by committed, trained members of your congregation who volunteer their time and talents as a ministry to the Lord and His church.

Someone in your congregation has interest and experience. A small amount of time and money may be wisely invested in getting them the increased training they need to do the job for you. Backup personnel must always be available for cameramen, directors, and others who may not be available on a given Sunday.

A prerecorded and edited production is normally in order if you intend to distribute your program to stations out of your area. But there is something special about a live Sunday morning telecast from your church to your city.

Frankly, I feel too many pastors may suffer from delusions of grandeur and are on nationwide television who would be better off simply broadcasting their morning worship services to their own city. A few television preachers may be worthy of national exposure. But are we doing more harm than good with hundreds of less-than-exceptional preachers filling the airwaves?

When we began televising our services in 1971, we were one of only two local television ministries in our city. Through the 1970s and mid-1980s, we determined by survey that fully 30 percent of our congregation had joined our church because they first began watching our telecasts.

Due to costs we went off the air for two years. But we entered the market again on an even larger and more prestigious station in the early 1990s. After two years of broadcasting on one of the largest stations in the South, nothing happened. I could not point to one person who joined our church during those twenty-four months because of television. There were, I believe, two reasons.

The first was an oversaturation of the television market with second-rate presentations, creating an increasing tendency to "turn it all off." But the second and perhaps most important reason may be laid at the feet of certain televangelists:

- Constant haranguing for money
- Claiming of miracles
- Bizarre, carnivalistic acts performed in the name of Jesus
- Exposure of the moral character of *some* televangelists

Five years before I retired, we pulled the plug on television. We began to put that money into buildings and staff, radio and missions, benevolence, outreach, and religious education. For us it was the right decision. God will lead you to yours.

Give your decision serious prayer and thought. But let me say frankly that television is not for every church or every pastor. Said another way, not every preacher should be on television. If you ask Him with a humble and sincere heart, our Lord will show you the way in this important decision.

Be aware that few unbelievers watch Christian television networks. In choosing a Christian network, we should honestly confront the question, Are we only preaching to the choir?

Try to purchase time on a local, secular station. And avoid the 5:30 and 6:00 Sunday morning times when no one is watching. Are you reaching people or stroking your ego?

And like it or not, you're competing with a secular society. It had better not look corny, homemade, or cheap, or you may do your church more harm than good.

Chapter 140

NEW MEDIA

New media is a term encompassing the latest in digital, computerized, networked information and communication technologies. Most are digital, often having characteristics of being manipulated, networkable, dense, compressible, interactive, and impartial. They include the Internet, Web sites, computer multimedia, online radio, online video, IM, social networking such as MySpace, Facebook, Word Process blog, LinkedIn, Twitter, computer games, CD-ROMs, and DVDs. They do not include television, traditional radio, feature films, magazines, books, or newspapers.

Initiating new approaches to make ancient truth more accessible is a time-sensitive issue in today's technology drenched and globally connected community. Television is entering a new era, subjugated to the popularity of the Internet and other major transitions occurring in the broadcast industry.

As of April 2010, five billion videos are streamed every month. Forty percent of all video consumption is online. Fifteen hours of video are uploaded every minute. Eighty-three percent of people under twenty-five watch some, most, or all of their TV programming online.

YouTube has become a monster influence on our culture with nearly ten million people visiting the site every day. The type of videos they watch and with which they interact has a huge impact on the way they view the world.

Unhindered access to anything and everything, created by anybody with a message, means one individual can have unprecedented influence when their videos go viral. And that one person should be you and your church. When the Holy Spirit inspired the apostle Paul to become "all things to all people, so that [he] may by every possible means save some" (1 Cor. 9:22). He foreknew the world today. Every possible means, means precisely that.

Never before has God placed within the hands of the church such total access to every person of every religion on every square inch of the earth. When Jesus said, "Into all the world," who could have envisioned the world of cyberspace and new media? Today such creative, cutting-edge ministries as MXTV are doing precisely that with overwhelming response. Join them. Get out there. It's where the world is today, and it's sitting right on your lap. If you can't do it, you've got a church full of teenagers that can. They would love to help you share Jesus with the world.

Chapter 141

PUBLICITY AND ADVERTISING

People cannot go to an event, attend an activity, or buy a product they do not know exists. The importance of good publicity cannot be overstated. The first Christmas angel publicized tidings of great joy.

The two-by-two, person-to-person witnessing taught by our Lord cannot be improved upon and is not inconsistent with mass publicity. As bombers soften the terrain for the foot soldier, so publicity through mass media makes people more receptive to a personal invitation to attend your church.

"Oh yes, I've heard of your church. I'll try to come," is more likely to be heard than, "Where's that again?" when you publicize.

Bumper stickers do little good. They're too small and move too fast. If used, they should contain only three or four words.

Attractive wrought iron signs in church members' yards are nice. Radio spots not exceeding thirty seconds with repeated exposure are good.

But don't quote Scripture, and don't preach sermons in spot announcements. Take a few seconds and get to the point.

Billboards continue to be an effective means of publicity. They should be lighted, on major freeways, colorful, on the right side of the road, and not cluttered with too many words.

Brochures should be done professionally. Do not distribute homemade invitations to anything. The world does everything first class and so must you.

Free publicity is often available. Most newspapers and virtually all Christian radio stations will carry announcements about your church's upcoming activities when neatly typed, well-written, concise reports are sent to them well in advance of the event.

Good newspaper ads should contain pictures and plenty of white space. Again, don't clutter. Get to the point and always purchase a right-hand page location in the main news section, if possible.

Creative TV advertising is excellent, but the cost is often prohibitive. A live Sunday morning radio broadcast is a good idea.

Get a slogan and get one that is justified and does not belittle any other church. Your publicity should emphasize what you can do for people, *not* what they can do for you. "Come help us grow" is not the message you want to convey.

Make your publicity truthful and make it positive. And don't expect it to pay off immediately. The effect of advertising is *cumulative*. It takes time to produce results, but it is well worth the wait.

Weekly church newspapers are virtually nonexistent. The Internet is the place to consider today; 87 percent of young adults read the newspaper online.

Many daily newspapers are struggling because of easy accessibility of information on the Internet. Many publish the full newspaper on the Internet as well as the traditional newspaper.

If you have a weekly church newspaper, offer the people the option of receiving it by snail mail or online.

> "How beautiful on the mountains are the feet of him the herald, who proclaims peace, who brings good news of things, who proclaims salvation; who says Zion, 'Your God reigns!'" (Isa. 52:7)

Chapter 142

Preparing for Retirement

Retirement is a good thing. Yes, I know, Moses didn't retire, or Elijah or Paul, but then they didn't have to make hospital calls, go to deacon's meetings, return phone calls, and counsel the same twenty people four hundred times. Oh yes, and fight the Houston traffic two or three hours every day. Retirement is great. Don't dread it. Get ready and enjoy it.

Life holds many wonderful serendipities. Hopefully by now you've learned what's really important in life. If you've got the Lord, your family, your friends, and your health, you've got it all. Everything else is just stuff. New car, old car, little house, big house . . . no matter, stuff is just stuff.

As a young pastor the most important thing in financial preparation is to start early.

- 10 percent to the Lord (or more)
- 10 percent in well-secured savings (don't speculate)
- 80 percent to budget

And don't touch that savings. By the time you reach retirement age, it will be huge. Be dead sure you're on track to retire with your home debt-free and everything else as well. Talk to a financial planner. Take the advice of people like Dave Ramsey. Totally debt-free by sixty-five or before is an absolute must.

If you have to downsize your home to do it, then do it. Your kids will be grown, and gone with homes and families of their own before you know it. Don't end up with too many extra empty bedrooms.

Retirement is great. It's a time to get up when you want, fish, golf, love on those grandkids, and just hang out. Look forward to it.

And don't get depressed because you feel unneeded. You've been faithful. Enjoy the fruit of it and find your security not in how often you are invited to preach but in who you are in Him.

Run errands with the wife of your youth. The richness of your marriage will be greater than you imagine. And look forward to mentoring young pastors. God will bring some into your life. Be a pastor to the greater kingdom of God beyond your church; it's wonderful.

And when? It doesn't have to be at sixty-five or sixty-six. It can be before. It can be after.

My friend Damon Shook of the great Champion Forest Baptist Church in Houston said, "The highlight of my ministry was the annual staff planning retreat where we cast the vision for the next year. I knew if the time ever came that vision was no longer there, it was time to retire." It came.

Today he finds great fulfillment in helping his son in his young and growing church. George Harris of the great Castle Hills Church in San Antonio enjoys the same experience with his son.

I knew when it was the right time for me. Three factors converged after thirty years at Houston's First:

1. After thirty years of growth, the church began to plateau.
2. My passion to minister to the greater kingdom of God was matched by an amazing increase in opportunities to do just that.
3. The calendar turned 2000.
4. I turned sixty-five.
5. My tenure at Houston's First turned thirty.

Retirement is great. Get ready and enjoy! Now I have time to write really good books. Like this one.

Part 12

ISSUES/
TAKING A POSITION

Chapter 143

ABORTION

Passion and politics must never determine our position on abortion. Nothing matters but the facts. Just the facts.

Fact 1: The issue of life goes to our creation. "God . . . breathed the breath of life into his nostrils; and the man became a living being" (Gen. 2:7b).

Fact 2: The issue of life goes to the heart of our faith. "I have come so that they may have life and have it in abundance" (John 10:10b).

Fact 3: The issue of life goes to our existence and purpose. "I chose you before I formed you in the womb; I set you apart before you were born. I appointed you a prophet to the nations" (Jer. 1:5).

"This is what the LORD, your Redeemer who formed you from the womb says" (Isa. 44:24a).

Fact 4: Abortion is a deadly wound in the soul of America.

- Approximately four thousand babies are aborted every day.
- More than fifty million abortions have been performed since 1973.
- In 2003 alone, more children died from abortion than Americans died in the Revolutionary War, the Civil War, World Wars I and II, and the Korean, Vietnam, and Gulf Wars combined.
- Only 1 percent of abortions are from victims of rape or incest.

Fact 5: The consequences are unquestionable.

- Ninety percent of pregnant women given a Down syndrome diagnosis terminate their pregnancy.

- The 10 percent who do not state their baby to be the *most precious gift of their life.*

Fact 6: Posttraumatic stress disorder manifests in serious symptoms:

- Eating disorders
- Relationship problems
- Guilt
- Depression
- Flashbacks of the abortion procedure
- Suicidal thoughts
- Sexual dysfunction
- Alcohol and drug abuse

Fact 7: The fetus is a child!

- The heartbeat can be heard at six weeks.
- The head is recognizable at ten weeks.
- The sex is determinable at sixteen weeks.
- One hundred percent of the time it becomes a baby!

Fact 8: One-and-a-half to two pound babies have been delivered, nurtured, and survived, growing into mature, fully functioning adults.

Fact 9: The child's ability does not equal the child's worth. Many of the greatest people in history were born with great physical impairment. Regardless of any physical or mental limitation, each baby is a precious gift of God, made in His image.

Fact 10: God has a special love for babies. He sent His Son, wrapped in swaddling clothes, born in a manger to save the world. The angels sang. The stars shone. The shepherds rejoiced. The wise men came. The kings knelt.

God sent His son in the likeness of every baby boy and girl that has ever come into the human family.

> For it was You who created my inward parts; You knit me together in my mother's womb. I will praise You because I have been remarkably and wonderfully made. Your works are wonderful, and I know this very well.
> My bones were not hidden from You when I was made in secret. (Ps. 139:13–15b)
>
> He counts the number of the stars; He gives names to all of them. (Ps. 147:4)

He who knows the names of every star knows the name of every baby—before the baby is born.

Chapter 144

HOMOSEXUALITY

Homosexuality will be an increasingly prominent issue. Gay and lesbian activists are organized, committed, and aggressive in their agenda to legitimize their behavior and legalize their marriages.

1. *Homosexuality is clearly presented as sin in Scripture* (Lev. 18:22–23; Rom. 1:26–27).

2. *The seed of all sin is in all human nature.* The banner of the homosexual community is, "I was born that way," and indeed they were. In fact, we were all "born that way."

Often we hear the term "latent homosexual." It is also true that we are all latent homosexuals. We are all latent adulterers, murderers, liars, thieves and rapists.

We are all latent everything. We are all born in sin. We are all "born that way." We go forth from the womb speaking lies in hypocrisy. We are indeed estranged from God from our mother's womb. The DNA of every sin is in every human being.

Some may be inclined more to one sin than another. When I drank, I was not inclined to drink. It was never natural to me. I drank for sociability. Some men are inherently pornography addicts and adulterers. Some are bent toward violence; some with nonviolent natures find gambling irresistible. But we all have the seed of all sin and are all latent everything.

3. *Every person is accountable to God for his own sin.* The fact that his propensity toward one sin is more prominent than another in the bent of his character and personality changes nothing.

Imagine the following court room setting.

Prosecutor: Your honor, the accused robbed Fourth State Bank, took $300,000 and murdered the teller in cold blood.

Defense Attorney: Your honor, my client pleads "not guilty." His defense is that he was born that way. In his crib he screamed at his mother. In his playpen he bit and scratched other little children. In first grade he beat up little kindergartners. He's always been fascinated with guns. He was obsessed with playing cops and robbers as a child. He's always been violent. It's in his genes. He was just born that way. I rest my case.

Judge: Guilty of murder in the first degree. Life without parole.

By any reasonable logic, in any court of law, in any civilized nation, "But I was born that way," as a defense against breaking the law, is ludicrous. All of us were *born that way.* All of us are capable of anything, and all of us are what we are and do what we do because we choose to do so. We are sinners by birth and sinners by choice, and we are accountable to God for our choices.

Our parents are not responsible for our sins. Our genes are not. Society is not. God is not. We are.

4. *The homosexual is to be treated like any other sinner.* Unrepentant, open, blatant sin is to be confronted like any other according to the Matthew 18 model. Unrepentant sin requires church discipline. Repentant homosexuals are to be dealt with as all repentant sinners. The church's attitude must ever be: "Welcome fellow strugglers. Come on in, we're all struggling with something."

The pervasive issue then becomes not only the homosexual's sin but his attitude toward it. Romans 1:32 warns of severe judgment to those who not only *commit* this sin but actually *glory* in its practice. And that is by far the prevailing attitude of the gay and lesbian community today.

5. *All sin, including homosexuality, must be confronted in love.* A holy God loves the sinner but hates his sin. So must we. Ours is a redemptive gospel. Born that way? Indeed! Jesus came that we might be born all over again.

Tender empathy and compassionate support is especially appropriate for the brokenhearted family dealing with a fallen child of homosexuality.

Chapter 145

PORNOGRAPHY

We are the first generation of pastors who must deal with point-and-click Internet pornography. In order to obtain pornography in the past, one had to drive to an adult bookstore, purchase the material, and attempt to get it home in secret. Many would avoid doing it only because of the possibility of being publicly seen.

Want to have some fun? Next time you see someone coming out of an adult bookstore, honk and wave like you know him.

Today all one needs is a computer and wireless access, and every variety of porn is available. The result has been catastrophic.

Sadly, too many studies have shown it is not simply a problem with the flock but one with which the shepherd must deal himself. I often receive a call or a visit from a minister who is struggling in this area. These are good people, caught in a bad addiction that will destroy them, their marriage, their family, their ministries, and possibly their very lives!

Why would a pastor, staffer, or layman who loves the Lord and loves his family expose himself to Internet porn? The reasons are many:

Curiousity—Movies, TV, music, magazines, newspapers, and spam create a curiosity that can easily lead to Internet porn exposure and addiction.

Breakdown of Modesty—For many reasons our modesty levels are being greatly compromised. Sex is viewed as a sport, not the deeply intimate, committed, and self-giving experience God created for a husband and wife. This has led to an obsession with anything sexual or sensual, which in turn can lead to curiosity and Internet porn exposure.

Stress/Unhappiness—Many men see Internet porn as an escape from the stress of their work. They actually think they *deserve* this outlet, when to the contrary it creates images and behavior that hinder and destroy them and their families.

Unhealthy Marriage—Some men view Internet porn as a "deserved escape" from an unhealthy marriage. What are the possible results?

Sexual Addiction—Internet porn never satisfies for long.

Sexual Deviancy—The "modeling effect" of Internet porn drives one to live out what he is viewing, leading to more varied and deviant forms of sexual behavior.

Memories and Non-Rational Behavior—In a report given to the U.S. Senate Committee Hearing on Internet Pornography on November 18, 2004, Dr. Judith Reisman stated:

> Pornographic images imprint and alter the brain, triggering an instant, involuntary, but lasting biochemical memory trail overriding the cognitive. Once new neuro-chemical pathways are established, they are difficult or impossible to delete these images cause secretion of sex hormones producing involuntary reaction. In 3/10 of a second, a visual image passes from the eye to the brain: the brain is structurally changed and memories created. These sexual images will always dominate, occupy, and colonize the brain and displace cognition.[1]

In other words, Internet porn will lead you to do things you wouldn't do if you thought rationally about it, like repeatedly exposing yourself to an activity that will destroy your ministry, family, and possibly your life. And it can lead to having unrealistic expectations of your spouse, in both appearance and behavior.

Address the subject openly and frankly with the men and boys in your congregation. Help them understand ten things.

1. If you have not started looking at Internet porn, don't! You cannot be tempted by what you don't know.
2. Read and understand 2 Peter 1:3–10. As a follower of Jesus, He has given you all that you need to "escape the corruption that is in the world." In other words you do not *have* to sin! Verses 5–10 give you the steps to take and close with, "You will never stumble."
3. Understand 1 John 1:9. Remember, confession includes stopping.

4. Don't think you're immune. Get rid of whatever tempts you: certain movies, TV programs, music, magazines, even your private access to your computer if need be. Everything of value is at stake.
5. Quit making excuses for your sin. It is still sin, and Psalm 66:18 and Galatians 6:7 are still true.
6. Give your spouse total access to your computer e-mails, history, passwords, etc.
7. Be accountable to another Christian man who has access to your Internet world.
8. Seek professional counseling that is godly and biblical if it persists.
9. Guard what you allow into your mind. Be tough. Job said, "I have made a covenant with my eyes. How then could I look at a young woman."
10. Be on guard! "Be serious! Be alert! Your adversary the Devil is prowling around like a roaring lion, looking for anyone he can devour" (1 Pet. 5:8).

Fact: There are more than four hundred million pornographic web sites on the Internet.

We are at war. Expect battles. Be prepared!

Endnotes

1. Judith Reisman, "The Science Behind Pornography Addiction," U.S. Senate Committee on Internet Pornography, November 18, 2004, www.drjudithreisman.com.

Chapter 146

COHABITATION

More young adults cohabitate than marry. Theoretically, trial marriage ensures success in real marriage: in fact, it ensures failure.

Only 26 percent of women and 19 percent of men marry the person with whom they cohabitate. The average cohabitant has several partners in a lifetime. Women who cohabitate before marriage are 80 percent more likely to divorce than those who do not. Cohabitants who marry experience significantly more difficulty with adultery, alcohol and drugs. The rate for "severe violence" in cohabitants is nearly five times as high as married couples. Cohabitating women are nine times more likely to be killed by their partner than married women. Cohabitating men are four times more likely than husbands to cheat on their partner. Cohabitating women are eight times more likely than wives to cheat on their partner. Women are 62 times more likely to be assaulted by a cohabitating partner than a husband. Males who cohabitate display a more accepting view of rape. Cohabitating women suffer twice as much from neurotic disorders as married women. They are more irritable, anxious, worried, and unhappy. They get sick more often and die younger. Only 10% of couples who cohabitate without getting married are still together after a period of five years.

With the average young adult male, sex, not potential marriage, is the underlying appeal in trial marriage. The "trial" part is not nearly as sincere with the man as with the woman.

The kind of person who will have sex *with* you, outside of marriage, is the kind of person who will have sex outside of marriage *after* you and had it *before* you. Your trial spouse is lying next to you not because you're some exceptional somebody; they're lying there because they're the kind of person who sleeps around. They cheated *for* you, and they will cheat *on* you.

As of this writing, there are thirty sexually transmitted diseases, ten of which have no known cure. The average thirty-year-old today has had 27.2 sexual partners. Big trouble!

The sexual union of two persons is the ultimate expression of two lives eternally committed to each other. God-blessed, sexual fulfillment does not grow out of trial marriage. It grows out of a sacred, lifelong marriage with, an "until death do us part" commitment. As fish can't breathe without water, marriage cannot breathe without commitment.

There's no such thing as *partial* commitment. You can't be *just a little* committed. Commitment is faithfulness. Faithfulness is fidelity, and fidelity is forever. You can't be *sort of* committed. You can't be *pretty* faithful. *Do you want to spend your life married to someone who is pretty faithful?* Commitment is to the end. Faithfulness is forever.

One of the defenses of cohabitation is that it is easier to separate when you cohabitate than when you marry. If you discover you are not compatible, you can terminate the relationship with little pain. Just the opposite is true.

Cohabitation is a union from which you can never fully be extracted. Glue two pieces of paper together and tear them apart. Neither will ever again be the same.

Here's the deal. When you have a sexual relationship with someone, you become *one person* with them. The Bible calls it *knowing* each other. You give to them and receive from them, each other's soul. Mix Dr. Pepper and Pepsi, and you can never fully separate them. You can never again be the two separate individuals you once were.

You can never give *all of you* to your lifelong husband or wife because you have already given *part of you* to another in your "trial" marriage. From now on, it's second best, at best.

In living together before the sacred commitment of marriage, you *lose respect* for each other. God's great gift of sex is cheapened and marginalized when it is not experienced as intended by its Giver.

Sex outside of marriage is using a painting by Picasso as a drop cloth in your garage. Not only does it devalue the gift, but it also devalues its giver and its recipient.

Sex outside of marriage is not just cautioned against, not simply forbidden; it is severely condemned by the God who created sex. The Ten Commandments are more than the backbone of the Judeo-Christian faith. They are the foundation of civilization, the warp and woof of life. And number seven is still on the list.

Break that commandment? No way. Break yourself on it? Way. No exceptions.

Completely apart from the issue of compatibility or incompatibility, physiologically, emotionally, psychologically, or socially, you must accept the fact that to openly, knowingly, blatantly defy the clearly stated will of God has devastating consequences. And that with no exceptions—none, nada!

Defy His law, blatantly disobey His clearly stated teaching, and you lose. Live in sin, and God will withdraw His presence from your life. Live like an animal and die like one. Game over.

Final score: Satan, 10; you, zippo.

And you *will* lose the game. You lose *here* and you lose *forever*.

There is no fornication without guilt. The only cure for guilt is a solid dose of repentance. And repentance means stop doing it.

Chapter 147

STEM-CELL RESEARCH

S tem cell research is a highly controversial subject. High-profile celebrities testify before congressional committees lauding the virtue of stem-cell research in order to find potential cures for dreaded diseases such as Alzheimer's, Parkinson's, diabetes, AIDS, and more.

Many entreat the government for funding for research with urgency. No doubt this area of research is promising and provides some hope for medical advancement because of the cell's ability to grow into any kind of needed cell. In other words, damaged or sick cells within a particular organ within the body can be replaced with healthy stem cells that can adapt to the area.

With so much potential for good through increased stem-cell research, why is the subject so controversial? And why are convictions so strongly held and apparently irreconcilable?

At the heart of the controversy, is *where* some stem cells come from and *how* the research is funded. There are three basic sources for stem cells in the human body: adult cells, umbilical cord cells, and embryonic cells. Bone marrow and the peripheral nervous system are the sources for adult stem cells. Bone marrow transplants have been used for years to treat such diseases as leukemia and lymphoma. While bone marrow is a rich source of stem cells, the medical procedure to extract the cells can cause damage to the marrow itself.

Extracting stem cells from the peripheral system avoids damage to bone marrow but requires more time. Since the adult stem-cell procedure takes the cells from the patient's own body, the DNA is an exact match, removing the fear of the body's immune system rejecting them. Of the three types of stem-cell research, adult stem cells appear to yield the most promising and least controversial results.

The umbilical cord is a second rich source of stem cells. These cells can be extracted during pregnancy without any harm to the fetus. They can then be frozen and stored for later use if needed.

The closer a family member is to a child, the less the chance for rejection of the cells. Of course, if the child should need his or her own cord cells later in life, there is already an exact DNA match with no chance of rejection. This process is similar to a patient's providing blood before surgery in case the need for it should arise. If not needed, it can be donated to another.

The third source of stem cells is from embryos. This is the *most controversial* and presents the most ethical and moral problems. Collecting the stem cells from the embryo, or blastocyst, requires the ultimate destruction of the embryo.

The cells that replicate from a single blastocyst are referred to as a "stem-cell line," and many exist due to the number of years that invitro fertilization made embryos available that were not used.

Most advocates of embryonic stem-cell research lobby for tax-payer funding of this research which they believe holds such promise. Proponents of embryonic stem-cell research argue that an embryo should not be considered a human being at this early stage because it does not yet have human features. Christians believe an embryo **is** a human life because life clearly begins at conception.

In addition, proponents say there are already stem-cell lines that will be wasted if they are not available for research, while opponents raise concerns that if this research is openly permitted and funded, science might begin to harvest life for the purpose of destroying it.

Even with the idea that embryonic stem-cell research could potentially help cure so many diseases or health issues, the idea of creating life to destroy life in order to make existing life better is an ethical and moral morass.

Psalm 139:13 describes God's forming our inward parts and weaving us together in our mother's womb. According to the biblical view of personhood, God is at work in the womb before embryos have outward features that would appear human. Therefore, holding to a foundational belief that personhood begins at conception, stem-cell research requires the destruction of a human being.

To ask people who hold this conviction to support tax-payer funding of this type of research only compounds the ethical problems associated with it. With the medical evidence supporting more beneficial results from adult and umbilical cord stem-cell research than embryonic, it would seem more constructive to pursue research in the former two, while avoiding the ethical and moral problems of the latter.

Chapter 148

EVOLUTION

In 1859, Charles Darwin wrote *The Origin of Species*. By the 1960s the monkey had leapt straight into the classroom.

Evolution is filled with many flaws.

1. *Evolution says that time and chance, not order, create life.* Am I to believe, if enough tornadoes swirl through enough airports, new airplanes will be created?

My wristwatch has only twelve moving parts. Am I to believe they just jumped into the case by chance?

On my desk is a newspaper. Am I to believe that it jumped out of an explosion in the print room of *The Houston Chronicle,* or hundreds of explosions, or trillions?

From order comes creation. From time and chance come disorder.

2. *Evolution teaches all life is traced to a common ancestry of one common cell:* amoeba, mosquitoes, ducks, alligators, buffalo—everything. What are the odds of just one cell forming in the universe and that cell being formed by space junk?

Renowned physicist and Cambridge professor Fred Hoyle attempted to calculate the possibility of an entire cell originating not just on earth but anywhere in the universe. Physicists say anything with odds of one in ten to the fiftieth power or beyond is considered impossible. He found the probability of this happening was over one in ten to the forty-thousandth power. Exponentially greater than impossible.

In his 1981 book *Evolution from Space* (coauthored with Chandra Wickramasinghe), he calculated that the chance of obtaining the required set of enzymes for even the simplest living cell was one in ten to the forty-thousandth power (one followed by 40,000 zeroes). Since the number of atoms in the known universe is infinitesimally tiny by comparison (one to the eightieth power), even a whole universe full of primordial soup wouldn't have a chance.

3. *In evolution there must be genetic mutations from one cell through ten mutations to produce man.*

- Nonliving matter
- Protozoans
- Metazoan invertebrates
- Vertebrates—fishes
- Amphibians
- Reptiles
- Birds
- Fur-bearing quadrupeds
- Apes
- Man

Each mutation would have to contain part of its predecessor and part of its successor. Darwin said, "Geology assuredly does not reveal any such finely graduated organic changes. This perhaps is the most obvious and greatest objection which can be urged against my theory."

In microevolution small changes do occur within species. There are cocker spaniels, basset hounds, and collies, but they are all dogs. Macro-evolution is change to a whole new species. No evidence of such change exists in all creation.

4. *Newton's Second Law of Thermodynamics states that left to itself, everything in fact devolves.* A brand-new Ford left in a pasture over enough centuries will devolve into a pile of rust, not *evolve* into a new Rolls Royce.

5. *If the Creator is removed, accountability is removed.* If I am not ultimately accountable to the God who created me, I am my own God. I can do as I please. Who does that sound like?

Without accountability I am on the throne of my own life. I do not sin against anyone. I determine what is true or false, right or wrong. Teach people they came from animals, and they will *live like animals*. And that's pretty much America without God today.

In the beginning God created the heavens and the earth.

Now the earth was formless and empty, darkness covered the surface of the watery depths, and the Spirit of God was hovering over the surface of the waters. (Gen. 1:1–2)

Then God said, "Let Us make man in Our image, according to Our likeness. They will rule the fish of the sea, the birds of the sky, and every creature that crawls on the earth." So God created man in His own image. He created him in the image of God; He created them male and female. (Gen. 1:26–27)

Then the LORD God formed the man out of the dust from the ground and breathed the breath of life into his nostrils, and the man became a living being. (Gen. 2:7)

Then the Lord God said, "It is not good for the man to be alone. I will make a help as his compliment. (Gen. 2:18)

So the Lord God caused a deep sleep to come over the man, and he slept. God took one of his ribs and closed the flesh at that place. Then the Lord God made the rib He had taken from the man into a woman and brought her to the man. (Gen. 2:21–22)

Chapter 149

GAMBLING

One of the more prevalent problems of a prospering society is gambling. Prosperity opens a door of opportunity for the green-eyed monster of envy. When someone *without* sees someone *with*, an overwhelming desire "to have" begins to grow.

Gambling usually affects the most those who can afford it the least. Gambling is nothing more than the pursuit of an image of prosperity that is in every way a mirage.

What is the real problem of gambling? Ethicists, economists, criminologists, and psychologists could each give valid arguments against gambling. Let me suggest four key areas that are spiritual in nature.

These are from my experience as a caring pastor.

1. *Gambling is wrong because it is poor stewardship.* We were raised on statements like, "Waste not, want not" and "A penny saved is a penny earned." These proverbs of stewardship led to the prosperity of a nation like none the world had ever known. To use scarce resources to produce an even more scarce gambling victory is simply poor stewardship of the resources with which God has entrusted us.

2. *Gambling displays an underlying lack of contentment.* Behind the purchase of the lottery ticket is a "what if" scenario that is spiritually unhealthy and will eventually negatively manifest itself in other realms of life.

I suggest you consider "get rich slow" schemes over "get rich quick" dreams. If you tithe off the top, live on what you have, spend less than you make, and save for your future, you will be content and you *will* have enough. Jesus promised it. "But seek first the kingdom of God and His righteousness, and all these things will be provided for you" (Matt. 6:33).

3. *Gambling is absent logic.* When you study the revelation of Himself God has given in nature, you see unbreakable sequence, tremendous order, and infinite logic. God has never revealed Himself as having characteristics of randomness. What God does, He does "decently and in order" (1 Cor. 14:40).

Why would a God of order lead us to participate in a game of chance? And why would a God of logic lead us to do something so terribly illogical? Just as God cannot lead us to deeds of darkness because "God is light, and there is absolutely no darkness in Him" (1 John 1:5b), He cannot lead us to the illogic of gambling because He is a God of precise order and logic.

One has a greater chance of being struck by lightning twice than of winning the "big ticket" in the lottery. That is poor logic.

4. *Gambling is problematic because it is symptomatic of misplaced faith.* Why take your offerings to the temple of Lady Luck when you could present your life as a living sacrifice to a loving God? A lottery ticket, poker game, or slot machine is an undignified and misdirected prayer for financial wealth. How much better to be faithful with little and trust the Heavenly Father, the Giver of all good gifts, to give you more.

Joyfully give the Lord His tithe and more, work hard, pay your bills, save for the future, and invest in yourself, your family, and your church. Jesus will pay great rewards, just as He promised.

> Give, and it will be given to you; a good measure—pressed down, shaken together, and running over—will be poured into your lap. For with the measure you use, it will be measured back to you. (Luke 6:38)

> For where your treasure is, there your heart will be also. (Matt. 6:21)

> The thief must no longer steal. Instead, he must do honest work with his own hands, so that he has something to share with anyone in need. (Eph. 4:28)

> When we were with you, this is what we commanded you: "If anyone isn't willing to work, he should not eat. (2 Thess. 3:10)

Gambling is stealing. It is taking something you do not deserve and for which you have not worked. If you gamble and win, you're a thief. If you gamble and lose, you're a fool.

Gamble: Lose-Lose.
Work hard. Tithe. Trust the Lord: Win-Win.

Chapter 150

SOCIAL DRINKING

I am well aware of the arguments for drinking. But let me tell you, not as a theologian or apologist, but from the heart of a caring shepherd across sixty years of ministry, alcohol has been by far the leading cause of broken homes, ruined children, and shattered lives.

The International Standard Bible Encyclopedia lists eleven Hebrew words translated "wine," some with an acknowledged degree of vagueness regarding alcoholic content. Everything from new grape juice to heavily aged wine is on the list. Admittedly we may not know everything historically or biblically about "the grape." Let's look at what we *do know.*

1. *Alcohol has a long history connected to debauchery, debased living, divorce, and death.* Abraham Lincoln said, "The liquor traffic has many defenders but no defense." Not one person in history ever negatively impacted their life because they *didn't* drink.

2. *Solomon, the richest man who ever lived, spent his life seeking happiness in wealth, sex, and alcohol.* At the end he wrote, "Vanity of vanities; all is vanity" (Eccl. 1:2 KJV). The word *vanity* means "empty-headed idiocy." Hear his pathetic cry, "Wine is a mocker, beer is a brawler, and whoever staggers because of them is not wise" (Prov. 20:1).

3. *Admittedly some drink in moderation and control their drinking all of their life.* Millions cannot. The tragedy is, once begun, no one can foresee who will be able to *control* their drinking and who will *be controlled* by it. Alcohol

is like leaving a loaded revolver on your children's dresser. You may use it in self-defense; your eight-year-old in *self-destruction*.

4. *Alcohol is deceptive.* It promises what it cannot produce. In spite of full knowledge of the destructive nature of alcohol on the history of the human race, most still choose to drink. Why? It gives a sense of security, sociability, relaxation, empowerment, exhilaration, and joy. All good things and all the fruit of the Spirit-filled life. Here's the catch: everything the Holy Spirit does for you, alcohol does for you but is a shallow and *deceptive* substitute for *the real*.

After alcohol's let down, it always happens: you not only are *as* empty as before you drank, but you are even *more* dull and flat than before. The nature of addiction is that it takes more and more of the same to equal the original high, and you become *addicted* to trying to duplicate the original. The result: you are an alcoholic.

Being filled with the Holy Spirit does the same thing but is more beautiful with each taste of the new wine of His power and person. That's why the apostle Paul said, "Don't get drunk with wine, which leads to reckless actions, but be filled with the Spirit" (Eph. 5:18).

The angels prophesy to Zechariah in Luke 1:15 makes the same connection. John the Baptist would not need the synthetic power of wine and strong drink: he would be filled from the womb with the true power of the Holy Spirit. Why substitute the fake for the real?

5. *Eroded influence is related to drinking.* Nothing more accurately reflects the soul of our culture than:

- Let's party.
- Eat, drink, and be merry for tomorrow we die.
- Let's go barhopping.
- Meet me at happy hour.

An unhappy, unfulfilled culture desperately searches for fulfillment and can't see it in the Spirit-filled life, of a satisfied, *all together* man or woman of God. How sad. If we drink, what have we which they have not? Where is our testimony for Christ as the salt of the earth that makes people thirst for the true wine of Christ? "It is a noble thing not to eat meat, or drink wine, or do anything that makes your brother stumble" (Rom. 14:21).

Unbelievers can greatly stumble over our negative testimony; "Christ is not enough." I have to look for meaning in the same glass in which you look.

In Proverbs, the king is admonished by his own mother, "It is not for kings to drink wine or for rulers to desire beer" (Prov. 31:4). Wine and "strong drink" cause men in places of responsibility to forget the law and pervert judgment.

When alcohol causes the liver to lose its ability to filter, it passes straight into the bloodstream and, within minutes, directly into the brain as acetylaldahyde. You know it by another name. Rat poison! Is drinking a sin? If not, it's sure a doggone dirty shame.

Scripture appears to present drinking as a personal choice, then shows it's a bad choice.

> "Look not upon the wine when it is red, when it gives its color in the cup, when it moves itself aright. At the last it bites like a serpent and stings like an adder." (Prov. 23:31–32)

> "Giving no offense in any thing, that the ministry be not blamed." (2 Cor. 6:3)

Chapter 151

CHURCH AND STATE

J ust this morning on ABC TV's *Good Morning America*, someone said, "Americans are angry at Glen Beck's constant reference to God at the Lincoln Memorial rally last night because the First Amendment clearly requires 'the separation of church and state.'" This "beyond absurdity" idea is the greatest perversion of truth in American politics.

Fact: The First Amendment says about religion, "Congress shall make no law respecting an establishment of religion, or prohibiting the free exercise thereof," and nothing more!

Clearly the intent of the First Amendment was to keep government out of religion, not religion out of government.

It was no accident that the First Amendment granted the freedom *of* religion. Had their intent been freedom *from* religion, they would have said so, and their public lives would have demonstrated it.

There was no separation of church and state when General George Washington was on his knees at Valley Forge, pleading with the Lord to rescue a struggling nation.

There was no separation when John Adams read five chapters of the Bible each day as did his son John Quincy Adams following his example.

There was no separation when Thomas Jefferson wrote, "God who gave us life gave us liberty."

There was no separation when Patrick Henry wrote in his will, "This is all the inheritance I can give to my dear family. The religion of Christ can give them one which will make them rich indeed."

There was no separation when Benjamin Franklin realized the need for God as the Constitutional Convention was falling apart and said, "And have we now forgotten that powerful Friend? Or, do we imagine we no longer need His assistance." With this he called the men at that convention to commit to prayer.

There was no separation when Abraham Lincoln pleaded with the Lord during the Civil War.

There was no separation when Benjamin Harrison had his morning devotions with his family.

There was no separation when Franklin Delano Roosevelt prayed on public radio in World War II, "Almighty God, our sons, pride of our nation, this day have set upon a mighty endeavor, a struggle to preserve our republic, our religion, and our civilizations, and to set free a suffering humanity."

There was no separation when Dwight D. Eisenhower added, "One nation under God" to the Pledge of Allegiance.

There was no separation of church and state when the founders signed their name to the Declaration of Independence, giving their agreement that, "we hold these truths to be self-evident: that all men are created equal, that they are endowed by their Creator with certain unalienable rights: that among these are life, liberty, and the pursuit of happiness."

Their intent was permanently etched in the capstone of the Washington Monument in Latin. "Laus Deo" translates to "Praise be to God." The cornerstone of the Washington Monument contains, among other things, a Bible, the Declaration of Independence, and the U.S. Constitution.

The U.S. Capitol has a chapel.

The Supreme Court has the imagery of Moses holding the Ten Commandments.

Of the more than 130 million items housed in the Library of Congress, only two are on permanent display in the Great Hall, the Giant Bible of Mainz and the Gutenberg Bible.

The separation of church and state issue was a *nonissue* to our founders. They saw their faith in the living God and His Son Jesus Christ inseparably tied to the beginning and sustaining of our nation.

Our Founding Fathers saw religion, and specifically the Christian religion, to be as necessary to good government as hydrogen is to water. They could not live, speak, or write without an inherent reference to the living God. He existed and they knew it.

They also knew that long after they lived, He would still exist, looking over the shoulders of their successors to see if they would be true to His grace and gift of this nation or if they would betray that gift and go it alone. Our nation stands at a great crossroads. Will we be true to the clearly revealed intent of our founding fathers and live or pretend it never existed and die. "Righteousness exalts a nation, but sin is a disgrace to any people" (Prov. 14:34).

Chapter 152

THE CHRISTIAN
AND POLITICS

Thomas Jefferson believed there are two basic requirements to sustain a democracy: a diffused majority (which we have) and an informed electorate (which we do not have).

Our country is facing critical issues while our population is focused on *American Idol* and *Oprah*. The question is, Who is going to inform the electorate concerning the issues of our day? In the early days of our history, it was the pastors, the proclaimers of God's Word.

John Adams said the Reverend Dr. Jonathan Mayhew and the Reverend Dr. Samuel Cooper were two of the individuals "most conspicuous, the most ardent and influential," in what he called, "the awakening and revival of American principles and feelings" that led to our independence. Today secular media and unfriendly courts would keep the Word of God and prayer within the walls of the church.

A recent assault from the courts involved the Santa Fe, Texas, school board policy of allowing voluntary prayer before football games if the student body chose to do so. In a chilling decision, the majority ruled that "worship is a responsibility and a choice committed to the private sphere." In other words keep religion sequestered. Don't allow it in the marketplace, specifically, not the public schools.

If ideas have consequences—and they do—and if high court rulings are the law of the land—and they are—it is only a matter of time until the idea of privatized worship is logically expanded beyond football games at public schools. Preachers must once again accept the responsibility of informing the citizenry, but it will require exceptional moral courage. Recently Franklin Graham opined that he expects to be persecuted for the beliefs he espouses. That threat must not silence the man of God or diminish his commitment to thundering forth with, "Thus saith the Lord!"

Who should educate our society about the great moral issues of our day? The government? Planned Parenthood? The media? I think not. You and I have the same responsibility to address the issues of our day as did the prophets of old.

There was a time when America was committed to protecting life because it was sacred. Today it is to be protected only if it is convenient. Who will speak for those who cannot speak?

Who is going to address the issues relating to marriage and the family? On a nightly basis television programs promote homosexuality and ridicule those who believe God intended marriage to be between a man and a woman.

We have watched as politicians, preachers, and citizens have trampled underfoot God's call to sexual purity. National figures are scandalized by their unfaithful sexual conduct. Homes are torn asunder by affairs and divorce. The majority of young adults cohabitate rather than marry. We must call our nation back to God and scriptural purity.

If not us, who?

The fact is that in modern-day America, the Christian faith is under attack by the elite institutions of academia and the media. Only the name of Jesus Christ is openly used as an expletive on American television, not Buddha, not Allah.

Whereas anything Christian is banned in public schools, some schools proudly teach about other religions in the name of diversity. Documented history has been revised on the altar of political correctness.

A philosophy that rejects truth is by definition a philosophy that cannot distinguish between a religion that encourages its followers to murder infidels and one that teaches every life is so important that God's Son gave His life for all.

We have been called by God to address society's issues.

- Proclaim the truth. The First Amendment simply says, "Congress shall make no law respecting an establishment of religion, or prohibiting the free exercise thereof." The purpose of the First Amendment was clearly to keep government out of religion not religion out of government.

- Get involved in the political process, particularly elections.
- Be bold in your pulpit. If you go to jail for preaching the truth, rejoice. Perhaps you'll meet the ghost of the apostle Paul.
- Lead your people seriously and earnestly to pray for revival in America.

"If . . . My people who are called by My name humble themselves, pray, and seek My face, and turn from their wicked ways, then I will hear from heaven, forgive their sin, and heal their land." (2 Chron. 7:14)

Chapter 153

PRAYER IN THE PUBLIC FORUM

Prayer in the secular arena is often preceded by the request, "Don't pray in Jesus' name. Jews, Muslims, and unbelievers may be offended."

Certainly God hears all prayer. He hears, sees, and knows all things. The Bible teaches that for prayer to be answered, however, it must be in His will, in faith, and in His name.

The fact that I pray in Jesus' name is an acknowledgement of who I am as a Christian and what I believe, and that is to be respected. If you wanted something else, you should have invited someone else to pray.

The fact that a Jew or other person does not pray in Jesus' name is likewise an acknowledgement of who they are and what they believe. They too are to be respected for their right to believe as they do. If you have the right to ask me *not* to pray in Jesus' name lest you be offended, I have the right to ask that you *do* pray in Jesus' name lest I be offended.

The only reasonable resolution to this impasse is, "let's respect one another enough to let everyone pray in the manner in which they pray." The God who knows all things and hears all prayers is really good at sorting out which ones He will hear and answer. And He has laid out those qualifications clearly in His Word.

And it's "in Jesus' name," not "for Jesus' sake," He tells us to pray. Certainly the phrase "in Jesus' name" is not simply three magic words to be tacked on at the end of our prayer. To pray in His name is to affirm that we come in faith, in His will, and on the merit of His atoning blood to our Father's throne.

> Jesus, oh how sweet the name.
> Jesus, every day the same.
> Jesus, let all earth proclaim
> The precious name of Jesus.

Politically correct gets you an audience with men. Biblically correct gets you an audience with their King.

> "Therefore, you should pray like this: Our Father in heaven, Your name be honored as holy. Your kingdom come. Your will be done on earth as it is in heaven. Give us today our daily bread. And forgive us our debts, as we also have forgiven our debtors. And do not bring us into temptation, but deliver us from the evil one. For Yours is the kingdom and the power and the glory for ever. Amen." (Matt. 6:9–13)

Chapter 154

MORAL ABSOLUTES

The Ten Commandments are the foundation of civilization. They are there in black-and-white. This is right; do this. That is wrong; don't do that.

Satan's earliest temptation to Eve was "You will be like God" (Gen. 3:5). To create a world without God, a world in which man is himself God, is the heart and soul of fallen human nature.

We live in a world without moral absolutes. God has been systematically taken out of government and public education until we have no moral moorings.

Man is now the arbitrator of truth. What I say, what I think, *is what is.* But what you think is different? Fine. Your moral code is yours; mine is mine. Mine is right because I say it is. Yours is right because you say it is, and we both have the right to our opinion of right and wrong.

The result of this kind of thinking is a world without absolutes and a world in moral chaos.

The simple heart of moral absolutes is that absolute truth is not just rooted in the Word of God. It's deeper than that.

The Bible records what God *said,* but absolute truth is rooted not simply in *what* God *says,* but *who* God *is.*

From God's character come absolutes.

- Truth is objective because God exists outside ourselves.
- Truth is universal because God is above all.
- Truth is constant because God is eternal.

From God's character come concepts.

- God is love.
- Life is sacred.
- Hypocrisy is unacceptable.
- People are important.
- Integrity is everything.
- Forgiveness is mandatory.
- Pride is despicable.
- God is fair.
- Might doesn't make right.
- All persons have value.

From concepts come commandments, moral absolutes.

- Character—God is pure.
- Concept—The highest and best is always unadulterated.
- Commandment—"Do not commit adultery" (Exod. 20:14).
- Character—God is true.
- Concept—Honesty and integrity are always right.
- Commandment—"Do not give false testimony" (Exod. 20:16).
- Character – God is faithful.
- Concept—Truth is not subject to change.
- Commandment—What was true on Mount Sinai is true in the twenty-first century.

Murder is not simply wrong because God says it is wrong. *That would be enough.* Murder is wrong because God is life.

Hatred is not simply wrong because God says it is wrong. *That would be enough.* Hatred is wrong because God is love.

Adultery is not simply wrong because God says it's wrong. *That would be enough.* Adultery is wrong because God is pure.

To say that is not to discredit God's Word. Every word is true, but it's true because God is true.

Any carpenter knows the necessity of sawing each new piece from the original pattern. Each patterned only from the last means that each gets farther and farther from the real.

In Severence, France, is housed the International System of Weights and Measurements. It is the final, exclusive, changeless standard for the world. It is correct, it is right, and it is truth. Saying there are thirty-five inches in a yard or fifteen ounces in a pound changes nothing!

Truth is inherent in the changeless. Jesus said, "I am the way, the truth, and the life." (John 14:6)

"The one who has seen Me has seen the Father." (John 14:9)

God is ultimate truth, and Jesus is the true revelation of God. In Jesus Christ you have the truth about the truth. And when you've got the truth about the truth, you've got the truth.

Chapter 155

THE SUBMISSIVE WIFE

E phesians 5:22 says, "Wives, submit to your own husbands as to the Lord." This greatly misunderstood verse is set in context of mutual submission. Verse 21 which precedes it says, "Submit yourselves one to another in the fear of the Lord."

A flawed hermeneutic leads to the dismantling of doctrine.

The key verse is 32, "I am talking about Christ and the church." Four images, each mirroring the other, may be seen in the text.

1. Jesus was submissive to the Father.
2. Christ's bride, the church, is submissive to Christ.
3. The wife is submissive to her husband
4. The local congregation is submissive to the undershepherd, their pastor.

Five principles must clearly be kept in focus:

1. In all relationships there must be order, and order requires headship.
2. Submission to headship does not denote inferiority.
3. In each there is mutual submission (Eph. 5:21).
4. The husband's selfless honor to his wife is even greater than is hers to him. "Wives, submit yourselves to your own husbands" is followed by "husbands, love your wives, just as Christ loved the church and gave Himself for her" (Eph. 5:25). The husband is to die for his wife;

the wife is not told to die for her husband. The honor, selflessness, giving, serving, and exaltation he demonstrates to his wife exceeds hers to him.

5. Headship is not demanded. Headship is deserved, earned by giving of oneself to honor his bride. In so doing, a husband receives more than he gives. What woman would not be only too happy to honor her husband as head of the home whose sole priority in every deed is "how can I lay down my life for you?" That's what the Paul meant when he said, "He who loves his wife: loves himself" (Eph. 5:28b).

We give our life to Christ not because He demands it but because He deserves it. The cross changes everything. What was true of Christ on the cross must be true of the husband and pastor.

Chapter 156

WOMEN IN MINISTRY

M uch of the beauty of the body of Christ is that we can agree to disagree on minor issues. I personally have been blessed by the ministry of women pastors in Nazarene, Methodist, and Presbyterian churches. My own dear mother-in-law preached in the absence of the pastor, my father-in-law, in a great Assemblies of God church before joining a Southern Baptist church in 1955.

Although the 2000 *Baptist Faith and Message* sets forth a different position, women serve as pastors in some Southern Baptist churches today. Let's look together at the reason behind the position of most Southern Baptists regarding women as pastors.

No one ever honored womanhood like Jesus. I am thinking of a prominent religion that greatly dishonors them, and it isn't called Christianity. Keep two things clearly in focus:

First, status or office denotes neither superiority nor inferiority. Jesus was subject to the Father but not inferior to the Father. Eve was Adam's suitable helper, his complementor, his completer. She was also his equal.

Second, in all things there must be order—government, church, family. Without order, there is only disorder and chaos. And God has clearly established order in His world.

The Holy Spirit of Christ speaks the mind of Christ through the inspired writing of the apostle Paul in 1 Timothy 2.

"I do not permit a woman to teach or to have authority over a man, but to be in silence" (v. 12). "For Adam was formed first, then Eve" (v. 13). "And Adam was not deceived, but the woman being deceived, fell into transgression" (v. 14).

The key to understanding the precept in verse 12 is clearly explained in verses 13–14. The copulative "for" which begins verse 13 explains the logic of verse 12. The fact that a man has the leadership is a picture of the beginning of sin and redemption from sin. Although Eve was first deceived, Paul writes in Romans 5:12, as the head, Adam must assume responsibility for sin entering the human race. Yet it was she who first succumbed to the voice of the tempter, enticed her husband, and opened the door to the process.

God's plan for leadership in the church is not some cruel punishment placed upon womanhood. It is divine genius from the mind of God to dramatize the most important message of all to mankind: the story of sin and redemption.

So important is the proclamation of the gospel about salvation from sin, that even the manner in which we conduct Bible study and worship services itself, portrays the gospel. The presentation of the gospel is so important God uses every means at His disposal to display it.

God even uses the universe. Romans 1 makes clear that no man can look into the heavens and not sense that Someone, somewhere created all of this, to whom he is responsible.

Music, pageantry, art, dance, preaching, teaching, puppetry, even how we "do church" should preach Christ. It's that important.

Generally, Southern Baptists believe a woman can hold any position and perform any ministry in church except senior pastor or deacon. The pattern for those who participate with the pastor in church leadership was clearly set forth in Acts 6 when the apostles directed the multitude to seek out seven good men as deacons.

First Timothy 3 also makes clear that deacons are men. Qualifications are given for four categories of individuals: pastors, deacons, pastors' wives, and deacons' wives.

"For Adam was first formed, then Eve." (1 Tim. 2:13)

Many believe Phoebe was a female deacon. "I commend to you our sister Phoebe, who is a servant of the church in Cenchreae. So you should welcome her in the Lord in a manner worthy of the saints and assist her in whatever matter she may require your help. For indeed she has been a benefactor of many—and of me also" (Rom. 16:1–2).

The word *servant* translates *diakonos,* the term from which we get *deacon.* The Greek word here is neuter and was used in the church as a general term for servant.

It is used of the household servants who drew the water that Jesus turned into wine (John 2:5, 9). Paul also used the term in Romans 13:4 to refer to secular government as "God's servant for your good" and even of Christ as "a servant of the circumcision," that is, to Jews (15:8).

When *diakonos* obviously refers to a church office, it is usually transliterated *deacon* as in Philippians 1:1 and 1 Timothy 3:10–13.

Chapter 157

SABBATH WORSHIP

Christians worship on Sunday to celebrate the resurrection of Jesus. The apostle Paul writes in 1 Corinthians 15:13–14, "But if there is no resurrection of the dead, then Christ has not been raised; and if Christ has not been raised, then our proclamation is without foundation and so is your faith."

The resurrection of Jesus most fully differentiate Christianity from every other religion, ideology, or philosophy of life. Christians gather together on Sunday to celebrate continually Jesus' offer of life His resurrection provides.

Those who disagree raise three points.

1. In creation God worked six days and rested on the Sabbath, the last day of the week.

2. God established a Saturday, end-of-week, Sabbath in the Ten Commandments.

3. The New Testament demonstrates that Jesus regularly taught in the synagogue on the Sabbath as was His custom (see Luke 4:16).

These can be compelling arguments. But they were under the old covenant.

Jesus' life, death, and resurrection instituted the new covenant which He transitioned from shadow to substance.

The author of Hebrews writes, "Since the Law has only a shadow of the good things to come, and not the actual form of those realities" (10:1). The law is a shadow. Jesus is the light. The law is the preview of coming attractions; Jesus is the feature event.

Paul writes in Colossians 2:16–17, "Therefore, don't let anyone judge you in regard to food and drink or in the matter of a festival or a new moon or a Sabbath day. These are a shadow of what was to come; the substance is the Messiah." The apostle Paul writes with a new covenant understanding.

In Colossae a form of Jewish legalism surfaced on two fronts, diet and days. He argues that obedience to these is not necessary for followers of Jesus. They are the shadows. Jesus is the substance.

The food regulations of Leviticus were shadows of holiness. Holiness is no longer found in maintaining a Levitical diet, but in the Bread of Life.

In like manner the Sabbath was established to formalize man's need for rest. But Jesus is the substance of rest. He promises in Matthew 11:28–30, "Come unto Me, all you that labor and are heavy laden, and *I will give you rest.* Take my yoke upon you, and learn of Me; for am meek and lowly in heart: and you shall find *rest for your souls.* For my yoke is easy, and my burden is light."

Man cannot attain the true substance of rest in *one* day. That can only be attained by resting in the Prince of peace *every* day.

Paul's argument necessitates that anyone who demands Saturday worship must also not eat meat! You cannot observe days *and not* observe diets. The Christian has been set free from both.

The writer of Hebrews further argues that New Covenant Sabbath is a promised lifestyle, not a day. He makes Sabbath rest one of his central arguments for the new covenant reality of Jesus in chapters 3 and 4. The author states:

"Again He specifies a certain day—'Today,' speaking through David after such a long time, as previously stated, 'Today, if you hear His voice, do not harden your hearts.' For if Joshua had given them rest, God would not have spoken later about another day. Therefore, a Sabbath rest remains for God's people. For the person who has entered His rest has rested from his own works, just as God did from His" (Heb. 4:7–9).

The Sabbath rest that remains is not a day but a life at rest made possible in Jesus. What the old covenant provided for, in external form, for a day, Jesus provides everyday, as a way of life.

Jesus, in His life, death, and resurrection, inaugurated the New Covenant. The new covenant is based in the *substance* of Jesus' fulfilling the *shadow* of the old covenant. Christians are no longer bound by diets or days. Sabbath rest is a way of life, not limited to a day.

Christians are free to worship on whatever day they choose, and some worship on *each* of the seven days of the week. Most Christians choose to worship Jesus on Sunday, to remember and celebrate His resurrection.

Often I am asked, "When did God change Sabbath worship to Sunday worship?" The answer is, He didn't. The Sabbath was never a day of worship in the first place. It was a day to rest and reflect on the greatness of what God had created the other six. It was only natural that as men thought of God's handiwork, they worshipped Him.

Just so, it was only natural that the disciples assembled to worship Christ on the day of His destiny-changing resurrection. Jesus apparently approved of the practice. In John 20:19, the disciples gathered on the first day of the week. Jesus blessed their assembly with His presence and peace.

In Acts 20:17 and 1 Corinthians 16:1–2, the New Testament church continued the practice of first-day worship. Not the last, not Saturday. The first day, Sunday, the Lord's Day.

Sunday is resurrection day, His day! Sunday is Sonday.

Chapter 158

ECUMENICISM

I t appears from Revelation that the Antichrist will control the world before Christ's glorious return, Armageddon and millennial reign. Two false systems will be in place that Jesus will harshly judge: the false world *economic* system and the false world *religious* system. Today we see the beginning of both.

To what degree then should we cooperate with other groups that may be gravitating toward a false one-world religious system? The first test is the necessity of not having to compromise our core values. The deity of Jesus, salvation by grace, His substitutionary death and bodily resurrection are nonnegotiables.

I can stand on the street corner and help my fellowman pass out bread to hungry people and not have to deny the cardinal doctrines of the faith to do so. Rushing to Haiti to help earthquake victims is always in order, regardless of the religious belief of the one who drives the ambulance.

The question then becomes, Do I appear to authenticate, or do I actually perpetuate the false teachings of another when I stand by him and feed the poor? For me the answer is no. You will have to find God's answer for you.

I should be able to lay aside secondary issues and cooperate, in at least *some things*, with Lutherans, Methodists, Assemblies, Presbyterians, such as Billy Graham crusades.

The core question becomes, Is there anything whatsoever incumbent upon me to compromise even slightly my personal or public stand for the cardinal doctrines of the faith?

Secondary issues are precisely that—secondary. If you get to know a fellow pastor of another persuasion, you might be surprised to discover how much you agree upon.

I have been invited to preach in many churches: Episcopalian, Bible, Nazarene, Church of God, CMA, Methodist, and Presbyterian. The things on which we disagree are far less significant than the great truths of Scripture upon which we heartily agree.

And I have been blessed.

Chapter 159

BIBLICAL INERRANCY

"All Scripture is inspired of God and is profitable for teaching, for rebuking, for training in righteousness" (2 Tim. 3:16).

The original autographs, the Dead Sea Scrolls, and the original languages are of little interest to the man on the street or in the pew. Most inerrancy debates are over his head and off his screen. He mainly wants to know the Book he holds in his hands is God's reliable Word. You can assure him that it is.

It is filled with hundreds of prophecies that have been and/or are being fulfilled right down to the last detail to this very hour.

Time has authenticated the Scriptures. The Bible says "the morning stars sang together" (Job 38:7). For years science scoffed at that. Today they know the heavenly bodies give off phonetic vibrations. With sophisticated listening devices astronomers can listen, not look, and determine which star they're hearing. The morning stars *do* sing together. Science was wrong. The Bible was right.

The Bible says, "God is enthroned above the circle of the earth" (Isa. 40:22). For years science said the earth was flat. The Bible said it was circular. Science has long since acknowledged its error. Science was wrong; the Bible was right.

And the beat goes on!

The Bible is self-authenticating. More than thirty-eight hundred times it says "Thus says the Lord," or, "And the word of the Lord came saying." It's unreasonable that thinking men everywhere would not have long since totally rejected a book fabricated on thirty-eight hundred lies.

For thousands of years men and women have claimed its promises, stood on its precepts, and risked their lives and eternal destiny to its teachings. I have heard thousands say, "I wish I were a Christian." I have never heard a Christian say, "I wish I were not." "God is a liar; He failed of His promises."

The Bible was written over fifteen hundred years by approximately forty different authors, most of whom never knew the others lived, let alone wrote. They lived in different lands, spoke different languages, and wrote on different subjects. Yet there stands before us one complete volume, one perfect Book with one God, one theme, one scheme of redemption. How do you explain the finished product unless there is one God who transcended those fifteen hundred years, and the Bible is His one perfect Book?

The Bible has life-changing power. Billy Graham was not seminary trained. More than 140 times in an average sermon, he said, "The Bible says," and millions of persons from every walk of life were transformed under his preaching.

Dr. Graham said, "There was a time it greatly disturbed me that I could not reasonably explain everything in the Bible. My uncertainty negatively impacted my authority. Then I determined, what I could accept by reason, I would accept by reason. What I could not accept by reason, I would accept by faith. Since that time," Dr. Graham stated, "the Bible has become a flame in my hand."

Simply stated "inspiration" in 2 Timothy 3:16, means "God breathed."

"By the Word of the Lord were the heavens made; and all the host of them by the breath of His mouth" (Ps. 33:6). (See Acts 1:16; 4:25; 13:32–35; Gal. 3:8, 16; and Heb. 37:10–15.)

The Southern Baptist Convention stands proudly with many other armies of the Christian faith on the inerrancy and infallibility of God's perfect revelation of Himself in Jesus Christ, as recorded in Holy Scripture.

You have only so long to minister in His name. I urge you to spend your time reading the Word, explaining it, and applying it to your people's lives, not debating and defending it.

If you have a lion, you don't need to defend him. Just turn him loose. He'll defend Himself.

Think on this: Is it important to God for me to know His truth? The answer is obviously yes. Since I wasn't around those fifteen hundred years it was being written, is it not incumbent upon God, who was, to preserve it for me in the form which I hold in my hand. Again the answer is obviously yes!

John 1:1 says, "In the beginning was The Word (Jesus), and the Word was with God, and the Word was God."

Jesus is God's *Living Word*. The Bible is God's *printed Word*. Jesus is God in a life. The Bible is God on a leaf. Jesus is God in a person. The Bible is God on a page.

Chapter 160

YOU AND YOUR DENOMINATION

T he potential impact of any local church is greatly enhanced when a part
of a greater fellowship of like-minded congregations. I urge you to be part
of such a body.

If your church is not, give it serious and prayerful consideration. The benefit
to your church, the larger group, and the kingdom expand immeasurably. And take
the time to understand clearly how your denomination or convention functions.

Most Southern Baptists identify themselves as such by the name of their
convention. Technically, *Baptist* is the denomination, *Southern Baptist*, the
convention or national association, the partnering group of thousands of local
Baptist congregations. The Convention of Southern Baptists was birthed in
Augusta, Georgia, in 1845.

Still strongest in the South, the Southern Baptist Convention now has
cooperating churches in all fifty states. Unlike other national bodies of
churches, that partnership holds no authority over any local church.

Each is an independent, self-governing, autonomous body, making its own
decisions with no outside controlling authority whatsoever. They call their
own pastor, and make all other decisions as they congregationally sense God's
leadership. The single unifying factor of their cooperation with the "convention
general" is the desire to fulfill the Great Commission.

Correctly, the assumption is that we can do more together than any of us can do alone, either as individuals or as congregations. The central ingredient in that cooperation is one central financial fund to which all Southern Baptist churches regularly contribute called the Cooperative Program. Out of it are funded thousands of missionaries, both national and international, as well as seminaries, universities, hospitals, evangelistic ministries, and social ministries to name a few.

After more than 170 years, the Southern Baptist Convention remains the most far-reaching such body of believers in the history of the Christian faith. Approximately sixteen million persons hold membership in approximately fifty thousand cooperating churches. Each is encouraged to give a minimum of 10 percent of its undesignated income to the Cooperative Program, but a stated amount is not mandatory for member status as a Southern Baptist church.

Southern Baptists are also bound together by the Word of God, the Great Commission, and *The 2000 Baptist Faith & Message: A Clear, Concise Declaration of What We Believe and What We Are About.*

At its core are the nonnegotiables of the Christian faith: the deity of Jesus, His vicarious death and bodily resurrection, salvation by grace through faith in Him, the inerrancy of Scripture, and the priority of the Great Commission. Persons sent from each church to the state or annual convention are designated "messengers" not "delegates" and are permitted to vote as they feel led of the Lord, *not* as directed by their church. Recent important matters have included: biblical inerrancy, women in ministry, refusal to recognize churches that accept the homosexual lifestyle, and "The Great Commission Resurgence Committee Report."

For years the spirit of the International Mission Board was "send your money, not your people on mission trips; the missionaries can do it better." Fortunately that philosophy has been completely reversed. It is the experience of actually having been there that most impacts the mission awareness and enthusiasm level of a local congregation and boosts cooperative giving upon their return.

The appeal to most young pastors is to lead their people in hands on rather than just send your money missions. It's not an either/or proposition. The former enhances the latter.

I urge Southern Baptists to do both things and do them through our North American Mission Board and International Mission Board. They get it right.

The Southern Baptist Convention is a really good thing, as are many other nationwide evangelistic bodies.

Chapter 161

YOU AND YOUR ASSOCIATION

Any successful army has battalions, divisions, companies, squadrons, etc. Christian soldiers march best in the same manner and Southern Baptists do it well.

Within the national body are many state conventions. In pioneer areas, smaller state conventions are often combined, such as Maryland-Delaware, Kansas-Nebraska, Washington-Oregon, etc.

Within state Baptist conventions are geographical associations usually consisting of thirty to sixty churches, though some such as Union Baptist Association in Houston may have as many as seven hundred or more. The same general structure is true of most other denominations.

Each association has its own executive director called the "director of missions," commonly called the DOM. He will have a staff, as will the state director called the executive director, normally with a much larger staff.

As with the larger Southern Baptist Convention, both state conventions and local associations will have a one- to two-day annual meeting where sermons are preached, reports heard, issues discussed, and business conducted. Local associations do a particularly good job in social ministries, Sunday school, Bible schools, lay training and evangelism.

Most associations have one or two prominent churches because of their size. Unfortunately, the attitude of too many pastors of large congregations is "the association can't do anything for my church." Dear pastor friend, that may be true, but what you *can* and *should* do for your association is tremendously important. I have found no greater joy than leading my church to help smaller congregations. Never forget the cross is still about laying down your life for one another.

Being a DOM can be as lonely as it is important. Just as important as your support at associational meetings is your personal encouragement of the DOM and his staff. Somehow I think God has a special love for smaller churches and their faithful shepherds. The DOM shepherds those shepherds.

The impact of that portion of the body of Christ called the Southern Baptist Convention on both the secular world and the kingdom of God is huge. But it is no more effective than the health of every cell, down to the smallest church in the most remote location.

Get involved with your association. Particularly if yours is a larger church. To paraphrase John F. Kennedy, "Ask not what your association can do for you. Ask what you can do for your association."

Chapter 162

A MISSIONARY CHURCH

At Houston's First, God built a truly mission-minded church. Each week over four or five hundred of our members serve in our local mission churches. Each summer, seven hundred to one thousand take off a week or two from their secular jobs to work in Mission Houston, our inner-city mission ministry.

Nearly eight hundred were ordained, went to seminary, and entered full-time Christian ministry; more than one hundred were on the international mission field.

Here's how God did it and continues to do it today. It all began in the heart of a pastor.

In 1971, I went to Nigeria for a citywide evangelistic campaigns in Lagos, Jos, and Port Harcourt. I never got over it. Upon my return I struggled for a year with the decision to resign my church and return as a full-time crusade missionary. Everything within me wanted to go except one: God would not release me from Houston.

Ultimately, I sensed a deep peace in my heart: I could do more by building a mission-minded church, calling out the called and sending many missionaries than by going myself.

Several factors went into that happening:

1. We built an atmosphere of missions by regularly preaching on full-time Christian service, particularly on the international mission field.

2. Testimonies were regularly given by those who had committed to go, had been on trips, or were career missionaries home on leave.

3. We provided a mission house where furloughing missionaries lived and intermingled with our people.

4. We increased awareness and emphasis on missions by combining the three traditional Southern Baptist mission offerings of one week each, into one major emphasis the entire month of December. For four weeks we preached on missions, had guest speakers from the mission boards and furloughing missionaries in every service and every Sunday school department, as well as videos, pictures, and a parade of flags, with people clothed in the national dress of more than two hundred countries.

5. We publicized missionary birthdays and prayed for them fifth-two Sundays a year.

6. We started sixty-seven local missions, mostly in transitional neighborhoods, and challenged our people to work in them.

7. Each adult Sunday school department adopted a mission.

8. We took our people on seven or eight international mission trips a year. Today the number is more than fifty.